# New England Must Not
# Be Trampled On

# New England Must Not Be Trampled On

## *The Tragic Death of Jonathan Cilley*

### Roger Ginn

**Down East Books**

Camden, Maine

Published by Down East Books
A wholly owned subsidiary of The Rowman & Littlefield Publishing Group, Inc.
4501 Forbes Boulevard, Suite 200, Lanham, Maryland 20706
www.rowman.com

Unit A, Whitacre Mews, 26-34 Stannary Street, London SE11 4AB

Distributed by National Book Network

British Library Cataloguing in Publication Information Available

**Library of Congress Cataloging-in-Publication Data**

Names: Ginn, Roger.
Title: New England must not be trampled on : the tragic death of Jonathan Cilley / Roger Ginn.
Description: Camden, Maine : Down East Books, 2016.
Identifiers: LCCN 2015038181| ISBN 9781608933877 (paperback : alkaline paper) | ISBN
    9781608933884 (electronic)
Subjects: LCSH: Cilley, Jonathan, 1802–1838—Death and burial. | Dueling—United States—Histo-
    ry—19th century. | Graves, W. J. (William Jordan), 1805–1848. | Legislators—United States—
    Biography. | United States. Congress. House—Biography. | Political culture—United States—
    History—19th century. | United States—Politics and government—1815–1861. | Cilley, Jona-
    than, 1802–1838—Friends and associates. | Bowdoin College—Biography.
Classification: LCC E340.C5 G56 2016 | DDC 328.73/092—dc23 LC record available at http://
    lccn.loc.gov/2015038181

Printed in the United States of America

# Contents

Introduction   1

1   Nottingham Square: A New Hampshire Hilltop   7

2   The Formative Years: Life on the Square   19

3   Bowdoin Years   29

4   Thomaston Years   45

5   First Term   63

6   Sent Home   75

7   Expelled   91

8   Mr. Speaker   105

9   U.S. House of Representatives   123

10   Confrontation   133

11   The Note   147

12   Rifle Practice   155

13   The Challenge   161

14   The Duel   171

15   Blame and Investigation   185

16   Wise and Clay   205

17   Mistaken Sense of Honor   211

Epilogue   219

Notes   225

Bibliography   243

# Introduction

On a damp cold Saturday afternoon, February 24, 1838, Jonathan Cilley, a thirty-five-year-old first-term Maine Democrat in the U.S. House of Representatives, was killed in a duel in a field outside Washington, D.C., by a Whig congressman from Kentucky, thirty-two-year-old William Graves. While in the early 1800s duels were not uncommon, particularly in the South, this duel grabbed national headlines. The political press talked of plots and conspiracies. It brought out, mostly in the Northern press, a cry for the abolishment of these so-called "affairs of honor," which were seen as only dishonorable to those involved.

When one today asks someone from Maine about the man from Thomaston named Jonathan Cilley, rarely have they heard of him. In Thomaston today, if you were to drive north through town on Main Street, you can spot on the left, just before the Mill River Bridge, a white house with the small sign over the front door that reads, "Jonathan Cilley House 1837." Also off Main Street, in the southeast corner of the Elm Grove Cemetery, stands a seventeen-foot granite monument erected by the people of Thomaston in 1841 at a cost of $500. At the top is found this inscription:

Hon. Jonathan Cilley
July 2, 1802–Feb. 24, 1838
Bowdoin 1825
Member of 25th Congress
"New England Must Not Be Trampled On"

Jonathan, a longtime supporter of President Andrew Jackson, arrived in Washington in the fall of 1837 as a new member of the 25th Congress at a time when the political climate was fiery and contentious. The issues of the day and the factional rivalries were seen as impacting the long-term survival of the new American experiment in democracy. The pro-Jackson newspapers characterized Jonathan's death as part of a plot by Southern Whigs who had conspired to rid themselves of a Northern Democrat they believed to be developing too much influence and thus posing a threat to their agenda. In March 1838, a decidedly pro-Jackson publication, the *Democratic Review*, offered what it claimed was a detailed account of the issues surrounding the duel, titled "The Martyrdom of Cilley." In it Jonathan was depicted as a man who stood up for the honor of New England. He was quoted as having said, "My name must not be disgraced, and I go to this field sustained by as high a motive of patriotism as ever led my grandfather or my brother to battle, as an unhappy duty not to be shrunk from, to my honor my principles and my country."

America was shocked by the death and distressed that a congressman had been killed. To some degree even the Northern *Whig* press was appalled by Jonathan's death. Sermons were preached on the evils and senselessness of dueling and the archaic gentleman's code of honor. Because the issues that precipitated the duel took place during a session of Congress, a congressional investigation was undertaken, though the only noteworthy result was that dueling was banned in Washington, D.C.

One thing that has made history so intriguing to me is that over time, through the many centuries, events have always been populated by people. These people had lives; they were at one time children, they struggled through their teenage years, they had goals and aspirations, they had fears and insecurities, and they experienced the joys and tragedies of their time. Often they are presented only as actors or actresses on the stage of the events of the day, but ultimately they were people with varying degrees of intellectual capability; they made choices and engaged in actions that impacted others as well as the world in which they lived. They had emotions—joy, happiness, sadness, fear, and anger. They had bonds (to varying degrees) with parents and siblings, as well as other family members, and also friends and rivals. They likely had spouses and children. They suffered losses. They grew old and died contemplating their legacy or sense of immortality, or they died young from sickness, accidents, or violence. History is made up of a long, unending series of lives.

As a psychologist, my work life regularly involved looking at the intimate experiences, the struggles, the joys, the successes, the fears, the heartaches, and the tragedies associated with the individuals with whom I worked. I attempted to understand where they came from, what guided their daily lives, and what might help them improve the quality of their lives or reduce their fears and despair. This involved an intimacy with others that would be uncommon in routine daily relationships. These lives have never ceased to fascinate me. They are all different, but often with many threads of sameness. All are unique and have their place in the human experience and the history of their time.

The only biography about Jonathan Cilley was a brief one hurriedly written a few months after the duel by his college friend Nathaniel Hawthorne. It is usually the source cited when Jonathan is discussed. But when you look past this brief sketch of Jonathan's life, a much more interesting and fascinating story unfolds. He was seen by some as a man who would have made an outstanding contribution to his country, in the mold of such contemporary Maine politicians as Hannibal Hamlin, Lincoln's vice president, and William Pitt Fessenden, Lincoln's secretary of the Treasury.

Beyond Hawthorne's sketch of Jonathan's life, there is an abundance of information available about Jonathan, his life, and his times. The most remarkable and poignant source of information is found in the Cilley letters, some five hundred of which were given to the Thomaston Historical Society in Maine. These letters were painstakingly transcribed and subsequently published in a 2003 book by Eve Anderson titled *Breach of Privilege*. They begin with a letter written by Jonathan to his younger sister, Elizabeth Ann, while he was attending a boarding school in Atkinson, New Hampshire, prior to entering Bowdoin College, and continue into the 1860s with letters written by his children. These letters provide an intimate and personal picture of Jonathan, particularly related to his family and his relationship with his wife. They give us insight into his aspirations and the struggles he encountered on his journey up the political ladder. For example, in a letter to his wife in 1832 during his first term in the Maine state legislature, he wrote, "The most unpleasant thing I meet with thus far in my political experience is political jealousy and rivalry among our friends. It is strange to me, that men who are engaged in a great contest for the maintenance of sound republican principles should be jealous of being outdone in so glorious a cause by any of their political friends."

More is learned about Jonathan's personal life during his early years in Thomaston from the journal of Hezekiah Prince Jr., which gives an enlightening daily account of early nineteenth-century life and activities in the small coastal town of Thomaston between 1822 and 1828. Prince was a close friend of Jonathan and eventually became his brother-in-law. The journal also provides a good glimpse of Jonathan's personal life and the development of his professional and political standing within the Thomaston community. The entries in the journal, along with the early letters, give added depth to the man who made national headlines in February 1838. They also provide important early insight into Jonathan's developing character and the positive rapport he had with the people with whom he lived.

Other significant information, particularly about his political life and the duel, is found in the newspapers of the time. His conflicts in the Maine legislature, as well as the conflicts within his own Democratic Party, are well documented.

Accounts of the duel are extensively covered in the newspapers of the time, as well as in the records of the U.S. Congress. *The Congressional Globe* provides a detailed report concerning the circumstances of the duel. There are also other firsthand accounts by those in Washington at the time. The letters of John Fairfield, also a congressman from Maine, and the letters of Reuel Williams, one of the senators from Maine at the time, provide firsthand information about Jonathan as well as the belligerent and contentious atmosphere in Washington at the time of his death.

The story of the fateful duel cannot be fully appreciated without consideration of the men whose actions were at the center of the challenge and its ultimate tragic outcome. These men in and of themselves were especially interesting individuals, most of whom had experience with dueling, and their involvement in the fatal duel adds depth and perspective to the Cilley tragedy. One was James Watson Webb, the New York newspaper publisher who took exception to a statement made by Jonathan in Congress. Another player was Henry Wise, a congressman from Virginia known for his fiery rhetoric and temper. Wise was the second to Graves at the duel and the one who took the brunt of the blame for Jonathan's death. Franklin Pierce, later the fourteenth president of the United States, was a confidante of Jonathan through crucial days leading up to the duel. A fourth notable player was Henry Clay, the distinguished senator from Kentucky and frequent presidential candidate. Finally, there was Congressman Graves himself, who was at times described as a pawn of his more influential colleagues. In all there were seventeen members of Congress involved, to varying degrees, in the affair. The tragedy was that, by all accounts, these two men, Cilley and Graves, had no real animosity toward one another, and under normal circumstances they would never have ended up facing each other with rifles at eighty paces.

The ultimate question for me in researching and subsequently writing about Jonathan Cilley was what was there about this man and the make-up of his personality that would lead him to choose to put his life at risk, to defend his honor and become in the eyes of some a martyr. At first glance, looking at his life, one would never predict that he would ulti-mately die in a duel or be held up as a martyr. But as we look at his life and the challenges he faced, it may not be so surprising. To the best of my knowledge, to date, there has been no objective look at the circumstances surrounding the duel and the people who were involved. The rhetoric at the time talked of plots and murder, but the real story is more complex.

Bringing understanding and meaning to a man's decisions and actions is a complex and multidimensional task. Some of an individual's behav-ior is the result of well-thought-out reasoning, but at other times an act would appear to be very impulsive and devoid of logical reasoning. Was Jonathan's decision to accept Congressman Graves's challenge the result of the former or the latter? One thing that helps explain and understand a man's behavior is the study of that individual's history, his personality, and his character An important factor to be addressed and understood in explaining a man's actions is the culture and the social climate of the time. The values, attitudes, and beliefs of a culture change over time. While today the idea of two men standing in a field, with friends watch-ing, pointing lethal weapons at each other would be abhorrent, in Jona-than's time dueling was, particularly in the South, the accepted means of settling personal differences among gentlemen. Central to what came to be called "affairs of honor" was the concept of honor as it was defined at that period of time and its importance among the influential men in early nineteenth-century America. While in present society the word *honor* is used in a more general context, back then a man's honor was of para-mount importance. It was a term used by men to assess themselves and judge others. An attack on a man's honor, either directly or indirectly, was something that required a response, for not to defend one's honor was in itself dishonorable.

The personality traits, values, and beliefs, the things that chart a per-son's course through life, are the products of cumulative life experience, or, as the psychologist would frame it, evolution through the stages of development. A decision or choice one might make at age ten or twenty in all probability would not be the same as the one made at thirty-six, and it may well be different from the one made at fifty. At any point in time, however, the only wisdom and understanding an individual has available is that which has been accumulated up to that point in his or her life.

While the main focus of this book is the short, fascinating life of Jonathan Cilley, it is also, to a lesser extent, the story of a proud New England family whose members lived through and played a prominent role in the American story from the middle of the eighteenth century through the Civil War. Jonathan's story can only be appreciated when looked at in the context of the Cilley family's contribution to the development of America and their commitment to public service both in peacetime and in war.

# ONE

## Nottingham Square: A New Hampshire Hilltop

Jonathan Cilley was born on Nottingham Square on July 2, 1802. He was the sixth child born to Greenleaf and Jane Nealley Cilley. He had three older brothers and two older sisters. Much of the foundation of Jonathan's character, sense of self-identity, and concept of honor (particularly as it related to his commitment to public service) was rooted in the role models of family members, by way of the stories, tales, and legends he frequently heard throughout his childhood and adolescent years as he grew up in Nottingham, New Hampshire.

Nottingham Square sits on a hilltop about twenty-four miles inland from the seacoast city of Portsmouth, New Hampshire, which had been a thriving seaport since the late 1600s. At the top of the hill today, at the intersection of two roads, there is a sign marking Nottingham Square. The origin of the Square dates back to 1721. It was here that Jonathan grew up among a large extended family. Remaining on the Square today are two monuments. On one are remembered Nathaniel Folsom, Robert Beard, and Elizabeth Simpson, who were killed in the Indian attack in September 1747 and buried somewhere on the Square. Elizabeth Simpson was likely a distant relative of President Ulysses Simpson Grant, since some members of the Simpson side of his family had moved from Nottingham to Ohio. Also on the Square is the large General Joseph Cilley Monument erected in 1917 by the Else Cilley (wife of Jonathan's great-grandfather) Chapter of the Daughters of the American Revolution. Additionally honored on this monument are Henry Dearborn, Thomas Bartlett, and Henry Butler, three other Nottingham men who were generals in the Continental Army. On one corner of the Square there remains the house of Jonathan's Uncle Bradbury. Hidden in the area are two cemeteries, where many Cilley family members are buried; unfortunately, both are in disrepair and grown over with brush. Gone are the churches, the school, the meeting hall, stores, and taverns that were once the hub of the Square.

One would not know in passing by that here, in the eighteenth and into the nineteenth centuries, was a small thriving community where the Cilley family, along with other families formed a close-knit community. Today the area is still surrounded by fields, farms, and woods. It was here that Jonathan lived, roamed, and learned. It was here that the roots of his commitment to public service began, where he would follow in the footsteps of his grandfather, uncles, father, and brother. With his roots firmly established, Nottingham Square was also a place to which he regularly returned over the course of his short life.

The first Cilley to come to Nottingham was Captain Joseph Cilley, Jonathan's great-grandfather, who arrived with his wife Alice (called "Else") in 1727, just five years after the town was founded. He was not one of the landowners who originally received plots of land surrounding the Square, but he did become an agent for those proprietors. He was also appointed captain of the local militia. A requirement of those granted the original tracts of land around the Square was that they had to clear some of the land and build on it; if they did not, they had to sell the land. This gave Captain Cilley the opportunity to acquire a significant amount of land; by the time he died in 1786, he had more than three hundred acres and was the wealthiest man in the area. He was described as a man with "an undivided interest in the welfare of his neighbors and in the progress of the community, an honest man." Captain Cilley had six children (four daughters and two sons), and this next generation of Cilleys continued the tradition of service to town, state, and country. The oldest son was Joseph, born in 1734, followed by Cutting in 1738.

Captain Cilley's sons received little formal education, as he believed that ultimately knowledge of the land would be more valuable. When the French and Indian War broke out in 1754, the twenty-year-old Joseph Cilley enlisted in the army and served with the famous Roger's Rangers along the northern frontier and into Canada. He started as a private, and when he returned to Nottingham a year later he was a sergeant. After his return, in spite of his limited education, he taught himself the law and provided legal services to the residents of Nottingham. He continued to be involved with the state militia and by the beginning of the Revolutionary War he had reached the rank of captain. In November 1756 he married Sarah Longfellow, a distant cousin of the poet Henry Wadsworth Longfellow. Her father, Jonathan Longfellow, along with Captain Cilley, was one of the men responsible for defending Nottingham from Indian attacks. Cilley and Sarah had ten children (seven boys and three girls).

Cilley, along with the other men on the Square, was well aware of the brewing conflict with England. They all certainly spent time in the taverns, Bartlett's store, and meeting halls discussing events such as the Boston Massacre in March 1770, and the Boston Tea Party in December 1773. The citizens of the Square provided financial assistance to the people of Boston after the British closed the port in retaliation for the dumping of the tea. Throughout the colonies people began to organize. They developed local and state committees of correspondence and public safety committees, which were to aid in the facilitation of communication and coordinate the brewing rebellion against Britain.

While Paul Revere is most notably remembered for his "the British are coming" ride on April 18, 1775, he made a less well-known ride to Portsmouth in December 1774, which placed the men of Nottingham at the scene of one the first hostile actions of the War of Independence. On December 13, Revere rode to Portsmouth with a letter from Boston for Samuel Cutts of the Portsmouth Committee of Correspondence. Just outside Portsmouth, in New Castle, at Fort William and Mary, the British had stored a large supply of gunpowder, as well as muskets and cannons. Revere's letter informed Cutts that the British navy was on its way to Fort William and Mary to reinforce the fort and possibly transfer the powder and weapons to a more secure place. The implication was that some action needed to be taken. On December 14 a group of local residents took control of the fort, but they needed help.

A call went out through the state for assistance, and on December 15 Cilley, then forty years old, along with other men from Nottingham Square headed for New Castle. Along the way they connected with other men from the surrounding countryside, under the leadership of John Sullivan, later a general in the Continental Army and a governor of New Hampshire. They joined those already in the fort and, with little bloodshed, were able to remove seventy-two barrels of gunpowder along with

some of the weapons. British troops arrived before they had time to dis-
mantle the cannons, so those were left behind. The powder was stored for
later use in various homes throughout the area—Cilley hid eight barrels
under his own house.

Following the Fort William and Mary raid, the men of Nottingham
Square began in earnest to prepare for the impending conflict. Under the
direction of the young local doctor, Henry Dearborn, who had married
Bartlett's sister Mary, the men gathered on the Square for drill. On April
20, 1775, when word of the battles of Lexington and Concord (which had
occurred on the previous day) reached the Square, Cilley, his brother
Cutting, and the other men of Nottingham were ready. Dr. Dearborn
called the men to the Square, and at 4 p.m. one hundred volunteers
headed for Massachusetts. In addition to the two Cilleys and Dearborn,
the group included Thomas Bartlett, Henry Butler, and Zephaniah Butler,
who was married to Cilley's sister Abigail. Traveling about sixty miles
throughout the night, the men astonishingly reached Medford, Massachusetts, by sunrise on April 21. Unfortunately for these men, who
wanted to be part of the action, the fighting had ended, and most of them
returned home to fight another day. It did, however, mark the beginning
of Cilley's meritorious military career. He, along with the other men from
Nottingham who served with distinction during the war, left in the
minds of future generations of Nottingham citizens a rich and notable
tradition of service to the country.

Dearborn, his medical career over, remained in Massachusetts following the overnight march and was instrumental in organizing the New
Hampshire regiments. Cilley initially served as a major in the Third New
Hampshire Regiment under Colonel Enoch Poor, whose two daughters
had married Cilley's sons, Bradbury and Jacob. The Third's initial responsibility was to defend the New Hampshire coast. The British had
attacked Portland, Maine, on October 15, 1775, bombarding it for nine
hours and setting three quarters of the town on fire. In New Hampshire
the fear was that the next target might be Portsmouth. Fortunately, no
attack took place.

While Cilley was in New Hampshire, Dearborn and other men from
Nottingham fought in the Battle of Bunker Hill. After Bunker Hill, then
Captain Henry Dearborn headed off through the Maine woods with
Benedict Arnold on the ill-fated expedition to capture Quebec City. Cil-
ley's regiment was sent to Boston and was part of the siege of Boston,

which forced the British to leave and head to New York City. Over the next six years Cilley was involved with his troops in many of the now-famous actions that ended with America's independence. After Boston, the New Hampshire men headed to New York.

With the failure in Quebec, the Americans were forced to retreat south. Washington, concerned about their safety, sent the now General Sullivan, of Fort William and Mary fame, and his brigade north to Canada to support the retreat. The newly appointed Lieutenant Colonel Cilley and the New Hampshire Third Regiment were part of this effort to get Benedict Arnold and his men back to fight another day. Dearborn was captured but later released as part of a prisoner exchange in March 1777. Cilley and his men were back with Washington in July 1776, when the Founding Fathers approved the Declaration of Independence. In the winter of 1776 Cilley was with Washington during the famous crossing of the icy Delaware River and at the badly needed wins in the battles of Trenton and Princeton.

Given the similarity between the name Cilley and the word *silly*, it has not been uncommon to find the words interchanged for the purpose of a little levity. In 1820 the *New-Hampshire Patriot* published the following:

> In the American Revolution a brave soldier was brought before a court martial and put on trial, charged with having uttered the following disrespectful words concerning the regiment to which he belonged, viz: "our regiment is the only damn, poor, silly regiment in the American Army." The soldier at his trial admitted the words to have been uttered by him, and relied on his justification of those words before the court by saying that the regiment was commanded by Col. Damn, Maj. Poor, and Capt. Cilley. The defense being true, instantly acquitted the prisoner, and for his wit, procured him ever thereafter the love and esteem of the whole regiment.

In April 1777 the now Colonel Cilley was given command of the First New Hampshire Regiment. Earlier in the spring he paid a visit home to Nottingham based on the birth of his last son in December 1777. He named his son Horatio Gates, after the once British officer who now was a general in the Continental Army. When he returned to action, Cilley and his men were sent back to Fort Ticonderoga because the British army, under General John Burgoyne, was marching south out of Canada. Dearborn, back with his New Hampshire brethren, now commanded the Third New Hampshire Regiment.

When Cilley headed off for his six-year tour of duty, he was accompanied by his second son Jonathan (our Jonathan's uncle), who was only fifteen years old when he left home. Part of the Cilley family lore has been young Jonathan's encounter with the British general John Burgoyne. In 1777, under heavy pressure from Burgoyne's forces at Fort Ticonderoga, located at the southern end of Lake Champlain, the American army, including Cilley's First New Hampshire Regiment, had to make a hasty retreat. Unfortunately, his son Jonathan was captured by the British. Legend has it that when General Burgoyne found out the young prisoner was the son of an American officer, he provided him with a pass so he could return to his father. He also gave Jonathan a horse to ride with two saddlebags packed with copies of a proclamation urging the Americans to surrender. Although certainly glad to have his son back, Cilley did not take kindly to the contents of the saddlebags. He reportedly ordered that all the proclamations be torn up. He tore one himself, threw it in the air, and said to his troops, "Thus may the British army be scattered." His son continued with the army until the end of the war, attaining the rank of lieutenant.

The two armies met in the area around Saratoga, New York, in October 1777. After several battles the American troops forced Burgoyne to surrender his army. The final result was hastened when the New Hampshire men outflanked the British. Cilley was named a hero for his perseverance in actions leading up to Burgoyne's surrender. After his men, following repeated attempts, captured British cannons on a disputed hilltop, a New Hampshire lieutenant in the First Regiment wrote in his diary that Cilley climbed on one of the captured cannons, "waved his sword over his head, dedicated the piece to the 'American Cause,' and turning it upon the foe, he opened its destructive energy upon the enemy with their own ammunition, amid an avalanche of applause from the New Hampshire brigade." This victory was immortalized in John Trumbull's 1821 painting, which includes Colonel Cilley, that to this day hangs in the rotunda of the U.S. Capitol.

The defeat at Saratoga was a major blow to what the British hoped would be a quick end to the American rebellion. With winter approaching, Cilley and the men of New Hampshire joined Washington at Valley Forge, where they remained until May 1778. As we all remember, the men at Valley Forge suffered for want of adequate food and warm clothing. The Continental Congress and the states were neglectfully remiss in their responsibility to provide even basic necessities. Even though the Valley Forge region of Pennsylvania was a prosperous area, the farmers and merchants preferred to trade with the British in Philadelphia because they could pay for the supplies with hard currency, while Washington had only the highly inflated and basically worthless Continental dollar.

At Valley Forge Cilley had the opportunity to establish a relationship with the Marquis de Lafayette. He and his men would have participated in the back to basics military training provided by the former Prussian captain, Baron von Steuben. The training gave the army a much-needed indoctrination to military order, procedures, and discipline. This was something for which the British army was noted, but the fledgling American army never had time to acquire. In spite of the cold, shortage of food, and inadequate clothing, when spring came the army left Valley Forge significantly improved. With spring also came word of the new alliance with France. This news buoyed the army's spirits and gave them a newfound sense of optimism.

By June Washington's troops were ready to engage the British, who had decided to leave Philadelphia and return to New York. The battle took place in Monmouth, New Jersey, on June 28, 1778. It was a fierce battle on a very hot day, which sapped the men's energy. The final result has historically been considered a draw. Cilley and his men fought coura-geously. In his brief 1921 biography, the *Life of Gen. Joseph Cilley*, John Scales wrote, "Colonel Cilley's regiment was closely engaged and he and his men behaved with such bravery as to merit the particular approba-tion of the illustrious Washington after the battle was over."

After Monmouth the men from New Hampshire did not see much action for a while. They ended the year 1778 as guards for the troops from Burgoyne's army who had been captured at Saratoga and were being moved to Virginia.

In May 1779, Cilley and his regiment, along with Dearborn's Third Regiment, in which Cilley's son was a junior officer, departed under fellow New Hampshire general John Sullivan for the Wyoming Valley in north-central Pennsylvania. In July 1778, the Wyoming Valley had been the scene of barbarous attacks by English-sympathizing Tories and In-dians against the settlers in the valley. Also, in November, the Tories and Indians attacked the Cherry Valley settlement in eastern New York, kill-ing forty-seven (mostly women and children), and took a number of prisoners, forty of whom never returned. The massacre of these settlers prompted Washington to send Sullivan and five thousand troops to the area to protect the settlers and put a stop to the attacks, and also to stamp out the threat along the Northern border. Washington specifically ordered Sullivan to completely destroy all the Indian villages and burn all their crops. This foray against the Indians of New York was probably the first major campaign in a strategy spanning more than a century to subdue and annihilate the Indians from this country in order to make room for expansion.

The campaign lasted about six months, with the troops marching through unsettled wilderness, constantly harassed by Tory rangers and Indians. The American troops significantly outnumbered the enemy and ultimately prevailed. The Tories retreated and the Indians were left to defend themselves. In the end, the Indians were subdued and their culture destroyed. More than forty villages were decimated, 160,000 bushels of corn and other crops were burned, and the orchards were cut and burned. Nothing was left, and five thousand Indians fled to the British held Fort Niagara, where there was little to sustain them over the winter.

The defeat of the Indians was hailed as a major victory, one that essentially put a stop to the raids on the settlers along the Northern border. This approach to dealing with the Indians would later be referred to favorably by then Congressman Jonathan Cilley in a speech in January 1838. Today, in some circles, the destruction of the New York tribes is not looked upon with admiration, but rather as a tragic example of the white man's campaign to remove the Indians from their lands. To this day, George Washington is remembered by the New York tribes not as the "father of our country" but as the "town destroyer."

Cilley's involvement in this action left him with some vivid memories. Scales wrote that "Colonel Cilley was accustomed to say, in after years that the sight of so many buildings on fire, the massy clouds of black smoke, the curling pillars of flame bursting through them, formed the most awful and sublime spectacle he ever witnessed." Scales added (likely echoing the prevailing attitude of the time) that as "awful as it were, it was trifling in comparison with the inhuman barbarities those Indians had inflicted on American citizens during the preceding years of the war."

After leaving New York, Cilley and his men spent the winter in Connecticut. In the spring they moved up the Hudson River to the West Point area. At that time, Cilley's son-in-law was in command of another New

Hampshire regiment stationed at West Point. Both men were involved in the protection of West Point after Benedict Arnold defected to the British. Cilley saw no more action after the Indian campaign. When the New Hampshire regiments were consolidated in January 1781, Cilley returned to Nottingham a hero after six years of service to the cause of American independence.

By the close of the war, Nottingham had contributed more high-ranking officers to the cause of American independence than any other town in the country. Most of those who left the Square to serve in the army returned to Nottingham at the conclusion of the war. The one exception was Dearborn, who initially settled in Maine. His ties to Nottingham likely ended with the death of his wife Mary, who had gone to Quebec with their children to serve as a hostage for him after his capture. She died in 1778. Dearborn went on to be secretary of war in Jefferson's cabinet and later served as a major general in the War of 1812.

Over the six years he was away, the colonel's wife, Sarah, and son Bradbury had maintained the family's business interests. On his return to New Hampshire, the state legislature appointed Colonel Cilley to a New England commission with the responsibility of providing much-needed supplies to the Continental Army. He was well aware of the supply issue from his winter at Valley Forge. He became involved in both local and state politics. He was a justice of the peace, served as a senator in the state legislature, and was a representative to the New Hampshire Convention, which revised the state's constitution. He continued to serve in the state militia, where he attained the rank of major general. Lieutenant Jonathan Cilley returned briefly, married Butler's sister Dorcas, and then moved to Ohio in 1804, never to return to the Square.

William Plumer, who had been governor of New Hampshire for six terms, wrote a brief sketch of General Cilley in 1830. This sketch captured the essence of the general's character, beyond his fame as a hero of the American Revolution. Plumer, born in 1759, was from Epping, New Hampshire, about six miles from the Square. He was involved in New Hampshire public life for thirty-five years, initially as a Federalist, but later he became what was known at the time as a Jeffersonian Republican. He was in the New Hampshire House of Representatives for nine terms, serving as Speaker twice. He was a Federalist U.S. senator from 1802 to 1807, and he voted, along with all but one New England senator, against Jefferson's Louisiana Purchase. When he returned to New Hampshire he served in the state senate, followed by his terms as a Jefferson Republican governor. He undoubtedly met the general when they served in the legislature, if he had not known him before. They both were members of the State Constitutional Convention. There were also family ties: Plumer's sister Hannah married the general's brother Daniel in 1790, and his brother Samuel married the general's sister, Elizabeth Cilley, in 1791.

Plumer wrote about the general as follows:

> He was a man of good judgment, a lively imagination, and of great decision of character. His passions were strong and irritable, his expressions quick and hasty: but he was humane and tender hearted. He was on all occasions open, frank, and explicit in avowing his sentiments; there was no vice he so much abhorred and detested as hypocrisy. His passions were too strong to be deceitful; he despised and condemned the artful cool, designing knave. He was manly and liberal — incapable of meanness: and his manners were not those of a courtier, they were easy, plain, and correct. His friendship was sincere and ardent; and his prejudices, for he had them, were the effort of strong passions and not of a depraved heart.

General Cilley was also described as a man who could work with people on both sides of an issue and who could facilitate compromise. He judged a man by his capabilities over political ideology; even if a man were a Federalist, the general would support him for public office if he believed the man was the better-qualified candidate. He spoke his mind and did not back down from what he believed to be important. He was devoted to his land and diligently worked to acquire more, and by the time of his death he passed on a sizeable inheritance, most of which went to his oldest son, Bradbury.

While Cilley throughout the war was an ardent supporter and admirer of Washington, he found himself disagreeing with the new president's politics and policies. Right from the beginning of the American experiment in self-rule, there was a decided difference of opinion regarding the direction the country should take and the roles and responsibilities of the new federal government. While rejecting the notion of political parties, which were believed to be too British and only for the selfish, unofficial opposition or factions were begrudgingly tolerated.

From the beginning and through the ratification of the Constitution in 1789, there remained significant differences of opinion about the relationship between the federal government and the states. The Constitution left this relationship ambiguous, thus opening the door to political disagreement. Cilley advocated for the common man and opposed a strong federal government, fearing, as did many others, that it would lead to an English-style monarchy, thus relegating second-class status on the average citizen, who would then likely carry an unfair tax burden.

Cilley was a fervent supporter of Thomas Jefferson and James Madison's republican concept of government, which advocated giving more power to the states and the concepts espoused in the Declaration of Independence: a government of the people, by the people, for the people. The responsibility of those who served in public office was to "protect citizens' political freedom and legal equality from any concentration of public or private power, and especially from law-granted privileges that gave advantage to some to the disadvantage of others."

When John Adams bested Jefferson for the right to succeed Washington as president in 1796, Cilley was disappointed and found himself continuing to disagree with what he believed was the pro-British course the government was taking. He was, however, in the minority in New Hampshire, as well as in Federalist New England, which had given all its electoral votes to Adams. In New Hampshire throughout the 1790s a Federalist governor had been regularly elected, never receiving less than 70 percent of the vote. Regrettably, Cilley did not live to see Jefferson elected president in 1800 and the Jeffersonians moving to the forefront both nationally and in New Hampshire.

Religion was not a significant factor in the lives of most of those on the Square, nor was it with the Cilley family. As the early settlers of New England came to the colonies in pursuit of religious freedom, those who later moved to New Hampshire came there in part to get away from the religious orthodoxy of old New England. Leon Williams, who grew up on the Square in the late 1800s and subsequently became a minister, wrote in his Nottingham history, *A New Hampshire Hilltop*, that those who came did so not "for conscience sake" but for secular reasons, most notably to make money. There were a number of different religions on the Square, and they coexisted without major controversy, and shared the meeting house. Williams lamented that "the godlessness of New Hampshire, of which we are so often reminded, is no new condition. It has been evident from the beginning, though never drifting to hapless immorality." General Cilley was not a church-going man. "His religion consisted more in practice of the moral and social virtues, than the articles of faith, the observance of ceremonials, or in attending the preaching clergy."

The general's thinking toward churches and religion carried over into succeeding generations. The Universalist church appears to have been the religious orientation preferred by Cilley family members. In 1827, a New Hampshire newspaper reported that Bradbury and his brother Daniel Cilley founded a Universalist Society in nearby Epsom. Universalists had little interest in salvation, tending to focus on service to the community. While Jonathan never mentioned in any of his letters any affiliation with a specific church, there was a reference in a newspaper at the time of his death that he told a woman he spoke to before the duel that he was a Universalist.

The man now known as General Cilley died in 1799 at the age of sixty-five, after a brief illness, three years before his grandson Jonathan's birth. Jonathan therefore would never know his famous grandfather, but he knew his grandmother. Many of the men, including Cutting Cilley, Bartlett, and Butler, who fought in the war, were still in Nottingham during Jonathan's childhood years, and he would undoubtedly have heard on many occasions the tales of the great war for American independence and the heroic stories regarding his grandfather.

# TWO

## The Formative Years:
## Life on the Square

At the time Jonathan was born in July 1802, Thomas Jefferson was in the second year of his presidency, with Nottingham, New Hampshire's Henry Dearborn serving as secretary of war, but Federalists were still in control of the New Hampshire State House. It was a time of relative peace; war with France had been averted at the end of the Adams administration, but significant issues still existed with England and Napoleon's France around America's unimpeded access to the oceans, with both countries continuing to interfere with America's overseas commerce. On the Square, the sons of General Cilley continued to work their land and produce children. Twenty-year-old Greenleaf had married fifteen-year-old Jane Neally in May 1787. Jane's father Joseph, also from Nottingham, had served as an officer during the recent war. Greenleaf and Jane Cilley already had five children before Jonathan arrived: Susanna was born in 1788, Joseph in 1791, Greenleaf Jr. in 1793, Fredrick in 1796, and Sarah in 1799. After Jonathan became part of the family, the last member of the family, Elizabeth, was born in 1804.

Little is known about Jonathan's father, Greenleaf. He owned land that he inherited from his father, which he and his sons worked to sustain his large family. He did, from time to time, hold some town offices and was a major in the state militia. Jonathan's time with his father was tragically brief, for Greenleaf died when Jonathan was five or six years old. Unlike present-day health care, medical knowledge and treatments were limited and unsophisticated, and any illness could quickly prove fatal.

Life expectancy was much shorter, and premature death from sickness or injury was much more prevalent then it is today. The loss of family members would not be an unusual occurrence; however, it was surely not something for which a young child would be prepared. It is not known what caused Greenleaf's death, or whether it was sudden or lingering or from illness or accident. In any case, the loss of a father was surely a painful experience for a young child who could not truly understand death but only know that Dad would no longer be at home. That same year Jonathan had to cope with a second loss, when his Grandmother Cilley also died. Fortunately for Jonathan, he had a large family support system to help him cope with these losses.

The loss of his father would have brought major changes in Jonathan's life. It could be assumed that Greenleaf had sustained the family (with the help of his sons) through farming and working his land. With him gone, there would have been a decrease in financial resources and the need to be more dependent on others. It is likely that Uncle Bradbury and Uncle Jacob, who also resided in Nottingham and had more substantial assets, made sure the family did not suffer. At the core of Jonathan's support was his mother, who by all accounts provided a strong and consistent foundation for the family. His six siblings also included three older brothers to look up to, providing him with male role models.

In the same year that Jonathan's father died, James Madison, who had been Jefferson's secretary of state, followed Jefferson as president. While Jefferson got New Hampshire's electoral votes in 1804, Madison was not popular in New England, and Charles C. Pinckney of South Carolina received all the New England electoral votes. By the time the 1812 election came around, Congress had authorized war with England. One of the military commanders for Madison was Henry Dearborn. The war was not popular in the predominantly Federalist New England, but in New Hampshire the support was divided, with those in the interior supportive and those along the coast opposed. The seaport towns of New England had been hard hit economically by Jefferson and Madison's 1807 Embargo Act, which prohibited trade with England and France and came as a response to British plundering of American vessels. The ship owners believed that a war would make matters worse for their business and preferred to take their chances on the open sea.

In October 1811, twenty-year-old brother Joseph enlisted in the state militia with the rank of ensign. Also in 1811, three years after Jonathan lost his father, tragedy again struck the Cilley family when eighteen-year-old Greenleaf Jr. died. The cause of his death is unknown, but most likely resulted from illness, an all too common occurrence in the days before the discovery of antibiotics. When war with England was declared in the summer of 1812, Republican Governor Plumer sent the New Hampshire militia off to war. Eight-year-old Jonathan watched his brother Joseph leave home, likely not fully realizing the risks involved, and still coping with the loss of Greenleaf. With Joseph responding to the call of battle and following the family commitment to military service, sixteen-year-old Fredrick and young Jonathan were left to carry on the male role in the family. In addition to schooling, Jonathan had to assume a larger share of the responsibility for the traditionally male functions within the household. At the center and undoubtedly the bedrock of the family was their mother Jane. It would be unimaginable that her children, so often touched by loss, could have persevered without this woman at the head of the household, whose resilience, courage, and guidance held the family together and allowed them to forge ahead in life.

In the regular army Joseph started as an ensign, and he fought in a number of major battles, ending the war as a captain. In 1814, reminiscent of his grandfather's action thirty-seven years earlier at Saratoga during the Battle of Lundy Lane, the young captain led a successful charge against British cannons, but while holding their new position Joseph took a musket ball in the thigh that left him with permanent damage and lameness. This injury, however, did not end his service, and he unfortunately later lost an eye at Detroit when a powder magazine exploded. He came home an acknowledged hero in the tradition of the other military men who originated from Nottingham, but with some disabilities that would plague him for the rest of his life. After the war Joseph continued in the army until 1816, but before he returned home death once more rocked the family when Fredrick died at age nineteen, most likely from some type of illness. After his return home, Joseph served in the state militia and then as an aide to Governor Benjamin Pierce (Franklin Pierce's father), finishing his military career with the rank of colonel.

Involvement in the political life of New Hampshire was a family tradition, if not an expectation. In addition to General Cilley's time in the state legislature, his sons also served in the New Hampshire House of Representatives. Daniel, who was a Republican, served in 1805, while brother Jacob served eight terms between 1802 and 1813, likely as a Federalist. It is also probable that they, as well as other Cilleys, ran for office and did not win. Right after Mr. Madison's war began in 1812, elections were held. Madison was seeking reelection, and his Federalist opponent was DeWitt Clinton from New York. In New Hampshire, the main issue was the war, and the newspapers pitted the war party against the peace party. Jonathan's Uncle Bradbury was part of a Federalist peace ticket seeking election to the U.S. House of Representatives. Madison won the presidential election, but the only New England support came from Vermont. The peace candidates won all the New Hampshire seats in the U.S. House, thus sending Bradbury off to Washington, D.C., for terms in both the 13th and the 14th Congresses.

In December 1814 New England Federalists sent representatives to Hartford, Connecticut, to discuss and formulate a strategy to deal with the war. New Hampshire did not send any official delegates because, even though the state had a Federalist governor, he was outvoted by his predominantly Democratic-Republican executive council. With the line between the rights of the states and the federal government's responsibility and authority continually debated, the option for some who believed the national government's policies were contrary to their interests was to remove their state from the Union, and thus a proposal was floated in Hartford that New England should secede from the United States. The resolution that came out of the convention did not recommend secession, but it did suggest seven new amendments to the U.S. Constitution. Two are of interest here. One recommended amendment—with New England frustrated that four of the first five presidents came from Virginia— would require that no president could be followed by one from the same state. The second new amendment would eliminate the "three-fifths rule," which allowed for representation purposes that each slave be counted as three-fifths of a person, thereby inflating the representation in Congress and giving slave-holding states an unfair advantage. (This continued to be an issue when Jonathan arrived in Washington in 1837.) The resolution's timing was inopportune because the treaty to end the war was signed on Christmas Eve 1814, and it was overshadowed by General Andrew Jackson's victory in New Orleans on January 8, 1815. The secession discussion at the Hartford Convention resulted in the Federalists being labeled traitors in the press, spelling the beginning of the end for the Federalist Party.

All references to Bradbury's time in the House suggest that he said very little. He was characterized as a "rich conservative patriotic country squire," an "unobtrusive backbencher," "quiet as a church mouse." While he undoubtedly took his responsibility seriously, he was not known to be a great orator. There are no records of any speeches. The voice in the House for New Hampshire came from a young lawyer from Portsmouth named Daniel Webster.

Webster honed his legal and debating skills in courtroom battles with the most famous lawyer in New Hampshire at the time, Jeremiah Mason, who represented New Hampshire in the U.S. Senate during Bradbury's terms in Washington. Webster, who primarily represented shipping interests, was a strong advocate of states' rights and an opponent of Jefferson's embargo and later Madison's war.

During the war New Hampshire returned a Federalist to the Governor's Office, but by 1816, with the war over, Plumer was back in office. America, the new member of the world community, had demonstrated that it could stand up for itself, and for the first time in its history a period of peace and economic prosperity settled over the country. The war party had prevailed and the peace party was fading. In the 1816 elections, Bradbury and his colleagues were voted out of office. The Federalist cause in New Hampshire was not helped when Webster decided the grass was greener next door and moved to Massachusetts.

In the 1816 presidential election, another Virginian, James Monroe, defeated Rufus King from Massachusetts and received all of New Hampshire's electoral votes. The state honored Joseph Cilley for his service during the war by selecting him to take New Hampshire's electoral votes for Monroe to Washington. Monroe was the first American president, and the last of the founding generation, to take office without the threat of war looming over his administration, and he guided the country through a period typically referred to as the Era of Good Feelings. Monroe was always concerned about the development of political parties, and had hoped during his administration to discourage their proliferation, but he failed. With the fading of the Federalist Party, a split was developing in the Democratic-Republican Party.

In 1816 the *New Hampshire Patriot*, from a decidedly Democratic-Republican point of view, drew a clear distinction between their favored ideology (vigilance and liberty, economy and national prosperity: "Moderate salaries, no unnecessary Taxes, no shackles to freedom, no arbitrary restraints on the rights of conscience, manful resistance to all foreign encroachment, a flourishing treasury, free trade and no impressments") and that of the fading Federalists (expensive government and royalty, enervation and slavery: "Exorbitant salaries, PERPETUAL Direct Taxes, a sedition law to abridge the liberty of speech and of the press, a law religion that shall compel all denominations to support the standing order, submission to foreign insults, a continually accumulating national debt—in fine, a government with all the tinsel and trappings of monarchy").

In early America, education was believed to be of paramount importance in order to ensure an informed and knowledgeable electorate. Nottingham was no exception in valuing the importance of education. Zephaniah Butler had been one of the town's first teachers. By the time Jonathan was ready to begin his education, there was a school on the Square. It would have been in this local school, along with the children of his large extended family, that he received his early education.

Having gotten all he could from the school in Nottingham, Jonathan left in 1820 to attend Atkinson Academy, in Atkinson, New Hampshire, about twenty-five miles from Nottingham. His brother Joseph had previously attended Atkinson. The school was established in 1787 and was one of the few co-educational academies in New England. It was considered a preparatory school for those who aspired to attend Harvard or Dartmouth, and the curriculum was in line with the admission requirements of those schools. Incoming college students at that time needed to demonstrate that they had the ability "to write Latin grammatically," as well as be "versed in Geography, and Welch's Arithmetic, Cicero's Select Orations, the Bulculus, Georgics, and Aeneid of Virgil, Sallust, the Greek Testaments, and Collectanea Grarca Minora." This was a college preparatory curriculum that would overwhelm today's high school students, but it was typical of the expectations of students entering college in the early nineteenth century. Some training in the social graces, such as dance—an interest right up to the night before Jonathan's death—was also part of the curriculum.

It was while Jonathan was at Atkinson that the initial letters found in the Cilley collection began. The few letters that survived were to his younger sister Elizabeth, in which he told her generally how he spent his day. He lived in a boarding house with six or seven other students and at least one faculty member. His days started early and were full of academics as well as the daily responsibility of household chores. Jonathan was not at Atkinson by himself. Also with him during his first year were two cousins. One was identified as Walker, but he was not a Cilley. The other was Enoch, the son of Jonathan's uncle Jacob. Sadly, Enoch died in December 1820 at the age of nineteen. Another blow to Jonathan, another death, although it was never mentioned in any of his letters.

While at Atkinson Jonathan had his first formal opportunity to develop his debating skills as a member of the school's debating society. This group met regularly to debate topics ranging from abstract issues such as honor versus shame and courage versus fortitude to topics of a contemporary nature, such as whether one's representative should vote according to his own will or that of his constituents.

Jonathan's opportunity to attend Atkinson would not have been possible without the financial support of his Uncle Bradbury, who paid all of Jonathan's expenses. In his last letter to Elizabeth, dated June 1821, just before leaving Atkinson, he noted his appreciation when he said, "To him I owe almost as much love and gratitude as I do a parent. The one indeed gave me an existence and support, but this was in some respects an act of duty. The other has of his own accord, put me in the way of obtaining that which can only make life honorable and truly worth processing."

With his education at Atkinson completed, the next step was college. The usual progression for New Hampshire young men was to attend either Dartmouth or Harvard, but Jonathan's choice was Bowdoin College, in the new state of Maine. The connection to Bowdoin came from more than one direction, but the main connection probably came from his Uncle Bradbury's friendship with Jeremiah Mason, who was in the U.S. Senate when Bradbury was in Congress. Mason's wife was the sister of Bowdoin president Jesse Appleton's wife, and Mason's son was also planning to attend Bowdoin.

During Jonathan's formative years, duels among some of America's most prominent men made the newspaper headlines. The most famous duel that occurred during Jonathan's young years was between Alexander Hamilton and Aaron Burr in 1804. Hamilton, who had been one of the authors of the *Federalist Papers* and America's first secretary of the Treasury, was back in New York with Jefferson, who was now president. Burr was vice president, but Jefferson was not going to support him for a second term, so Burr was looking to run for governor of New York. Hamilton and Burr had been in constant conflict for fifteen years, always avoiding a duel. Hamilton did not hesitate to let anyone who listened know that Burr was not worthy of being New York's governor. When Burr heard that Hamilton had made some particularly disparaging remarks about his (Burr's) character, he had had enough and wrote to Hamilton demanding an explanation. After a series of letters, Burr was not satisfied with Hamilton's responses and believed that he had no choice but to issue a challenge, which Hamilton quickly accepted. The two men met in Weehawken, New Jersey, on July 11. Hamilton did not wish to kill Burr, so he intentionally missed, but Burr's aim was sure and Hamilton was struck in the abdomen. He died the next day.

Hamilton was intimately aware of the risks of dueling. His son, Phillip, had been killed in a duel in 1801 over a trivial matter. Hamilton, while in theory opposed to dueling, believed he had no alternative but to accept. If he refused (or so his thinking went), his public image and usefulness would forever be destroyed.

In the same month in which Jonathan was born, DeWitt Clinton, then a U.S. senator from New York, was challenged to a duel by John Swartwort, a political ally of Aaron Burr. In a squabble over political patronage Clinton called Swartwort "a liar, a scoundrel, and a villain"—all words that called into question a man's honor. Thus Swartwort demanded satisfaction.

Like Hamilton and Burr, the two men met in Weehawken. Standing ten yards apart, they exchanged shots five times. After each exchange, Swartwort refused, as the offended person, to acknowledge satisfaction. On the fourth shot he was hit in the leg and on the fifth hit in the ankle. He was still not willing to quit, but Clinton, believing he had done enough damage, walked off the field. Clinton later became mayor of New York City and a candidate for president in 1812, and then governor of New York.

William Crawford, an 1824 presidential candidate, was involved in two well-documented duels during his early years in Georgia politics. As a young lawyer, Crawford moved to Georgia from Virginia. He quickly became involved in the local political scene as a Jefferson supporter, which was extremely confrontational and aggressive and where affairs of honor were a regular occurrence. In 1802, Peter Van Alen, a henchman of

General John Clark, challenged Crawford to a duel. Clark was famous for his actions during the Revolutionary and Indian wars and was asserting himself into Georgia politics. Crawford was reluctant to be drawn into a duel, but assumed the challenge was part of a conspiracy to force him out of the political arena. If he refused the duel, he believed his political career would be over. Crawford accepted the challenge and Van Alen was killed on the second shot.

Clark was not done with Crawford, and in December 1804, after Clark had accused Crawford of misusing his position to win favor for a relative, Crawford challenged Clark. Friends mediated the dispute and a duel was averted, but the animosity continued. Two years later they were back on the dueling grounds. This time Crawford received a disabling wound to his wrist. Clark, still not satisfied, again challenged Crawford in July 1807. Crawford declined, citing the terms agreed upon for the previous meeting. Crawford soon thereafter was appointed to the U.S. Senate and went to on be a minister to France, as well as secretary of the Treasury under both Madison and Monroe, before running for president.

The most notorious duelist and brawler of this period was Andrew Jackson. Estimates have suggested that he was involved in over one hundred altercations, shootouts, and duels over the course of his life. He was a man who took quick offense and would not back down from anyone. At the time Jackson married his wife Rachel, they believed she was divorced from her previous husband, but in fact she was not. The whole matter was straightened out a few years later, but disparaging remarks about Rachel's immoral behavior were something Jackson would not tolerate. In 1803 he got into a dispute with John Sevier, Tennessee's first governor, over who should be appointed to lead the state militia. During one confrontation Sevier commented that the only notable thing Jackson had done was to marry another man's wife. Jackson naturally pulled out his pistol and shots were exchanged in the street.

In 1806 Jackson was involved in a dispute in Nashville over a horse race with Charles Dickinson. Dickinson called Jackson a worthless scoundrel and a coward. He made some remarks about Mrs. Jackson as well. Jackson responded with a duel challenge. When they met, Dickinson fired first with no noticeable results; no one realized that Jackson had been shot in the chest. By the rules Dickinson was required to stand and receive Jackson's shot. Jackson coolly aimed at Dickinson, but his pistol misfired. He re-cocked his gun and fired again, killing Dickinson. Dickinson's bullet remained in Jackson's chest for the rest of his life, and it always affected his overall health. Ever after, Jackson's opponents labeled him a cold-blooded murderer, and the affair would follow Jackson for his entire political career, used as an example of his callous character.

In 1813, Thomas Hart Benton, later a long-term influential U.S. senator from Missouri (along with his brother Jesse), was involved in a shootout in a Nashville hotel with Jackson. Jackson, along with some friends, got in a dispute with the Benton brothers, and Jackson threatened to horsewhip Tom. When Jackson encountered them on the streets he pulled out his horsewhip, pistols were drawn, shots were fired, and Jackson received a severe wound to his left arm. So, along with a bullet in his chest, he now had a severely damaged left arm.

Benton was back in action a few years later, this time with Charles Lucas, a Missouri lawyer. The conflict arose during a trial in 1816 where they ended up calling each other liars in court. Things continued to fester into 1817, when Benton accused Lucas of spreading false rumors during a political campaign. Lucas then challenged Benton to a duel. They met in August on a sandbar in the Mississippi River that carried the label Bloody Island because of its frequent use as a dueling location. Armed with pistols at thirty paces, both men were wounded. Lucas wanted to decrease the distance to ten paces but changed his mind. Their conflicts continued, and they were back on Bloody Island on September 27. This time Lucas was killed, in what newspapers called an honorable murder.

Henry Clay, in 1809, when he was in the Kentucky legislature, got into a dispute with Humphrey Marshall, an outspoken member of the legislature. Clay had proposed a bill that would require members of the legislature to wear only suits made of American cloth. Marshall objected, and in the ensuing debate he called Clay a liar. Clay, his honor thus offended, issued a challenge. The combatants met on the shore of the Ohio River. Three shots were exchanged, and both men left with minor injuries.

# THREE

## Bowdoin Years

On a fall morning in September 1821, Jonathan left New Hampshire and his family on Nottingham Square and headed for Bowdoin College in Brunswick, Maine. He traveled to Maine in a mail coach that regularly traveled between Maine and Boston. There were three other young men in that coach, who were also heading to Brunswick. Franklin Pierce was returning to Bowdoin for his sophomore year. Jonathan would have been familiar with Pierce, because Pierce's father, Benjamin, was involved in New Hampshire politics. Also riding in the coach was the future author Nathaniel Hawthorne. The third passenger was Alfred Mason, who would be Hawthorne's roommate.

Horatio Bridge, a member of the Bowdoin class of 1825 and a lifelong friend of Hawthorne, noted in his *Personal Recollections of Nathaniel Hawthorne* that the coach was pulled "by strong, spirited horses, and bowling along at the average speed of ten miles an hour. The exhilarating pace, the smooth roads, and the juxtaposition of the insiders tended in a high degree, to the promotion of enjoyment and good fellowship which might ripen into lasting friendships." Jonathan, Hawthorne, and Pierce did become life-long friends.

Bowdoin's class of 1825 has long been considered one of the more eminent classes to graduate from Bowdoin. In addition to Hawthorne, this class included Henry Wadsworth Longfellow. Three members, including Jonathan, would become members of the U.S. House of Representatives, and one would become a member of the U.S. Senate. As one of

Hawthorne's biographers has suggested, "there must have been quite a fermentation of youthful intellect at Bowdoin between 1821 and 1825."

Early in his first year Jonathan made an impression on one of his fellow freshmen. George Washington Pierce from Maine commented in a November 1821 letter that he saw two members of his class being noteworthy. The first was Josiah Little, who in 1841 and 1856 would be Speaker of the Maine House of Representatives. He then remarked that "Cilley is also a fine fellow, some think he will get the first part [be at the top of his class]."

After Jonathan's death, those who knew him during his Bowdoin years remembered him from a variety of perspectives. Hawthorne described him as not being a prominent scholar at the top of his class, but as someone who "probably derived all the real benefit from the prescribed course of study that it could bestow on so practical a mind." John Abbott, another member of the class of 1825, and later a minister, remembered Jonathan "as a young man of exceeding ambition" and as having "great powers over others." He further commented that Jonathan "was not a man of high moral instinct. But he led the class. If he wished to win anyone to his side he would take his arm, and the work was done." He seemed to be describing Jonathan as someone who could, in a sense, twist someone's arm to get the person to side with him, although the person would not be aware that his arm was being twisted.

In addition to Jonathan's leadership skill, Hawthorne wrote that in interpersonal relationships Jonathan "possessed a remarkable fascination. It was impossible not to regard him with the kindliest feelings, because his companions were intuitively certain on a like kindliness of his part." Jonathan was seen as having a strong capacity for empathy "which enabled him to understand every character, and hold communion with human nature in all its varieties." He enjoyed talking to people and was always eager to interact with others—a trait that in the long run would enhance his popularity even among those of a different political ideology.

Brunswick, Maine, settled in 1627, lies alongside the south bank of the Androscoggin River and about twenty-seven miles north of Portland, Maine's largest city. In the 1820s approximately 3,500 people lived in Brunswick. There were numerous sawmills as well as cotton and woolen mills. Bowdoin College today is at the heart of Brunswick. It is one of the foremost small liberal arts colleges in the country, with a large campus and over 1,600 students. By contrast, when Jonathan entered Bowdoin, the campus was made up of just three buildings, a chapel, and the president's house all to accommodate its roughly 150 students. The campus was situated in the southeast corner of the town, and it was described as "a hideously ugly college set in surroundings of great beauty and charm."

Jonathan, in a letter home, described the Brunswick area as "one of the most pleasant, delightful, barren and dusty places that I have ever seen. The dust, when agitated by the wind, sweeps in clouds along the street, veiling all in obscurity and driving like snow into the windows."

> Just back of the College buildings, the plains which are perfectly level and extended two miles, are shaded with a fine grove of pine fir and spruce with very little or no underbrush. The soil, though not fertile, produces the greatest abundance of blue-berries, which are now ripe, and although the pigeons are, comparatively speaking as numerous as grasshoppers in harvest time, and although the students peruse and pick them off with eagerness and avidity of a flock of turkeys, yet the former do not lessen the number of blueberries, nor the latter in the number of pigeons. Nothing can indeed be more delightful than this grove, if I may so call it, which affords such coolness and shaded for those who wish to walk, so much game for those who wish to recreate themselves with a gun, and such abundance of the most delicious kind of plums for those who wish to gratify the palette.

From his description of the landscape around the Bowdoin campus, one can see that Jonathan had an appreciation of nature and the calmness and quiet it could provide. This environment was reminiscent of his boyhood home on the hill in rural New Hampshire.

At age nineteen, Jonathan was one of the oldest of the thirty-eight entering freshmen, for it was not uncommon for students entering college to be as young as thirteen. Half of his class was sixteen or younger. Longfellow was fourteen, while Hawthorne was seventeen. With Jonathan being older and likely more physically developed than his classmates, it would make sense that he would gravitate toward a leadership role.

Given the youthful age of many of the young men on campus, there was an expectation on the part of the families of these students that the college administration would exercise a good deal of control over their children's daily lives. This was expressed in a letter written to one of the faculty members by Longfellow's father, who explained that his sons,

Henry and Stephen, were "rather too young to encounter the temptations of a college life, without being under the immediate care of a father, or friend who would stand *in loco parentis.*"

With Jonathan being older than most of the other students and already having had experience living away from home, he was probably somewhat less prone to the excesses of youthful enthusiasm. It should be assumed, however, that Jonathan was not totally unlike the typical student. While he never got into any serious trouble for his behavior, he was not above unwinding during breaks from study and getting involved in a few of the student pranks. He described the rigors of college as filled with "uniformity and sameness" and offering "little variety of matter or incident." There were opportunities to play tricks "on some unpopular student, on officers of government, or upon the doughty yogger-hammers who dwell by the riverside round about the factories," and occasionally "making a bonfire or cutting off the bell rope." He also noted that students seldom mixed with the local people, and that should one of the college boys be seen with a young lady from the town, it would likely be "made the talk of half the old women in the village."

*In loco parentis* was the order of the day at Bowdoin in the 1820s. The faculty attempted to exert control over the lives of their charges across three segments of student behavior; religious, academic, and social. During Jonathan's time, the control came through the Executive Government (faculty), who met regularly to discuss student behavior and issue consequences. Fortunately for the researcher interested in the lives of the young men who passed through Bowdoin, meticulous minutes of these meetings were taken and still exist. At the first level, an in-depth system of fines was available to be assessed over a wide range of misbehaviors. The fines typically ranged from three cents to a dollar. More severe transgressions could result in having the guilty student apologize for his behavior in front of the whole faculty and student body. Various forms of suspension were also available for those who amassed an abundance of infractions.

Indeed, the life of the student was quite rigorous, and the days were full. Possibly because the Bowdoin campus was so isolated, students had no choice but to submit to the arduous academic demands of college life. Each day began before sunrise in the unheated chapel and also ended in the evening with chapel. Attendance at chapel was mandatory and fines for improper behavior during chapel could be expected. A particular concern was the habit of students falling asleep during services. Of the six fines incurred by Jonathan while at Bowdoin, four were related to chapel. The worst was a fifty-cent fine for "sleeping at public worship." He was also absent from prayer or public worship on three occasions. His friends, Hawthorne and Horatio Bridge, on one occasion were each fined twenty-five cents for "walking unnecessarily on the Sabbath." After morning chapel there was a one-hour recitation before breakfast and then study hours from 9 a.m. to 12 p.m. Study hours also went from 2 p.m. to 5 p.m. The day ended with prayers again before the evening meal. For Jonathan, it was likely, given his minimal religious background, that this part of his education was not something he valued, but something he tolerated.

Unlike today, with e-mail and our ability to travel from Bowdoin to Nottingham in about two hours, in the early 1820s the distance was formidable and the mail moved slowly. When one was away from home and family for long periods of time, the letters from those at home were anxiously awaited. His years on the Square among his large family and circle of friends forever bound him to home. Throughout the course of his student life he tried to get home at least once a year. At one point while at Bowdoin he talked about walking home, a walk that would certainly take three or four days. On another occasion he said he could come home if someone would send him money to cover the cost of the trip. Even though he was occupied with his life at Bowdoin, he at times, in his letters, sounded lonely and was "heart sick" when he would trudge through the snow and slush to the post office and ask, "Is there a letter for me?" only to receive the reply "No Sir." While the surviving letters are mostly to his youngest sister Elizabeth, it was apparent that he expected his letters to be shared with the other family members. He also communicated regularly with his brother Joseph, and probably his uncles, as well as other family members and friends. Unfortunately, those letters have not survived.

When they had time away from their studies, the young men at Bowdoin in the 1820s were not unlike college men of today. Being on the cusp between adolescence and adulthood, they were eager to push the limits, to do what was forbidden, to enjoy the pleasures of drink, smoking, gambling, and possibly the company of young women who would not be seen as having the highest moral character. A student could be fined for playing cards for money, smoking cigars on the streets, or associating in

Brunswick or Topsham with any person of known "dissolute morals." Jonathan's friend Franklin Pierce, during his first two years at Bowdoin, was described as being "somewhat of a playboy," and by the end of his sophomore year he was at the bottom of his class. Hawthorne was fined in July 1823 for being at a tavern. William Pitt Fessenden, later a senator from Maine and secretary of the Treasury for Abraham Lincoln, was fined for "irregularity of eating and drinking at Wardsworth Tavern without permission." The Wardsworth Tavern was a very popular place with students, and it is quite likely that Jonathan found his way there, probably in the company of Hawthorne. It was also a place with which the faculty had lost all patience. In July 1823 the faculty voted "that students be prohibited from frequenting the house of Mr. Wadsworth— a tavern keeper in Brunswick, and from calling there on any pretense whatsoever."

Because the faculty looked disparagingly on the students frequenting local taverns, groups of students formed their own clubs, typically on the pretext that the club was a dining group or one that purported to foster some type of learned activity. The faculty was always alert to the formation of these clubs and believed, probably rightly, that they were fronts for drinking, smoking, and other activities upon which the faculty would have frowned. During Jonathan's early years at Bowdoin, an organization called the Law Club had a short existence and was prohibited when the faculty ruled in October 1822 that "whereas there exists in College a Club recently established called the Law Club, which society, to the dishonor of the college, held a meeting on Saturday evening last, at which meeting liquors of various kind were drunk, and whereas the tendency of the Society appears both from its constitution and the manner of conducting it to be unfavorable to science and morality."

Hawthorne, along with Jonathan and four other classmates (Alfred Mason, George W. Pierce, Jeremiah Drummer, and David Shepley), established their own club: the Pot-8-Club. Part of the challenge for these young men was to create a club or group that, on the one hand, would give them an excuse to socialize and share some forbidden beverages while, on the other hand, putting something over on the administration. The club's constitution, handwritten by Hawthorne, began with these words: "We the undersigned subscribers being convinced that it is beneficial both to the health and understanding of Man, to use vegetable diet, and considering that the Potatoe is nutritious, easy of digestion, and procured with less difficulty and expense than most other vegetables do hereby agree to form ourselves into an association under the name of the Pot-8-O Club."

The group would meet once a week with a menu that was required to include "roasted Potatoes, Butter, Salt, and Cider or some other mild drink." A hint, perhaps, to the underlying and main purpose of the club lay in the phrase that Hawthorne wrote (and underlined) in the text: "but ardent spirits shall never be introduced." At each meeting one member was required to present "an original dissertation or poem," and if the assigned individual did not come prepared, he was fined "a peck of Potatoes." The presentation requirement, given the social nature of the club, was certainly not difficult to fulfill, since all that was required was fourteen lines. Any fines imposed on members were undoubtedly used to acquire more "ardent spirits." Hawthorne, along with Jonathan and others, also founded another group called the Androscoggin Club that was "dedicated to card playing and drinking."

While Hawthorne's closest friend through college was Horatio Bridge, he also had a strong friendship with Jonathan. He was said to have looked up to and admired Jonathan, seeing him as an older brother and as someone with whom he could talk freely. After the Bowdoin years Jonathan would be quoted as saying that he loved and admired Hawthorne but thought that he kept his real thoughts and feelings at bay. Given Jonathan's noted ability to put people at ease, he and Bridge were able to get the closest to the standoffish Hawthorne.

Both Jonathan and Hawthorne took pleasure in the rural, open nature of the Brunswick area, and when the opportunity presented itself they would walk, berry pick, hunt, or fish. Jonathan described for Elizabeth an occasion during a vacation when he and Hawthorne went fishing on the Androscoggin River and caught "between forty and fifty fish apiece," and then enjoyed some of the fish the next morning for breakfast. Jonathan also took time for "gunning," which was his favorite pastime.

As has always been the case, not all students had the financial resources to cover the total cost of their education. Jonathan's family had limited resources, but it is believed that Uncle Bradbury, as he had done for Atkinson, contributed a large part of the money that was needed for Jonathan's education at Bowdoin. Even with this, letters home during his time at Bowdoin reveal that Jonathan's mother and his brother Joseph sent him money. One way Jonathan earned additional money to cover his expenses was to teach school during breaks from college. This was a common practice throughout New England, and a good way for towns to staff their schools.

In December 1823 Jonathan started teaching in the town of Topsham, Maine. He wrote Elizabeth that he had "procured a school and entered upon the duties of a pedagogue this morning. The school is in Topsham Village, about a mile and a quarter from College." He obviously was surprised by his reception:

> There were fifty scholars came to me today and ten of fifteen will be added to the number in a few days. And a more noisy and roguish set of little urchins never had existence. I let them have their own way this morning for some time without saying a word to them. And such a higgledy-piggledy, hurly-burly and harrum-scarrum as there was, you nor nobody else in the world but myself ever saw or heard of. But pretty soon I put on a dignified school master look and with as much authority and importance as I could crowd into one-word I demanded "Silence" nodding my head as little as was natural.

The reaction to his demand was as follows:

> The little whitehead urchins not much higher that the pen I am writeing with, turned out the white of the eye and glared at me with sort of a vacant stare, whilst the larger ones eyed me archly and with keen and scrutizing looks to the intent that they might read some thing in my countenance where by they might discover what kind of an animal their new master would be to deal with.

Jonathan must have adjusted to teaching, and his students to him, for he returned to teach the next year.

A notable component of the curriculum in the colleges and universities during the 1820s was the development of the students' skills in public speaking and debate. Daniel Howe, in his recent book *What Hath God Wrought*, where he examined the transformations that occurred in America between 1815 and 1848, noted that in male society at that time "elocution was practiced as an art form and oratory constituted a branch of literature." All those who described Jonathan during his time at Bowdoin commented on his oratorical and debating skills. Hawthorne recalled that Jonathan had a "free and natural eloquence" that allowed "a flow of pertinent ideas, in a language of unstudied appropriateness, which seemed always to accomplish precisely the result on which he had calculated."

Opportunities to hone his debate skills came in "class-meetings when measures, important to those concerned were under discussion." There were mock trials where Jonathan, "played the part of a fervid and successful advocate." Hawthorne went on to relate, "Nothing could be less artificial than his style of oratory." And "After filling his mind with the necessary information, he trusted every thing else to his mental warmth and the inspiration of the moment, and poured himself out with an earnest irresistible simplicity." These traits in his friend were aspects of Jonathan's personality of which Hawthorne stood in awe. These types of interactions and debates were occasions that Jonathan relished but Hawthorne did not enjoy, was uncomfortable with, and would, if given the chance, avoid.

Another arena in which Jonathan had the opportunity to develop and sharpen his verbal and debating skills came through his involvement with the Athenaen Society, an organization he joined his freshman year. During Jonathan's stay at Bowdoin, the Athenaen Society was one of two societies that competed for members. The other was the Peucinian Society, which was the older of the two. The Athenaen Society was formed in 1808 by a disgruntled Peucinian. The purpose of these literary societies was to promote intellectual interchange among members as well as to provide opportunities for social interaction. Both groups had their own libraries. They were basically the forerunners of modern-day fraternities.

Each society had its own personality and drew different types of members. The Peucinian members tended to be more urban, stiff, and aristocratic. Politically, they were more likely to identify themselves as Federalists and later National Republicans. They were also somewhat stifled by having faculty actively involved. To modern readers, it sounds like they were a group of young men who were rather scholarly and did not have much fun. In sharp contrast were the Athenaens, who tended to come from a more rural background and were described as rowdy and more dissident. Politically, they gravitated toward the developing Democratic Party and supported Andrew Jackson for president in 1824. Along with Jonathan, other Athenaens were Hawthorne, Pierce, Bridge, Fessenden, and Stephen Longfellow, Henry's older and rowdier brother. Longfellow was a Peucunian, as were Mason and G. W. Pierce. It was within the Athenaen Society that Jonathan "regularly trained himself in forensic debate" and developed into a campus leader.

It is unlikely that Jonathan spent much time with Henry W. Longfellow. They belonged to different societies, and Longfellow by all accounts was a rather serious and diligent student. Abbott recalled Longfellow as "then a poet of no mean note—very handsome, always well dressed, with no taste for any but refined pleasure." This was not Jonathan. A Longfellow biographer described Jonathan from what could be Longfellow's perspective as one of "unquestionable genius" and speculated that, had Jonathan not "indulged in habits . . . into which he was drawn by his fine social qualities," he may have placed much higher in his class ranking. Jonathan did, however, reach the upper tier of his class and graduated *phi beta kappa*.

As they moved into their junior year, in the fall of 1824, the topic of women and marriage came up in conversations between Jonathan and Hawthorne, as well as others. Given Hawthorne's shy and reserved nature, Jonathan teased Hawthorne about the likelihood of his ever getting married. What came out of these conversations was a bet. The bet was whether Hawthorne would be married ten years from the day of the wager, November 14, 1836. Jonathan bet that Hawthorne would be married or a widower by the appointed date, and if he were not, Jonathan would provide Hawthorne with a "barrel of the best old Madeira wine," but if Hawthorne was indeed married or a widower at that time, he would owe Jonathan the barrel of Madeira. The written wager was given to Horatio Bridge with the following instructions: "If Hathorne [how he spelled his name at the time] is married within the time specified he shall transmit intelligence to him [Bridge] immediately. And the bet, whoever shall lose it, shall be paid within a month after the expiration of the time." Bridge faithfully kept the unopened bet until November 1836.

When Jonathan entered Bowdoin, James Monroe was heading into his second term as president and the country was in the period labeled the "Era of Good Feelings." Monroe had nearly unanimous support throughout the country's now nineteen states, with the exception being one New Hampshire elector who cast his vote for John Quincy Adams. The 1820 election was the first for the newest state, Maine, and all their electoral votes went to Monroe. During his years at Bowdoin, Jonathan continued to maintain his interest in politics, regularly reading, when he could get them, both Maine and New Hampshire newspapers, and he encouraged family members to keep him abreast of the political scene in New Hampshire. There was only occasional mention of politics in his letters to his sister, but he without doubt discussed political affairs with his brother, cousins, and uncles.

A hot topic debated on campus throughout the fall of 1824 was the upcoming presidential election. With Monroe concluding his two terms, a new president would be elected. The two leading candidates were John Quincy Adams, supported by the Peucinians, and Andrew Jackson, supported by the Athenaens; also in the race were Kentuckian Henry Clay, Speaker of the House of Representatives, and William Crawford of Georgia, who was serving as Monroe's secretary of the Treasury. Crawford had narrowly lost out to Monroe for their party's presidential nomination in 1816.

J. Q. Adams, son of the country's second president John Adams, was highly educated and intelligent, and he had spent his formative years in Europe with his father, who was acting as an American envoy to France and later the Netherlands. Because of his proficiency in French, at age fourteen J. Q. Adams headed to the Russian court in St. Petersburg to serve as interpreter and private secretary for newly appointed envoy Francis Dana. After returning to the United States he attended Harvard; was minister to the Netherlands, Portugal, and Prussia; and served in the U.S. Senate. He only lasted one term in the Senate because he lost favor with Massachusetts Federalists by supporting Jefferson's Louisiana Purchase and the 1807 Embargo Act. During the Monroe administration he was secretary of state, the position that had been normally the stepping-stone to the presidency. General Andrew Jackson from Tennessee was most notably remembered for the victory at New Orleans against the British in 1815 to close out the War of 1812.

The election was close and had to be settled in the House of Representatives. While Jackson had the most popular votes and the most votes in the Electoral College, they were not enough to give him an absolute majority. Adams ultimately carried the day when Henry Clay, knowing he could not win, urged his supporters to vote for Adams. With Adam's victory Clay then became secretary of state. The Jacksonites were outraged by what they called a "corrupt bargain," and the campaign to sabotage Adam's presidency and get Jackson elected in 1828 began as Adams was sworn into office. All of New England had supported Adams, although in Maine and also New Hampshire support for Jackson soon experienced a rapid rise.

Among the treasures found in the archives in the Bowdoin Library are the senior commencement compositions, handwritten by the graduating seniors. In this collection are two essays written by Jonathan. Both of these papers provide some insight into his thinking and beliefs, at this point of his life, concerning human nature and the nature of society. It would be hard for the modern student with a computer and spell check to appreciate the tremendous amount of work required to produce a final, neatly written, mistake-free, handwritten paper. For those looking to read Jonathan's subsequent writing, his handwriting unfortunately went downhill from here.

In his essay on fictional writing prepared for presentation at graduation, Jonathan discussed the role of the novel in the society of the 1820s, suggesting that the majority of people did not have the intellectual capacity to comprehend more learned or intellectual literature, and fiction would be the best vehicle to teach the masses. He used the example of the fable as a "vehicle of truth" and suggested that they could be used to illustrate "moral and political doctrines which the multitude could not in any other way so readily comprehend." He saw the common man as "not well-qualified for argument." He appeared to believe that the essence of human nature in his contemporary world was "a thing of petty interests, selfish, overreaching, deceitful and perishable." He also appeared to see the common man as not very bright or virtuous. For him, the author of the novel could produce characters that could inculcate by example virtue, goodness, greatness, and heroism. Additionally, Jonathan implied that to escape into fiction would be an appropriate and valued way to temporarily escape the negative reality of basic human nature. Here we get an early glimpse from Jonathan that the world outside academia may be a harsh place.

A second, more consequential composition written by Jonathan in 1824 was titled "Satirical Compositions," where he began by commenting that "the strongest barrier, perhaps against the inroads of vice, among the more cultivated part of our species, is well directed ridicule. They, who fear nothing else, dread to be marked out and exposed to the contempt and indignation of the world." He further advanced the idea that "to expose to the world, therefore, the false pretensions of counterfeit virtue, is to disarm it at once of all power of mischief, and to perform a public service of the most advantageous kind." He went on to say that the use of satire had generally been thought of as "a sort of supplement to the legislative authority of the country, as assisting the unavoidable defects of all legal institutions for regulating morals, and striking terror even where the divine prohibitions are held in contempt. The object, which satirical writing professes to have in view, is information of manners. To accomplish this it assumes the liberty of boldly and publicly censuring and ridiculing the prevailing of vices and follies of the ages."

Jonathan then credited Cervantes and Don Quixote with being responsible for the end of the "extravagances of chivalry and knighterantry." He followed this with a wish and ultimately a very prophetic desire that "may we not hope, that at no very distant period, a Cervantes may arise in our own country, who, in a similar manner, consigning, to undying ridicule and contempt the impious but fashionable practice of modern dueling, shall acquire an imperishable fame, and be hailed as the benefactor and reformer of this age?"

He went on to suggest that satire had a role in monitoring the behavior of public officials: "All public men, however distinguished, must in their turn submit to it if necessary to the welfare of the state. The altar and the throne, the minister and the statesman, may feel and own its influence. Honest satire is always the patroness of virtue and the avenger of vice, and as such it will ever prove a powerful and successful instrument, in maintaining and enforcing public order, morality, religion, and good manners, in those cases, in which the pulpit and the courts of law can seldom interfere and rarely with effect." Unfortunately for Jonathan, as his political career progressed he did not fall victim to much satire, but rather to attacks which were direct and personal.

During the time that Jonathan was at Bowdoin, there is no information to suggest what he had planned to do when he left college. In March 1825, he was annoyed because his brother Joseph had got married at a time when Jonathan was unable to attend. He wanted to be sure that his sisters, both of whom intended to be married soon, planned their weddings when he was home. He wrote that they should "wait if not too impatient, till I graduate, and there I shall be, the Lord only knows where, I don't." So six months before graduation he was up in the air about his future, and possibly contemplating returning to Nottingham.

It was likely that he talked with his friends at Bowdoin who also needed to make decisions about their own futures, and he would have likely corresponded with his brother and uncles about post-graduation plans. It would be safe to assume that he did have some sense of what he wanted to do, and therefore it would not be surprising that he would move toward a career in law, given his proclivity for argument and debate. He certainly had, during his years at Bowdoin, developed a reputation as a leader and as a young man with sound skills in persuasiveness and debate. It is unclear whether he had choices or had actively sought out lawyers under whom he could study law.

The only record of the choice he pursued came from the letters he received from John Ruggles, a Thomaston, Maine, lawyer who offered Jonathan the opportunity to come to Thomaston to study law and help with Ruggles's new newspaper, the *Thomaston Register*. At some time prior to graduation Ruggles had talked with a B. F. Deane, who must in some way have been familiar with Jonathan's abilities and suggested to Ruggles that Jonathan might be interested in studying law. At some point Deane, in his conversations with Jonathan, likely gave him some information about Ruggles and Thomaston. Jonathan may have heard of Ruggles, given his interest in politics, and may also have known that Ruggles at that time was a member of the Maine House of Representatives. We do not know whether Jonathan had ever been to Thomaston or how much traveling he had done in Maine. Thomaston is about fifty miles from Brunswick. In one of his letters home he did mention that he had gone to the home of his roommate in Hallowell, Maine, in 1823 for Thanksgiving, so it is possible that Jonathan had been in Thomaston or done some traveling in the state.

Ruggles initially thought that he would be at Jonathan's Bowdoin graduation, but when he was unable to attend he made arrangements for Hezekiah Prince Jr., who was planning to attend the graduation, to bring Jonathan back to Thomaston. When Prince arrived in Brunswick on September 6, he met with Jonathan and gave him a letter from Ruggles. From a note in Prince's journal, it seems that he was not yet sure whether Jonathan had committed to come to Thomaston, but after the meeting it was clear he did intend to go. At that time Jonathan accepted Prince's invitation to travel back to Thomaston with him. This was the first meeting between these two men, who quickly became friends.

Bowdoin graduation was spread out over three days. Prince gave a firsthand and interesting description of the main graduation exercise. Apparently the graduation was very well attended and people lined up well in advance of the doors opening. There is no note that any of Jonathan's family attended. Prince related that "many hundred had collected at the doors and stood crowded together with their gallants in the midst of them like a vast flock of sheep when gathered before the shearer. It was absolutely disgusting to see delicate females and those, too, of the first respectability crowded and jammed and pushing and shoving like lusty fellows and keeping their stations near the door or endeavouring to obtain as near position as possible." He wrote that when the doors opened at 9:30 there was a rush, and "the utmost exertions of the several door keepers were hardly competent to regulate and prune the flood of ingression of many a tall, straight or comely lad which the flow of females bore along with it."

The graduation exercise did not start until 11:00. Prince noted that the meetinghouse was very crowded, and he also commented on the number of attractive young ladies in attendance. The exercises lasted about three hours. Seventeen of the graduates had speaking parts, one of whom was Jonathan, who presented his paper on "Fictitious Writing." There was a ball in the evening, at which Prince said there were 150 ladies present. Jonathan was likely at the ball, inasmuch as he was one of the managing organizers; however, Prince commented that because he was not feeling well, he did not attend. The next day there was an assembly for those members, including Jonathan, of the Phi Beta Kappa Society.

Hawthorne described Jonathan at the conclusion of his years at Bowdoin as being

> a young man of quick and powerful intellect; endowed with sagacity and tact, yet frank and free in his mode of action: ambitious of good influence, earnest, active, and preserving; with an elasticity and cheerful strength of mind which made difficulties easy, and the struggles with them a pleasure. Mingled with the amiable qualities that were like sunshine to his friends, there were harsher and sterner traits which fitted him to make headway against an adverse world; but it was only at the moment of need that the iron framework of his character became perceptible.

All of these positive and negative traits would be put to the test as Jonathan entered the world of politics.

At sunrise on the morning of September 9, 1825, Prince and Jonathan left Bowdoin for the long horse-and-buggy trip to Thomaston. On the way there was a stop in Bath, and later they stopped in Wiscasset for over an hour to visit Prince's seventeen-year-old sister, Deborah, who was a boarding student at Miss Tinkham's School for Young Ladies. This was

Jonathan's first encounter with the young woman who would in 1829 become his wife. The trip to Thomaston was long and Prince, who still was not feeling well, needed Jonathan to drive some of the way. After a long and tiring trip of eleven or twelve hours, they arrived in Thomaston as the sun was setting. Prince left Jonathan at the O'Briens' house, where he would be boarding; it was just three houses away from the Prince home. And thus Jonathan began in his new life and career in the downeast town of Thomaston, Maine.

# FOUR

## Thomaston Years

When Jonathan arrived in Thomaston, Maine, in the fall of 1825, it was a bustling, active, and prosperous seaport community, located about seventy-five miles up the rockbound coast from Portland. It sits about twelve miles up the St. George River at the end of one of the many fingerlike inlets along the Atlantic coast of Maine. It is also here that both the St. George and the Mill rivers merge and flow toward the ocean. Captain George Weymouth first explored the Thomaston area in 1605. What impressed him at that time was the large number of tall pine trees throughout the area, which, in his sailor's mind, would be ideal for the masts of English ocean-going sailing ships. Thus the Thomaston area quickly became a major source of the wood and masts for British ships.

By the time Jonathan arrived in Thomaston, the town, which bore the motto "The Town That Went to Sea," had become one of the main shipbuilding sites in the United States. At the time Thomaston had 3,500 residents and included the areas that would become the towns of Rockland and South Thomaston. By the time Jonathan left for Washington in 1837, the area had grown to 5,200 residents. The Thomaston area was also known for its extensive deposits of limestone, which was mined and then burned in numerous kilns throughout town to produce lime. An unfortunate side effect of this burning, in more than one hundred kilns in the Thomaston area, was significant air pollution, which undoubtedly impaired the overall health of those who lived there. The lime, however, became one of the major exports for Thomaston's shipping industry. In 1824 Thomaston also had the dubious distinction of being the new site for the Maine State Prison. It was built along the St. George River on land that had been purchased from former Governor King. The prison was built with local granite, and for a time the convicts were made to cut and prepare granite for shipping.

When Jonathan arrived in Thomaston in 1825 with Hezekiah Prince, the Prince family was well established. Hezekiah Prince Sr. had come to Thomaston in 1792 at the age of twenty-one. He left for a brief period to travel in the South but returned and settled permanently in Thomaston in 1794. He initially did construction work, mostly involved in building houses. Prince Sr. married Isabella Coombs, and they had ten children. Hezekiah Prince Jr. was born in 1800. In 1814 Prince Sr. built his house on Main Street in the Mill River area of Thomaston. He was a founding member of the Masonic Lodge in 1805 and was involved in the Temperance Society. During the War of 1812 he was responsible for the defenses of the area, believed to be necessary because British warships were patrolling the coast of Maine. Early on he dabbled in a number of businesses, including a cotton and wool mill as well as a shoe factory. In 1817 he was appointed deputy customs collector, a position he held until 1840. In 1821, with the help of Ruggles, he was appointed postmaster of Thomaston. At one point he served as a local judge and was involved in politics. He regularly served as a town selectman, at one point as a state senator, and he also served on the governor's Executive Council.

Hezekiah Prince Jr. was two years older than Jonathan, and the first male in the family. His education was limited to the local schools, but he always had an interest in books. From an early age he was plagued with rheumatoid arthritis, and periodically suffered significant flare-ups. One of his means of making a living was serving as the local customs inspector, likely working for his father. Later he became an insurance agent. Much of his journal writing was devoted to his activities on the Thomaston waterfront, providing an excellent picture of the busy and picturesque life on the docks of Thomaston. He noted that before Jonathan came to town, he spent a lot of time in Ruggles's law office, particularly during the times when Ruggles was away at the legislature or out of town at court. This served the purpose of keeping the law office open, and Prince collected fees and performed other tasks that Ruggles requested. Ruggles's office was also a place where the young men in town gathered in the evenings, regardless of whether Ruggles was in town.

While there were quite likely taverns in the town, they are not mentioned by either Prince or Jonathan.

Deborah was born in 1808, the fifth of the Prince children. Her father clearly valued education for women and when she was seventeen, after she completed local school, he sent her to Miss Tinkham's boarding school in Wiscasset. It was a popular school for the girls of Thomaston, where, in addition to regular academic subjects, the young women also received instruction in needlework, lace work, and painting on velvet.

The man under whom Jonathan was to study law, John Ruggles, came to Maine in 1817. He was originally from Westboro, Massachusetts, and graduated from Brown University in 1813. He moved to Skowhegan, Maine, in 1815 after studying law in Massachusetts. Two years later, at age twenty-six, he came to Thomaston, where he remained until his death in 1874. At one point he boarded at the Prince house. He was actively involved in local politics and was a regular member of the local school committee. He served in the Maine House of Representatives from 1824 through 1831. At the time of his first election to the House in September 1823, it would appear that he was not completely popular with all the Democrats in town. Prince wrote in his journal that there was "considerable excitement in this town with regard to the candidate for representative." And the old guard in particular was "straining every nerve to destroy his election." After his election, Prince commented that there were "many, very many sorry faces on account of Mr. Ruggles being elected."

The developing animosity within the local Democratic Party could in part be attributed to what was labeled the Post Office Affair. In 1821 J. D. Wheaton, who had been postmaster in Thomaston since the post office opened, was unexpectedly replaced by Prince Sr. While Wheaton had not been especially competent at his job, his friends saw him as a loyal Democrat and were infuriated by the change. They viewed Prince Sr. as someone who was already a successful businessman in Thomaston and therefore did not really need the job.

Because Ruggles had played a significant role in obtaining the position for Prince Sr., he also took a good amount of the blame, "which his political adversaries endeavored to make the most of." Prince Sr. had opened a store in the Mill River area, and the post office was located in the store. In 1823 a judge forced Prince Sr. to relinquish the postmastership back to Wheaton. Prince Sr., along with Ruggles, was also accused of taking money from the mail, and a court action was brought against them. In October 1824 they were exonerated by a jury, which reportedly deliberated for only five minutes. Prince concluded his comments about this affair by saying, "Thus is this subject which has caused so much excitement throughout this part of the country and by which a few individuals have endeavored to destroy Mr. Ruggles and my father, put to silence and by the investigation they have been honourably acquitted and their persecutors are viewed with the contempt they deserve."

The young men of the town, seeking to socialize and to discuss and debate issues of the day, formed a group called the Alpha Society. According to Prince, it was formed "for purposes of improvement in declamation, argument and other branches." They typically met weekly, often in one of the local schoolhouses. Prince and Ruggles were founding members. They debated issues that even today, 185 years later, continue to be of relevance. One question was "Is the great influx of foreigners beneficial to the United States?" After a lively discussion, the group decided that foreigners were not beneficial. Another topic deliberated was "Are the miseries of human life commensurate with its pleasures?" The conclusion in this case was that life's pleasures indeed outweighed its miseries. Meetings occasionally sparked the interest of the members of the community, and on one occasion, when the topic for debate was "Which is the most productive of happiness, anticipation or participation?" the schoolhouse was "filled with spectators—men, women and children." At the conclusion of the discussion, they voted in favor of anticipation.

In 1825, when Jonathan arrived in Thomaston, John Quincy Adams had just begun his term as president, and Prince believed the town was pleased with President Adams, even though Prince had originally preferred Andrew Jackson.

In January 1825 Ruggles was elected Speaker of the Maine House, a post in which he served through 1831, during all the sessions when the Democrats were in the majority. In March 1825 Ruggles partnered with Edwin Moody to establish a local newspaper called the *Thomaston Register*. Ruggles had editorial control and looked to Jonathan to assist with the newspaper, particularly during the time of the year when Ruggles was either sitting in the legislature or out of town at court. The first issue was printed on May 17, 1825. Initially the paper was politically neutral, but "under the editorial care of Mr. Cilley, it became a warm political paper in support of the Jackson's administration." Prince Sr. had added space to his store in order to accommodate the new printing press.

With his arrival in Thomaston, Jonathan opened a new chapter in his life, one that would significantly impact future events. In the 1820s the study of law involved a three-year apprenticeship under the supervision of a member of the local legal community, which typically involved "clerking in the office, copying legal documents, running errands, studying a few classics and whatever other books might be around, observing the business of the office." The apprentice typically paid a fee for the privilege of learning the profession. In Jonathan's case, Ruggles acknowledged that the local bar group frowned on any sort of atypical arrangement, but if the rules were not flagrantly violated, no one would pay any attention. Ruggles therefore agreed to waive the fee and compensate Jonathan up to $150 a year for editorial help with the *Register*, but Jonathan was urged to keep this arrangement to himself. The $150 could not cover all his expenses, and through his first three years in Thomason he continued to rely on family members for financial support, but he was occasionally chided for not acknowledging receipt of money. At one point, his brother Joseph suggested that if Jonathan was not more prompt with his acknowledgment, the money might stop. As an additional means of supplementing his income, Jonathan continued to teach school in the nearby town of Warren.

Jonathan quickly settled into his new life in Thomaston. Three days after his arrival the local Democratic Party held its September caucus, where, among others, Ruggles was reelected to the House of Representatives. Since the Princes and Ruggles were in attendance, one would assume this was Jonathan's first introduction to local politics. Prince played a significant role in introducing Jonathan to the community. Throughout his journal entries there are numerous references to the things he had done with Jonathan. He took him to a regimental muster, showed him the lime quarries, and included him in the social scene. Jonathan related that someone had taken him to a local meeting of the Masons, though he was not impressed with what he saw. He noted that there was "too much pomp and ceremony," and he thought that what he called the grand priest in his robes looked more like a "grand great fool than a reasonable being." It would appear that perhaps he was being encouraged by others, judging from this comment: "Silly said of Masonry, it may be a great deal better than it appears to be, and I hope it is." Still, there is no evidence that he ever became a member, even though his grandfather had been a Mason. It is likely that the formality and rituals of Masonry did not appeal to him.

One gets a glimpse of Jonathan's character and his compassion for others through his response to Prince when, in October 1825, Prince's arthritis flared up and he had serious difficulties with his knees, and for a time he was confined to home. Prince mentioned a number of times that Jonathan came to the house to spend time with him, just talking or playing checkers or chess with him. Prince wrote in his journal, "Mr. Cilley frequently calls and I esteem him very much. He is an excellent young man."

The young people of Thomaston had a very active social life. Groups of up to twenty or thirty couples, married and singles, regularly gathered for a variety of different activities. Balls were very popular. Two or three of the young gentlemen would serve as managers and make all the arrangements, and Jonathan was one of these managers on a regular basis. There were also picnics and berry-picking excursions; on occasion, they would find themselves a ship large enough for them all and then sail and party up and down the St. George River. In the winter, when there was enough snow, sleighing was popular.

As 1826 began, Ruggles was off to the House of Representatives in Portland, the last year before it moved to the new capital under construction in Augusta. That year the young men of Thomaston revived the Alpha Society, which had been dormant for a while, and Jonathan was elected its new president. One of the first topics discussed was "Are the mental capacities of women equal to those of men?" Jonathan concluded for the group that women's mental capacities were not equal to those of men. This is not to suggest that he in any way was demeaning of women, but when one looks at his letters it is apparent that he conversed with women on a different level than he did with men. He saw the societal roles of men and women as being different. While equal in many ways, men were the citizens, the political people, while a woman's place was in the home and her role was to be a good neighbor.

Jonathan's early years with Ruggles appear to have proceeded smoothly. Ruggles did not hesitate to involve Jonathan in the day-to-day office activities. He relied on Jonathan to manage the office and work on the newspaper, particularly when he was away in the legislature or at court. There are a number of letters from Ruggles to Jonathan that typically contained news of the politics of the day as well as instructions for things he wanted Jonathan to do regarding the law practice and direction on what to include in the *Register*. It would appear that Jonathan also had some responsibility to look after Mrs. Ruggles and to assist if needed or provide her with transportation. Their letters were cordial and business-like.

After only seven months boarding at the O'Briens, Jonathan felt he needed to find a new place to live. The reason he wanted to leave, he awkwardly explained to his sister, was because of Mrs. O'Brien's monthly mood change. He said that when she "was breeding," her disposition totally changed and she became "cross and ugly," and "instead of being a kind, submissive, and loving wife, she became by fits a real termagant and made the house quite too hot for any quiet people to live," so it was time to move. He related that he had discussed the issue with Ruggles, who had himself at one point boarded at the O'Briens' and had the same experiences. He added in his letter, "Pray God it may not have such an effect on my wife if I have one."

Jonathan immediately made an impression on the community, and after being in Thomaston for only ten months he was asked to give the annual speech at the Fourth of July celebration. The Fourth was a major local event—sometimes partisan, sometimes not. The year 1826 was especially noteworthy because it was the fiftieth anniversary of the signing of the Declaration of Independence. The festivities typically started with a large outdoor meeting, where one community leader would read the Declaration of Independence, and another would give a lengthy speech commemorating American independence. This was followed by a large community feast, often attended by people from both political parties, depending on the tenor of party politics in the town at the time. The day often ended with a ball. The honor of speaking on the Fourth had to have been highly satisfying for Jonathan, and it would have given him an opportunity to impress his new lady friend.

Jonathan believed that the Fourth should be a nonpolitical occasion. Writing about the Fourth of July celebrations to his Uncle Bradbury, he declared, "No American feelings should be outraged on the day of our Nation's Jubilee by ill humored allusions to present or past party differences. In the hour of peril the great of both parties were united heart and hand. On the day of rejoicing then why should not their descendants be of one mind and one feeling."

Jonathan spoke for about half an hour and kept with his view of honoring those who gave their all to reject what he termed enslavement by a foreign power. The speech was at times wordy and confusing to follow, though it received positive reviews in the local press, and it allowed Jonathan to hone his public speaking skills. In line with his belief that the celebration should honor those who fought politically and militarily to break the bond with England, he focused on being "mindful of a gallant people," undoubtedly reflecting on the experience of his grandfather and the other heroic citizen soldiers from Nottingham who left their homes and families to fight for their country's freedom. He told his audience:

> It was the American cause, its holy foundation in truth and right, its strength and life in the hearts of the people, that converted those who would otherwise have been peaceful and industrious husbandmen, into more than veterans, into high-souled, unaffected, citizen heroes. A people less firm, less high-minded, less proud of their rights might have hesitated to measure their weakness with a powerful array set against them, they might have hesitated ere they closed forever all avenues to an honorable accommodation. But the men of the revolution did not stop to calculate the danger of defending their freedom. In the fearful moment of impending danger they lost none of their firmness, they resolved to set fortune at defiance.
>
> The cause called the sturdy yeomanry from the thousand hills of New England to share the danger and glory. Led on by this spirit they moved forward to scenes of battle without orders, acted together without previous combinations and dared the fiery blasts of war. But in the spirit and strength of the cause alone they persevered, they fought, they bled. The struggle though glorious, was long and doubtful. There were times when the most ardent and patriotic feared that the tomb of independence would not be far from the cradle and more than once, when the great cause of freedom seemed lost and the dawn of the republic over shaded forever, that army, whom distress only rendered more terrible, gathering new resources from danger, drove back before its enemies the clouds of misfortune.

Jonathan reminded the crowd that in 1826 there were only a few of those patriots still alive. But for those still "amongst us, their lives have been graciously lengthened out by heaven that their eyes might be blessed with the sight of our present prosperity and happiness, ere the grave should close upon them forever." At the conclusion of his speech, he asked that while the veterans were "dropping around us like the leaves in autumn, while scarcely a week passes, that does not call away some member of the veteran band already so sadly thinned, let us this day form a determination to make a strong and united effort to light up on their aged and war beaten countenances, one grateful cheerful smile of pleasure, one parting beam of joy, ere they are gone from us forever."

In his speech he made a point of urging those gathered to remember Presidents Jefferson and Adams for their contribution to the founding of the country. Sadly, he had no way of knowing that on this momentous fiftieth anniversary of the Declaration of Independence, first Jefferson had died at Monticello, and a few hours thereafter Adams passed away in Massachusetts.

Jonathan was quickly immersed in the day-to-day life of a lawyer and found it somewhat overwhelming, particularly with Ruggles out of town at the legislature. He related to Ann, "'Tis a vexatious life, to be a Lawyer—shall be heartily glad when Mr. Ruggles returns. His clients are eternally calling on me for advice and they think I know as much law as if I had studied twenty years." After only a few months as a law student, he was presenting cases before a local justice. He said he liked what he was doing but found it discouraging when he had a verdict go against him. He told Ann that it was "strange how justice decides sometimes—but it can't be helped."

Early on, in addition to throwing himself into the study of law and working for the newspaper, he found himself hopelessly attracted to the young Deborah Prince. There must have been something memorable in that brief first meeting with her on the way to Thomaston that sparked his interest. There is no evidence that he had any previous involvement, interest, or experience with young women. There was never any mention of ladies in his letters home. It would be hard to imagine that growing up in Nottingham, with so many young people present, Jonathan was never bitten by the love bug. But if Deborah was his first love interest, even at age twenty-three, and past the raging-hormone adolescent years, he was truly smitten by this young woman.

As early as February 1826, in his first surviving letter home, he confided to his sister how disappointed he was that there was not enough snow to go sleighing because there was "a pretty, really pretty girl" who had been planning to accompany him. This unnamed young woman, who he said was an elegant dancer, had also accompanied Jonathan to a ball the previous week. He revealed to Ann that he was not at all versed in the ways to charm and woo a young lady, and that it must be an art that came with experience, of which he unfortunately had none. For a young man mastering the arts of debate, persuasion, and law, talking to women about feelings was a skill with which he struggled, increasing his anxiety.

At the same time the women at home had been discussing Jonathan's need for a love interest and apparently came up with the names of young ladies they believed would be right for him. It does not appear that they ever shared their choices with him, likely because he had been subtly letting them know he had a romantic interest, but he had also told them that he had no intention of being swayed by the local eastern beauties and "that at the present I am a learner—a student of the law and therefore have but very few hours to spend among the lasses."

He continued to spend time with Deborah, and she became his partner at all social events in the Thomaston area. He was reluctant to tell his family Deborah's name, declaring, "I am a modest youth and hardly dare trust myself to write the name here, for fear my hand might tremble." He did not reveal her name until the fall of 1828, during a home visit. While his family undoubtedly knew he had a love interest, it is surprising that they did not press him for details. Joseph's wife thought Jonathan was infatuated with his cousin Harriet, but he told Ann that he would sooner become a Shaking Quaker than marry a relative.

Jonathan did not have a strong interest in formal religion or in attending church, though at Bowdoin attendance at chapel had been mandatory. The Prince family, however, was much more pious and were regular churchgoers. If Jonathan was attending church, it was probably because it provided an excellent opportunity to see Deborah. In a letter he wrote to Ann one Sunday, he quipped that he probably should be going to church, "where I should hear a good sober orthodox sermon, if I could keep awake." But he then added that the only likely thing that could keep him awake was the presence of the young ladies, particularly one.

In his letters to Ann, unlike in his correspondence with others, he would from time to time blurt out a comment that revealed thoughts and feelings he would not share with others, particularly men. He seemed to think about life and its purpose and how one moved through it. Given the losses he experienced in his early years, he would have needed a method for reconciling them to the path of his life. One time he mused, "We poor mortals are strange beings—made up of strange compounds—

full of notions—good, bad, indifferent and queer, possessing but little light and knowledge, yet knowing still less of ourselves than of almost any other subject. The world jogs on: and all things in the end turn out for the best. At least it is a consoling doctrine to believe, and one to which at times we recur with particular satisfaction." It was as though he was saying that if things look overwhelming or problems appear unsolvable, you just do your best, and if your intentions are honest and honorable, things will turn out well. He was, however, struggling with this feeling of love, and he almost embarrassingly looked to Ann for guidance. He confided, "I never was *in love* in my life, though I have loved forty—who could help it? Yet I always keep dark—I don't mean that I court in the dark, for I do not court at all. Only that I say just nothing at all about it to any but you and I say this much in confidence."

Early on he described Deborah as being "pretty though and always looks so pleasant when she sees me, that I can't for the life of me help feeling mighty pleasant also." He then asked Ann, "Is that the way love acts?" By August 1827 he finally revealed to Ann, with the caveat that she was to tell no one, that "I am in love, yes Jona, is in love as sure as the world is flat and the moon made of green cheese, so sure is it that your brother Jona is clean gone for it. There is no help, no remedy, no balm. How it happened or came to pass I know not. I am quite sure I never dreamt of such a thing."

It was such a new and unknown feeling for him that he had difficulty putting a label on the feeling and figuring out how it occurred. He was also at a loss as to how to deal with this emotion: "I told you I was in love—yes that is it in LOVE—deep in love—up to the very tip of my nose in Love. When-where-how, who with do you ask? She must have caught me napping as it were, had no idea of it myself. Am fast bound—no escape, I could not if I would and I would not if I could. I thought of it and thought of it again last night going to bed and finally on the whole concluded—it was best concluded. I was really bona-fide heart and soul in the pickle aforesaid." However, he admitted that she was "not so very handsome either, but I like her for all that most confounding-most shocking-most terribly-most-oh you can't think how most." She was "one of the most modest, unobtrusive, demure looking creatures you ever saw."

In the fall of 1827 Jonathan paid his yearly visit home, and while there he attended his sister Sarah's wedding. After he returned to Thomaston he received letters from his brother Joseph and his cousin, also named

Joseph (the son of Uncle Jacob), and was dumbfounded to learn that he was the talk of the town for his scandalous behavior at the wedding. The story was that a young family friend, Martha Crows, who was also at the wedding, had broken off her engagement to a Colonel John Rogers because Jonathan had lavished attention and affection on her to the point that she then preferred Jonathan to the colonel.

Jonathan wrote his brother and vented his anger about "the ten thousand false and ridiculous reports about me." The letter to his cousin added a new twist to the rumor and alleged that Uncle Bradbury had put Jonathan up to wooing poor Martha in order to break up her relationship with the colonel, and that there was in some fashion a financial advantage for Bradbury if the marriage did not take place. "How people love to lie and make mischief," Jonathan wrote, but he was not surprised that "Martha had dismissed the Col. As it was a natural result after what took place at Mother's the night Sally was married." Jonathan was more annoyed that Uncle Bradbury had been accused of being the precipitator of the whole affair: "It is passing strange how ingeniously people will reason to make out a lie. One grain of truth in the grossest of falsehoods will be sufficient to make the falsehood current among most people. There are not wanting those who will greedily seize it and make the most out of it they possibly can—whether they believe it or not."

Jonathan, however, was not totally guiltless in the affair. In a previous letter he had wondered to Ann whether Martha would not be happier if she had loved a "younger man stronger and longer." He had, and perhaps others had, talked to Martha at the wedding. As he put it to his cousin, "What a damnation fuss Jo—I thought it would be so—but who cares. We told her no more than the truth—plain truth—and what she most wanted to hear, though few would have spoken so plain. Let it work—I have nothing to accuse myself of, or to regret." Jonathan believed Martha did not really love the colonel, was looking for a way out, and needed to be reminded of that fact.

In another letter to Ann, after he had some time to let his irritation subside, Jonathan quipped to her what a terrible person he must be and "how slick and cunningly he cut out Rogers, how triumphantly he wooed and won his beloved and lovely betrothed." He hoped, however, that the story had not progressed to the point where he and Martha had married, because, he reminded Ann, as he had been suggesting to her these past months, his affection lay with another. It surprised him that he could court and impress a young lady in such short order, given his naivety and bumbling approach in his relationship with Deborah.

The upcoming presidential election of 1828 was an important event in Jonathan's burgeoning political career. Jackson was the clear favorite of Maine Democrats, but Adams, who had carried the state in 1824, was still strong in Maine. In addition to his law studies, which were coming to an end, Jonathan had the main responsibility for the editorial page of the *Register*. Ruggles had directed him not to give Adams negative press, but rather to focus on emphasizing Jackson's positives. The campaign was the bitterest and most contentious to date. The Adams side, without the involvement of Adams himself, attacked Jackson's dueling history (and what they called the cold-blooded murder of Dickinson) and referred to Jackson's wife Rachel as an adulteress because she had married Jackson before she was divorced from her first husband. The Jacksonites labeled Adams elitist and anti-Catholic, as well as charging that while he was serving in Russia he had procured prostitutes for the czar. Unfortunately, none of Jonathan's political editorials have survived.

By this time Jonathan was boarding in the Prince home and so had ample opportunity to spend time with Deborah. On July 18, 1828, Deborah and her father departed from Thomaston on a ship bound for Boston, which was the first leg of a trip to visit Deborah's oldest sister Eliza and her family in Spencer, Massachusetts. When they reached Spencer on July 25, they learned of Eliza's tragic death, and that of her baby, due to complications from childbirth. Prince recorded in his diary that at the door "they were informed that Eliza was a corpse within. A sudden and dreadful reverse of feelings entered our family. For the first time we are called to put on mourning for a deceased member of it."

In addition to her husband, William Pope, Eliza left two young daughters, Lucretia and Sarah. It was decided that Deborah would remain in Spencer for a while to help with the children. Prince Sr. returned to Thomaston on July 31, and his son commented that "the poor old gentleman looks and speaks as though his feeling had been somewhat lacerated since he left us, as indeed they must have been." Prince Sr. returned with a letter from Deborah for Jonathan that informed him of the loss, but he had already heard what had occurred from Lucy, Deborah's younger sister.

Jonathan quickly responded and fittingly empathized with the pain she had to be experiencing, as well as the deep sense of loss, particularly given the shocking emotional shift from joyful anticipation of seeing her sister, and being totally unprepared "for the greatest of human calamities, the loss of a near and dear friend." Despite being no stranger to heartbreaking loss, he was not sure that "since my feelings have ripened" he could endure such a tragic experience.

At the same time that he acknowledged her pain and grief, he also wanted to let her know that he missed her. He was having difficulty writing what he termed a love letter, something he had no real experience doing, and this awkwardness showed when he apologized to her for addressing the letter to "My Dr. Deborah" instead of "My Dear Debby," but he noted that he was writing the letter in the office and was concerned others might see he was writing a very personal letter: "I don't like to have any lookers on while writing." Additionally, he was concerned that she might get too attached to the children and not want to come back to Thomaston: "You must not be too good and kind a Mother to the little ones, if you do they will love you too well and you them: so much so that you may, forget some of your good friends Down East." He further voiced concern that he might be taking up too much of her time: "I know I used to plague you a little too much sometimes but I could not well help it." It is unlikely that she was at all bothered, given her infatuation with him.

Deborah was a small, frail young woman who was prone to sickness, particularly of a respiratory nature, and her health was regularly mentioned in her letters. Jonathan had a fairly strong constitution, but, typical of the times, when bleeding and leeches were the apparent treatment of choice for most illnesses, when one did get sick the illness tended to linger and keep one out of action for often three or four weeks. Jonathan was sick during the time Deborah was in Spencer, and he suggested to her that he had not been getting much better. Deborah lamented that she was not there to nurse him back to health, and was concerned he would push himself to work when he should be resting. She strongly urged him to leave Thomaston and go to visit his mother in Nottingham, so she could "restore you to health." Given what had just happened to her sister, an ostensibly healthy young woman, Deborah pleaded that he should go, "if not for your own sake, do so for mine. Oh I could not bear to part with you too." A secondary motive was that if he went to Nottingham, he could stop in Spencer to see her and possibly take her to New Hampshire.

In Deborah's letters to Jonathan, it is apparent that she was having difficulty coping with the complexities of her situation. In addition to grieving over the sudden and unexpected loss of her sister, she was now acting as a maternal figure to two young girls who had just lost their mother. It was unclear how long Deborah was to stay in Spencer, and that ambiguity had to have been a source of stress. She also missed Jonathan and the time she would spend with him. She did have a friend, Julia Draper, in Spencer, but her most difficult time was when she was alone. Among other things, she had a strong tendency to view the world from a melancholy point of view.

In his letters Jonathan always encouraged Deborah to freely express her thoughts and feelings, but she was reluctant, indicating her fear that she would say something that he might criticize by commenting, "what a critic you naturally are." Deborah had a long history of apologizing for her thoughts and feelings, and Jonathan would regularly counter that she need not worry about that type of thing. An example was her comment in a letter to Jonathan from Spencer, in which she wrote, "I am afraid I have tried your patience, or shall with this long letter. I should be sorry to have you impatient to get to the close." Through the years she needed regular reassurance from Jonathan that he was not displeased or irritated by what she wrote. And he always encouraged her to put negative thoughts out of her mind.

Just as Deborah was concerned about what she wrote, Jonathan, not a poet, found it difficult to elegantly express his love and affection for Deborah. Playing on the Cilley name, he inquired of Deborah whether she may "not be afraid [that] by reading silly letters and writing a silly beau" she might turn silly herself. She responded, "I like my silly beau very much and his letter does not make me silly but very happy and I am very willing to become so Cilley."

Another issue undoubtedly on Deborah's mind was what Jonathan planned for himself after he finished his legal studies, which were to end soon. While it appears that he made a natural transition into a legal practice in Thomaston, he may have been considering other options. While it was undecided when she would return to Maine, it appeared to some degree that Deborah's return depended on what Jonathan's future plans were. She told him, "I am very anxious to hear where you determine to settle." Even though he was solidly established in Thomaston, it would also have been possible, given his bonds in New Hampshire and with his family, that at some point he would seriously consider returning to New Hampshire. None of his letters to New Hampshire, however, discussed this issue.

In a way, it appeared that this unexpected, emotionally trying separation solidified Deborah's and Jonathan's relationship. Deborah returned to Thomaston in October and was accompanied by one of the Pope girls. In a March 15, 1829, letter to Ann, Jonathan informed his sister that he would be marrying Deborah, who was "a rose and a lily and everything else that is sweet and pretty," and thus make her his "partner for life, the sharer of his joys and sorrows." Jonathan further mentioned that he had not envisaged being married so soon, but had changed his mind, and attributed the change to having grown older and wiser. The unmentioned factor that likely contributed to his rush to marriage was that Deborah was pregnant. They married on April 4, and their son Greenleaf, named after Jonathan's father, was born on October 27. In spite of Deborah's Baptist upbringing, the closeness of their living situation, and the longing that was the result of an emotional two- to three-month separation, evidently kindled forbidden passions.

Jonathan and Deborah, along with Greenleaf, moved into their own home in 1830. The house was located between the home of Deborah's parents and Ruggles's house. As was common, they had a young girl named Mary living with them to help Deborah with household chores, mind the fire, help with the children, feed the cow, and clean the barn when Jonathan was gone.

Jonathan's emotional attachment to Greenleaf was strong. When he wrote to Ann in February 1830, after she had given birth to a son, Jonathan shared his own feelings: "I love to look at the little innocent faces and round mouths myself. It gives the feeling of so sweet and tender a joy. I can't describe it in any other way you have felt and do feel it every time you look at your little quiet babe. You may call the feeling love and so it is, but a different kind of love from that we feel for anything else. It is a love for babies."

With his legal studies completed and his marriage, the question of whether Jonathan would remain in Thomaston was determined. He soon had his own office and told family he had "a very tolerable sum of business" and that he liked being in Thomaston but regretted not being able to see his friends in New Hampshire. At that time a lawyer's practice mostly involved civil suits dealing with debt collection, contracts, titles, foreclosures, and bankruptcies. Early on he continued to share some cases with Ruggles. It is not known how long Jonathan continued with the newspaper. The life of the lawyer during this era also involved blocks of time away from home when court was in session. Court was more than just a series of legal sessions; it was also a social occasion. The judges, lawyers, clients, and witnesses converged in whichever town court was being held and shared the hotels or boarding houses, as well as socializing in the taverns.

Legend was that Jonathan was a sort of after-court companion. One story had it that Jonathan's "old friends would assemble evenings and listen to his mirth-providing jokes and amusing stories." He was supposedly someone with a large repertoire of stories and anecdotes. Once, when friends requested one more story at the end of an evening, Jonathan was said to have replied, "If I do, it will be a silly one." There is no other mention of Jonathan being the life-of-the-party type, but he was certainly popular and well liked and had the ability to interact in an amicable and friendly way with people of all interests and backgrounds.

The election of 1828 saw Jackson defeat Adams, which ultimately changed presidential politics forever. Much to the disappointment of Jonathan and the other New England Democrats, New England unanimously supported Adams. The only electoral vote Jackson received came from Portland, Maine. However, the Democratic Party maintained the governor's seat and a majority in both branches of the state legislature. Ruggles continued as Speaker of the House. The new Jacksonian Democrats felt optimistic about their future.

Over the next two years Jonathan continued to be involved in local politics, practiced law, and enjoyed his family, adding Jane in July 1831. He returned to Bowdoin at least twice to give graduation speeches before the Athenaen Society. In July 1831, he was again the featured speaker at the local Fourth of July celebration. Also in 1831 he was admitted to practice before the Maine Supreme Court. He remained a staunch supporter of Jackson and noted in one letter that his mother also backed Jackson, but he lamented that, along with some of his uncles, his brother Joseph had "turned fed. I tried hard to reclaim him, could not, told him he would repent it in dust and ashes ere long." The Cilley family's commitment to public service spread to their relatives in Ohio when Jonathan's cousin Jonathan was elected to the Ohio Senate in 1830.

The year 1831 also marked two major losses, when Jonathan's uncles Jacob and Bradbury died. When Ruggles was selected to be a judge in the Common Pleas Court, it was not surprising that Jonathan was elected to succeed Ruggles in the Maine House of Representatives.

In 1827, the then twenty-three-year-old George W. Jones, who would in 1838 serve as Jonathan's second, was living in the rough and tumble Arkansas territory. He had aligned himself politically with a faction that had supported Clay in the 1824 presidential election and would be opposing Jackson in 1828. This faction was led by Robert Crittenden, the brother of Senator John Crittenden from Kentucky, who would later be one of William Graves's friends. Loyalties were constantly shifting, often accompanied by accusations in the press of corruption and the inappropriate use of public funds.

During this period, Henry Conway, who at one time had been a friend of Robert Crittenden, served as the Arkansas delegate to Congress. After the 1827 election in which Conway easily defeated Crittenden-supported candidate Robert Oden, tempers flared. Ambrose Sevier, Conway's cousin, made loud and disparaging remarks about Crittenden on a street in Little Rock. Thomas Newton, another Crittenden crony, took on Sevier's insult to Crittenden and challenged Newton to a duel. Jones served as Newton's second. The first shot missed both men, and Jones pushed for another shot, but cooler heads prevailed. The following month, Crittenden's conflict with Conway ended up on the dueling grounds, and Conway was killed. Sevier then replaced Conway in Congress.

# FIVE

## First Term

The beginning of 1832 saw Jonathan off to Augusta for the first of his five terms in the Maine House of Representatives. It was the first year that the Maine legislature met in Augusta, and it did so in a new capitol building designed by John Bullfinch, who had also designed the National Capitol in Washington, D.C. For its own unique reasons, Maine held its annual, approximately three-month-long legislative sessions during the coldest, snowiest time of the year. It was often a struggle for members of the legislature to make their way to Augusta over frozen or slushy roads. Once they got to Augusta most of them were unable to get home during the course of the legislature's session. Members stayed in boarding houses, frequently with roommates. Sessions often went well into the evening.

For Jonathan, the trip was only about forty miles, but it does not appear that over the course of his five years in the House he had his own source of transportation, and so he relied on others to get him back and forth. He must not have had his own horse or sleigh (a typical Maine requirement in the winter). If the snow was melting, the roads would have been nearly impassable because of mud and slush. While he was in what two-and-a-half-year-old Greenleaf called "Gusty," Deborah was at home with Greenleaf and six-month-old Jane. Fortunately for her, during this first year, her family was right next door, and Jonathan's mother was visiting from New Hampshire most of the time. Deborah also had what she called "a girl" staying in the home to help. This first year was probably the easiest and least stressful of the six years that Jonathan was away from home.

During the 1832 legislative session Samuel Smith, a Democrat from Wiscasset, was serving his second term as governor. Both branches of the legislature were also in Democratic hands. Even in the 1830s the proceedings of the legislature were well documented in state newspapers. In perusing the records, one sees that Jonathan settled right in and actively participated in the proceedings. At some point in early January he left Augusta for a brief visit to Nottingham, most likely related to the death of his uncle Bradbury, who had died the previous month at age seventy-one. When he returned, Jonathan brought his mother back to Maine for a lengthy visit.

The only letter from Jonathan to Deborah during this first session that survived came in late February, two weeks before the end of the session. This letter gave a good overview of his first year's experience. He wrote that he had not made many speeches, mainly because there had not been issues on the agenda "worth making a long speech upon." If he were reelected, he hoped she would come to Augusta so she would "have the opportunity to ascertain if your heart will still be quick and warm at the sound of my voice in the Halls of Legislation." Perhaps one of the things that attracted Jonathan to Deborah was that he saw her as being impressed by his oratory skills. After all, it is very satisfying to one's self-image to have others reinforce those aspects of character that one has worked hard to master. Jonathan clearly believed that participation in the legislature meant that he would be actively engaged in the debates, and he intended to do so with eloquence and persuasiveness.

At some point prior to embarking on his political career, Jonathan and Deborah had a conversation about his aspirations and ambitions, and they agreed that he should move into the political arena. What were his goals? Where did he see himself going? How far up the political ladder? He seemed to clearly have had a plan in mind. The February 26, 1832, letter suggested that Deborah had concerns about how difficult the road might be to travel. She may have heard something about difficulties he was having in Augusta. Jonathan reassured her that, while there might be difficulties, they would "climb the Hill together." He reminded Deborah that "political eminence," which was undoubtedly part of his thinking, "is hard to be attained," and he added that one in a thousand would be successful. He was, however, beginning to be aware that some of those who attained eminence might not be worthy and might have pursued it in less than honorable ways. He went on to tell Deborah that "Ambition causes me no sleepless nights or anxious days," and he was "determined so far forth as I know to do what is right, come what may."

Jonathan was a representative in Augusta with the blessing of Ruggles, who was now a judge in the Common Pleas Court. Ruggles, as we shall see, had other plans for his own political future. It would be natural for Jonathan to strive to comport himself in the legislature in a manner that would please Ruggles. His February letter stated that he believed Ruggles, who had recently been in Augusta, went home satisfied with his (Jonathan's) performance. Jonathan was concerned, however, that "Gross misrepresentations were made" to Ruggles while Jonathan was away in Nottingham "by those from whom I did not expect it." He was puzzled as to their motives. There is no record as to what those statements were, but they marked the beginning of the conflicts Jonathan would have with members of his party who saw him as a threat to their own goals and aspirations.

One thing that Jonathan told Deborah he found disturbing was the "jealousy & rivalry among our friends." For him, staying within the principles of the "so glorious cause" around which the new Democratic Party had been organized was of paramount importance. In other words, Jonathan believed that principles should come before personal ambition. While he believed the vast majority of his colleagues were "determined to do right, and give credit to those who deserved it," there were "a few restless and truly selfish individuals" within the party who could "cause a great deal of trouble." He gave no names.

It is unclear whether Jonathan had any inclination about what would transpire when he came up for reelection in September 1832. Surprisingly, his friend Ruggles came after Jonathan with a vengeance that never relented; Ruggles did everything in his power to keep Jonathan from regaining his seat. Things had been brewing within a faction of the Democratic Party that affected not only Jonathan's reelection but also events that followed him for the next three years, constantly impacting his capacity to persevere and do what he believed right.

The politics of Maine in 1832 were not unlike politics that came before and after, and not unlike national politics. In addition to philosophical differences between the parties, there were always regional and sectional differences. In Maine there have always been differences between the southern and northern areas of the state; between the city business-oriented people and the rural "dirt farmers and down-east fishermen"; between those at the top of the party hierarchy and those who aspired to be at the top. Compounding the picture were personal ambitions and self-interests that clouded the motivations and actions of those in the forefront, as well as those who worked and conspired behind the scenes.

All of these issues came into play beginning in 1831. One of the destabilizing conflicts within the Democratic Party was the dissatisfaction with what was labeled the "Preble Junto," which was composed of a group of older party men who ran the party and did not allow the younger Democrats into positions in government. William Pitt Preble was from Portland and was at the time the owner of the Portland newspaper *Eastern Argus.* He was a strong supporter of Governor Smith. Reuel Williams and Ether Shepley, both of whom subsequently became U.S. senators, were also considered part of this junto. At the vanguard of the opposing group, comprising mostly lawyers from the Portland area, was a Portland lawyer named F. O. J. Smith, whose political aspirations and ambitions were vast, though his ethics were always believed to be questionable. He rose fast in Maine politics, serving in the Maine House in 1830 and the Maine Senate in 1832 (he was also president of the Maine Senate in 1832). He likewise served in the U.S. House of Representatives from 1833 to 1839. Ruggles was part of this group, with his own personal aspirations. Another member was Robert Dunlap of Brunswick, a former Federalist who had recently switched parties.

Why any of these men believed they had not had opportunities within the party is an open question. Ruggles had been Speaker of the House five times, Dunlap had been president of the Senate four times, and Smith had been president of the Senate once. This group also claimed to be truer Jacksonian Democrats, but the assertion was rather weak, inasmuch as both Ruggles and Smith abandoned the party when it benefited them to do so.

The issues that brought Jonathan into conflict with the party began brewing as early as 1831. At that time Ruggles had resigned his position as Speaker of the House in order to become a judge in the Common Pleas Court. He did it because he was under the impression that the change would be a stepping-stone to his election to the U.S. Senate in January 1833. Apparently others had assured him that they would support his candidacy. Also brewing in 1832 was a plan to replace Governor Smith with Dunlap.

After F. O. J. Smith was defeated in his bid to be reelected to the House in the fall of 1831, he set his sights on the Maine Senate, with the specific goal of gaining the position of senate president. Failing that, he then aspired to a seat in the U.S. House of Representatives. An essential part of his strategy was to wrest control of the Democratic Party from the Preble Junto and also obtain control of the Cumberland County Democratic Caucus. Cumberland County was Maine's most populous county and included Portland, Maine's largest city. He also saw the U.S. Senate seat coming up in 1833 as a possibility.

Ruggles had accepted the seat on the bench with the understanding, at least from his point of view, that there was a faction of the party that would support him for the upcoming Senate position. If Smith were to succeed in changing the party hierarchy in a direction that favored his ambition, he would need the support of men outside of Cumberland County, men such as Ruggles. So if he were to let Ruggles strive for the Senate, his own goal would need to be the House of Representatives. The *Portland Advertiser*, an opposition newspaper, reported that Robert Dunlap was also interested in the House seat. The paper additionally wrote that Smith's plan was to replace Governor Smith with Dunlap, thus opening up the way for him to seek a seat in Washington.

Jonathan must have known Ruggles was looking toward the Senate seat, but there appears to be nothing concrete suggesting that Jonathan was not supportive of Ruggles's aspiration. There was also nothing to suggest that Ruggles was displeased with him when Jonathan returned to Thomaston at the close of the 1832 legislative session. Jonathan was aware that negative comments had been made to Ruggles, but we do not know exactly what those comments were. Jonathan likely assumed that all he had to do was to assure Ruggles that what he had been told was untrue, and the matter would be forgotten. Unfortunately for Jonathan, that did not happen.

When September arrived and it was time for local elections to select the representatives from the Thomaston area to the state House of Representatives, Ruggles, along with some of his friends, made a direct frontal assault on Jonathan's character and worthiness to serve in the legislature. Ruggles clearly believed that Jonathan was opposed to his winning the Senate seat and based his beliefs on what he had been told by others.

Vengeance was now Ruggles's chief motivation, and it would bring an end to the seven-year relationship between these two men. Ruggles went so far as to forbid his wife from even associating with any of the Cilley family, which was difficult given that the two families lived next to each other.

After three months and numerous meetings that attempted to elect two representatives, finally, on December 4, Jonathan, along with Elkanah Spear, supposed they had been officially elected for the 1833 term. At some point after the December 4 meeting, a group of Thomaston Democrats, including Prince and other friends of Jonathan, was appointed by the Democratic Party of Thomaston and asked "to draw up a full statement of facts in relation to the unpleasant division among the Democrats in this town, and to the several trials to elect representatives." Their detailed report provides a significant amount of information about what prompted Ruggles to change his attitude toward Jonathan, and how he systematically worked to bring a quick end to Jonathan's budding political career.

At the first meeting of the party caucus on September 4, it was clear right from the beginning that Ruggles had come prepared to sabotage Jonathan. At this meeting Prince commented that "reports had been circulated, injurious to the political reputation of Cilley." Prince then asked Ruggles about the basis for the charges made against Cilley and why he was working against Jonathan. Ruggles replied that "he had been the friend of Mr. Cilley; he had voted for him last year . . . because he thought it for his interest so to do." Ruggles went on to say "that he opposed him this year, because he had not found him so friendly to his views as he had expected, and that he had made up his mind to vote against him." He then stated, "Men, generally acted as their interest dictated; and although he might have other reasons," the reason he had given should be sufficient in the present situation.

Jonathan picked up on Ruggles's reference to his personal interests and countered "that, as the representative of the town, he had endeavored to discharge his trust faithfully; that he had thought he owed his election last year to the Democratic Party, and that he was the Representative of that party and the town, and not merely the representative of one man." Jonathan did not know what Ruggles meant "by his interests and his views." Jonathan was aware that there had been rumors in town that during the last legislative session he had supposedly told people that he was opposed to Ruggles's election to the U.S. Senate. Jonathan denied making any statements hostile to Ruggles while he was in Augusta, and he was certain that his friends and colleagues would vouch for his behavior. He then asked Ruggles "for proof of his being unfriendly to his interests and views."

Ruggles responded by saying "that he had been told by prominent members of the Democratic Party, in different parts of the state that Mr. Cilley was unfriendly to his election to the U.S. Senate." He was astonished at first but upon reflection recalled that Jonathan had never told Ruggles that he fully supported his desire for the Senate seat. Ruggles named four men who had stated they had heard Jonathan make derogatory statements about him. The only individual to support Ruggles's assertion was a gentleman named John McCrates, who lived in the neighboring town of Noblesboro and had served in the House with Jonathan. The committee report contained a letter from McCrates written on September 7, three days after the first election caucus. He apparently had been asked by a Ruggles supporter to provide information about Jonathan's actions in Augusta. He wrote that he was initially reluctant, but he was "aware that in so doing I might incur the bitter hate and unrelenting hostility of some who have been ranked among particular friends." He concluded, however, that "the acts of a man in public trust are the property of the people," and then he proceeded to conclude that Jonathan's behavior in the recent legislature "was often a source of mortification to many of our political friends." He was not sure whether Jonathan had been suffering from a lack of experience or whether he had "less worthy reasons." He gave no specifics as to what Jonathan was supposed to have done.

McCrates went on to claim that Jonathan betrayed Ruggles by not supporting his bid for the U.S. Senate, adding, "In almost every instance he was found among those who opposed rather than urged the claim of Judge R." If Jonathan were to be returned to the legislature, McCrates believed, Jonathan would make use of his position "to oppose the election of that gentleman to the seat in the U.S. Senate." McCrates believed Jonathan was someone of whom the party should be cautious. He saw Jonathan as deserting a person who should have been "eminently entitled" to his wholehearted support. (Interestingly, McCrates closed his letter by stating that "a man who can forget his obligations to his benefactor is but a poor supporter of his party; like Webb of the N.Y. Courier and

Enquirer—he deserts whenever it becomes his interest to do so." This is
the same Webb who later would a major fermenter of the fatal duel.)

It had to be disappointing and perplexing to Jonathan that McCrates
would be so hostile toward him. During the last legislative session, when
Jonathan's behavior supposedly mortified many in the party, McCrates's
right to hold his seat had been challenged because he also held a federal
government position as a commissioner of insolvency. It was suggested
that McCrates should not hold both positions, and a committee was appointed to investigate whether a court opinion should be requested. Jonathan was on that committee, and he reported to the legislature that an
opinion was not necessary and thus McCrates should keep his seat. In
subsequent debates on the issue, Jonathan continued to support
McCrates. So much for the notion of standing by one's friends. Other
than McCrates, everyone whom Ruggles had suggested would substantiate what had been said about Jonathan denied that Jonathan had behaved in ways disparaging of Ruggles.

After the first meeting regarding the House seats for Thomaston on
September 4, a resolution was passed by the thirty-six individuals
present to support two other candidates for the legislature. The very next
evening another meeting was held "for the purpose of entering into a
more full investigation of the charges made against Mr. Cilley." There
were close to one hundred men at this meeting. Also present were two
gentlemen from the neighboring town of Warren who had been members
of the previous legislature. They were there to give their opinion that
Jonathan's behavior had in fact been appropriate and in line with the
party as a whole. The group resolved to support Jonathan and Spear in
the upcoming general election—coming up in five days. It was not stated
whether Ruggles was present at this caucus. The report did state that
after the caucus, Ruggles and his supporters distributed pamphlets in
town "denouncing Mr. Cilley and his friends," as well as the two gentlemen from Warren, "in the most virulent and abusive terms." Those who
wrote the report decided that the pamphlets contained such "a complete
tissue of falsehoods and vulgar abuse" that the committee would not
report it.

By the time the next meeting took place, Ruggles had been conspiring
with the opposition National Republican Party to sabotage the election,
but their efforts failed when the vote was taken. Jonathan and Spear
received the most votes; however, election rules required the winners to

receive not only more votes than any other candidate but also a majority of all the votes cast. Another election was required; it was scheduled for October 1, and once again Jonathan and Spear received more votes than the other candidates, but not a majority. Jonathan's supporters wanted to schedule another vote for the next day, but the town selectmen, believing they had the authority to schedule the next vote, reminded Jonathan's allies that Ruggles had advised them they could schedule a meeting any-time they wished. In concert with Ruggles, the selectmen did not sched-ule the next vote until the first Monday in December. This was getting close to the start of the next legislature session, which was scheduled to begin in January.

By the time December came the McCrates letter had been circulating around town and the selectmen manipulated the hours the polls were to be open. At the appointed time for the polls to close, Jonathan and Spear had enough votes to be elected, but the selectmen allowed the polls to remain open for two more hours so more voters could be rounded up to vote against Jonathan. When the polls finally closed, there were still not enough votes for any candidate to be declared a winner. The next election was scheduled for the next day, but, at the appointed time, none of the selectmen appeared and the voter list had disappeared. After waiting until noon, those in attendance chose the necessary officials and pro-ceeded with the election. It was also decided that on the previous day the selectmen had incorrectly counted the votes and that Jonathan had in-deed won a seat, and Spear also received enough votes to earn a seat.

A second source of negative remarks concerning Jonathan came from Dunlap. These comments probably occurred during the summer, when the lawyers of the area were gathered at court. It is not specifically stated what Dunlap told Ruggles, and it is not known exactly when Jonathan learned of the remarks, but Jonathan insisted they were without founda-tion and would not go unchallenged. As would become a core aspect of Jonathan's nature during the period from the first election in September to the last election in December, he pursued an explanation from Dunlap concerning the derogatory statements Dunlap had allegedly made, par-ticularly statements made to Ruggles. Jonathan was not the type of man to let untruth or unwarranted and defaming accusations pass by without a challenge. There were letters exchanged between Jonathan and Dunlap during the fall of 1832. Only one of the letters, dated November 3 from

Jonathan to Dunlap, survived, and that letter provides a good summary of the issues involved.

Jonathan initially wrote to Dunlap requesting that Dunlap state whether he had made a "severe" remark to Ruggles, a remark that Ruggles was using "to destroy my political standing with my townsmen and defeat my reelection to the House of Representatives." The exact nature of the remark is unknown, but it involved statements Jonathan allegedly made when he returned to Thomaston after the legislature had adjourned. It was alleged that Jonathan had spoken "in very disrespectful terms of many of our prominent Republican appointees" and "of endeavoring to bring into contempt and ridicule our men and principles." Jonathan told Dunlap that he and his friends could not believe Dunlap would make such a comment. In response to Jonathan's inquiry, Dunlap replied that he had made the remark, but he would not say where he got the information, stating that he would need the permission of those responsible before divulging his source.

Jonathan did not believe that Dunlap's refusal to name his source was acceptable or gentlemanly. Given that the accusations were so condemning of Jonathan, and because he believed he had some sort of collegial relationship with Dunlap, he questioned why Dunlap failed to ask him whether the information was in fact true. Jonathan assured Dunlap that he could easily prove that what Dunlap had heard was false, and it had been intentionally spread to injure Jonathan. He was further perplexed as to why Dunlap had not consulted him before making the comment to Ruggles, since Jonathan had been at court at the time. Jonathan had perceived Dunlap to be friendly to him that day and wondered why, even after disparaging him, Dunlap still invited Jonathan to his house.

Jonathan concluded that since Dunlap would not reveal the source of the information, there was likely no other source, and Dunlap's actions were calculated to do damage to Jonathan. Jonathan was not about to take this lying down and allow himself to be treated unfairly. He told Dunlap that "it is a duty that anyone owes himself, his family, and his friends to defend his character and standing whenever and by whomever it is unjustly assailed." No one was going to trample on him without him defending his character and honor. Jonathan told Dunlap that his first step would be to lay out their correspondence to the public and let them be the final judge as to whose reputation had been tarnished. It is not known whether Jonathan in fact made his letters public. When Dunlap was proposed for governor in 1833, it is not surprising that Jonathan was not one of his supporters.

While a plot was in the works to replace Governor Smith in the 1833 election, he was easily reelected in the fall of 1832. Also in the fall of 1832 President Jackson handily defeated Henry Clay for a second term. Jackson's vice president would be Martin Van Buren from New York. Van Buren was known as the "little magician" for his political astuteness and ability to make things happen. He has been credited by some as the one who brought partisanship to party politics.

On the national scene, in November, South Carolina, in opposition to what it believed to be oppressive tariffs, held a Nullification Convention. The South Carolina government believed the imposition of federal tariffs to be unconstitutional and insisted the federal legislature rescind them. It also asserted that any state should be free to choose which federal laws it wanted to follow. The South Carolina legislature authorized the raising of a 25,000-man militia. If Congress did not eliminate the tariff, South Carolina threatened to secede from the United States.

At the forefront of the nullification proposal was John C. Calhoun, who had been Jackson's vice president during his first term. Calhoun had resigned his vice presidency in order to return to the U.S. Senate. Calhoun had previously suggested a similar nullification proposal in 1828, also prompted by displeasure with tariffs. At that time nullification was also paired with threats of secession.

Part of the struggle in the early life of the new United States was the proper balance between the rights of individual states and the rights of the federal government over the states. When a state or a group of states believed that their interests were at odds with those of the federal government, one option contemplated was secession from the Union, just as the Federalists in New England had threatened secession when they believed the War of 1812 ran contrary to the business interests of the people of New England.

Jackson's responded quickly to the South Carolina threat. On December 10 he issued a lengthy proclamation that stated that nullification of federal laws and secession were not options. He urged the citizens of South Carolina to clearly evaluate the course in which they were headed, and the consequences they would incur.

As 1832 came to a close, Ruggles was clearly not happy with Jonathan retaining his seat in the House. He must have also had inklings that he did not have enough support to gain his desired U.S. Senate seat. After the final meeting, when Jonathan's election was confirmed, Ruggles wrote to a political friend that while Jonathan had claimed his seat, Ruggles did not think he would be able to keep it. He alleged that Jonathan had heaped abuse on some of the prominent members of the party at the last election meeting and had denounced Dunlap "as a federalist, and everything else but an honest man."

Jonathan was aware of the rumors and innuendos circulating, but it was unlikely that he was prepared for what Hawthorne described as "the first act and declaration of a political hostility which was too warm and earnest not to become in some degree personal," which made Jonathan's "subsequent career a continual struggle with those to whom he might naturally have looked for friendship and support."

# SIX

## Sent Home

Maine, which had supported John Quincy Adams over Jackson in 1828, gave its support to Jackson in 1832. In the Maine legislature in 1833, the Jackson Democrats controlled both the Senate and the House. F. O. J. Smith was elected, as he had planned, president of the Senate, and one of his cohorts, Nathan Clifford, became Speaker of the House. Having assumed that he was again a representative from Thomaston, Jonathan was in Augusta in January 1833. While Jonathan was in Augusta, he and Deborah regularly exchanged letters. Unfortunately, only one of these 1833 letters has survived, but its content reflected the increasing conflict and strain Jonathan experienced in the House over that winter.

In earlier letters he had confided to her the problems he encountered upon his arrival in Augusta, and there was a reply from her that he said touched him emotionally. While he had colleagues in Augusta whose support he valued, it was with Deborah that he shared his deepest feelings. Moreover, it was Deborah on whom he relied for understanding and empathy. It would be one thing for Jonathan to maintain an outward public image as one who was strong and confident and who could handle whatever adversity came his way, but the more personal, intimate recesses of his thoughts and feelings would be shared only with those with whom he had a strong emotional bond and trust.

Soon after the start of the session, he discovered that those in Thomaston who had opposed his election had challenged his right to his seat. The House referred the issue to the Committee on Contested Elections, which had the charge of determining the validity of his election. This committee did not report to the full legislature until the end of January, and the final decision did not come until February 21. He was not sure how the challenge would turn out, but until the issue was resolved, he wrote that he would be at his post. He did not intend to violate the trust of the people of Thomaston, and he was going to take consolation from doing his duty to his state, his country, and his constituents.

Ruggles was in Augusta in early January lobbying for his selection to the Senate. Jonathan wrote Deborah that right from the beginning of the session, Ruggles, whose bitterness toward Jonathan was still festering, along with Smith and his cronies, were unrelentingly heaping "continual misrepresentation and persecution" on him. He told Deborah that he had "suffered much more than" he ever believed he would have had to endure, and he felt that he deserved better treatment from those in the party. Jonathan never mentioned the exact nature of what was being said about him. Undoubtedly, the talk was related to Ruggles and the upcoming selection of a new senator to represent Maine in the U.S. Senate. There is no record that Jonathan had ever said he would not support Ruggles. Clearly, Jonathan was perceived as a man who had growing influence in the party, an influence that the Ruggles/Smith faction wanted to stifle.

In spite of the assault on his character, he reassured Deborah that he had "borne it all as a man" and he was "determined never to give up till justice" was achieved. He added that he had been developing political power and "I know that by many here I am hated and feared," going on to say that "I am hated because I am feared."

He was feared not by those in the opposition party but by some within in his own Democratic Party—more specifically, by Smith, Ruggles, and their cohorts, because they believed Jonathan was working to oppose their agenda. Ruggles was looking for a U.S. Senate seat and, given his opposition to Jonathan's reelection, had to assume Jonathan would oppose his Senate bid. Jonathan must also have known about the plan to replace Governor Smith with Dunlap. Most likely, with the move to get Jonathan's election reversed, the hope was to have him back home in Thomaston by the time the party caucus met to select the gubernatorial candidate. This would thus negate Jonathan's opposition and any influence he would have with others.

In mid-January, the legislature was ready to take up the appointment of the new senator. With the Democratic Party in control of both branches, its caucus selection would get the seat. The opposition press did not care for any of the suggested candidates. They described Ruggles as a person with "the low cunning of mere animal instinct, and a kind of mock dignity that is truly farcical." When the Democrats assembled to choose their Senate candidate, Ruggles came in second. The Smith/Ruggles group had not achieved enough power to get Ruggles elected. The choice was Ether Shepley, who, at the time of his selection, was the U.S. attorney in Maine, a post he had held since 1821. With Shepley elected, Ruggles begrudgingly returned to his court bench and would need to wait until 1835 for another chance to gain a Senate seat.

Jonathan believed that in spite of the animosity toward him, he could be "useful to the cause of republicanism" and that he could be helpful to the cause of the party. So, while awaiting a decision regarding his seat, Jonathan actively engaged in the issues before the House, but his anguish over the attacks against him was beginning to take a toll. In assessing his own style of dealing with others, he compared himself to Hezekiah Prince. Jonathan described Hezekiah as a person who, when he found an individual lacking in principle, would ascribe the same lack of principle to all others with like opinions. Jonathan, however, thought each individual should be judged individually and not by the group to which he or she belonged.

Early in his political career Jonathan found it hard to believe that anyone who set out to serve the people could be less then honorable, and not have the people's interest as their priority. He naively assumed the goodness in people and was thus blindsided by those from whom he did not expect it. This would change over the course of the next five years. Hawthorne wrote that Jonathan "was slow to withdraw his confidence from any man whom he deemed a friend, and it has been mentioned as almost his only weak point, that he was apt to suffer himself to be betrayed before he would condescend to suspect. His prejudices, however, when once adopted, partook of the depth and strength of his character, and could not be readily overcome: he loved to subdue his foes: but no man could use a triumph more generously than he."

Even though the right to his seat in the House was in jeopardy, Jonathan did not back off from doing his job. Early in the session Governor Smith requested that the legislature make known their support of Jackson's stand against South Carolina's nullification threat. A committee was appointed to prepare a resolution, and the one they returned was not totally supportive of the president's proclamation. The resolution put forth by the committee affirmed Jackson's stand against nullification but spoke against the federal government's right to impose tariffs. Jonathan argued, much to the irritation of those who were trying to send him home, that those in the legislature who were true Democrats should support Jackson without any deviation. He said that unless the part of the resolve that strongly denounced tariffs was removed, he would not vote for it. He also criticized the resolution for not speaking out strongly against secession. A vote for the resolve would allow South Carolina and states with a similar determination to sabotage the Union and encourage putting their own agendas ahead of the nation as a whole.

On January 31, the Committee on Contested Elections' report concluded that Jonathan was not entitled to his seat. The committee's reason for denying him his seat was different from those presented by the men who challenged the election. Jonathan protested that he had never been informed about the possible objections and was not given time to prepare a defense. When the report's recommendation was brought up again on February 5, Jonathan asked the House to postpone discussion because he had been sick and unable to prepare. It agreed to give him another week, but it was to no avail.

Finally, on February 19, the matter came before the House for a vote. The reasons the committee gave to support their position were not related to anything Jonathan had done, but were based on what they believed was an inappropriate scheduling of meetings on the part of the selectmen, two of whom had been seeking the House seat. The vote on the motion to deny Jonathan his seat passed by a ratio of 2 to 1. Every member from Cumberland County, both Democrat and National Republican/ Whig, voted against him. So Jonathan was given his pay and travel allowance (about $200), and he returned to Thomaston. Two days later, the House also decided that Spear should not have his seat. The two seats were not filled.

The National Republican/Whig press painted Jonathan's removal as the work of Ruggles, who used his tools in the legislature to gain his revenge because Jonathan "had the independence to oppose his ambitious schemes of self-aggrandizement." The *Argus* shot back and pointed out that most of the National Republican Party had also voted to remove Jonathan. In either case, both factions had at least temporarily sidelined Jonathan, whose rising political fortunes they feared.

With Jonathan no longer part of the legislature, he missed the caucus that traditionally met to nominate the party's gubernatorial candidate for the upcoming September election. The customary procedure was to re-nominate the incumbent, unless he made it known that he did not wish to stand for reelection. For their own reasons, the Smith/Ruggles faction wanted to replace Governor Smith with Robert Dunlap. In order to push their agenda they manipulated the Democratic caucus into not nominating a candidate, but instead pushed for a statewide nominating convention to be held in June. The reason given for the convention was to allow more people to have a say in who should be the party's candidate for governor. It was clear that they believed they could more easily push Dunlap forward in a convention setting. The convention was intentionally scheduled for June 26, at a time that ensured low attendance, particularly by those people from rural agricultural areas. Had he been there, Jonathan would not have supported this change in the nominating procedure. With Jonathan back home in Thomaston, his opposition would not be heard until later.

Even after Jonathan left Bowdoin he continued to maintain contact with Franklin Pierce. After Pierce graduated in 1824, he returned to New Hampshire to study law. George Washington Pierce (not related to Franklin) was in Jonathan's class at Bowdoin. He had been a member of the Federalist-leaning Peucinian Society along with Longfellow and he later married Longfellow's sister Anne. Soon after leaving Bowdoin he relocated to New Hampshire to study law in the same practice as Franklin Pierce. The two Pierces became close friends and exchanged many letters. G. W. Pierce subsequently returned to Maine. He, along with his brother Josiah, served in the Maine legislature during the same period of time that Jonathan was serving. Franklin Pierce was aware of the developing conflict between Jonathan and Ruggles in early 1833 and in a letter to G. W. Pierce asked whether Jonathan's political future was in jeopardy because of his conflicts with Ruggles. We do not have a response from G. W. Pierce. What Pierce may not have been aware of at the time was that G. W. Pierce, who was from the Portland area, was aligned with the Ruggles/Smith faction. Over the next few years the tension between the two Bowdoin classmates intensified, with Franklin Pierce serving as a mediator.

Throughout the spring rumors circulated that Dunlap's nomination had already been secretly assured. The *Argus*, the main press outlet for the Ruggles/Smith faction, initially denied that any arrangement had been made. They assured their readers that they would support anyone who was nominated, and they championed the use of a convention as a true reflection of Democratic principles. Also in March the *Jeffersonian*, a small newspaper in Paris, Maine, edited by Horatio King, moved to Portland. The intent of the move, to the much larger Portland market, was to bring greater readership to its opposition Democratic voice. The *Jeffersonian* would also be a stalwart friend of Jonathan over the next two years, coming to his defense when he was attacked and condemned by the *Argus*.

There is no record prior to the upcoming June convention as to Jonathan's activities concerning the proposed selection of Dunlap. Based on his actions after the convention, it can be assumed that he sided with Governor Smith and believed he was being unfairly pushed out of office. By April the *Argus* realized there were members of the Democratic Party, including Jonathan, who were not going to let the Dunlap plan go unchallenged and pass quietly into the night. The *Argus* charged that those who did not support the change from Governor Smith to Dunlap were not true Democrats. The will of the majority was all that mattered. The man selected did not matter as long as the newfound principle was upheld. By scheduling the convention in June, they had increased the odds that their agenda would go through. The more agriculturally oriented people would be involved with their land and less likely to attend. As one newspaper put it, they wanted the right to make or unmake governors, while the people "are shoving jack planes or hoeing their corn."

On June 26, the Democrats convened in Augusta. As had been arranged, Robert Dunlap was nominated by an approximately 2–1 margin. The pro-Dunlap papers relished what they saw as a harmonious convention where the will of the people (those who could get away to attend) triumphed over individual self-interest. At the convention Jonathan was the most outspoken voice in opposition to the Ruggles/Smith attempt to control the party. He charged that the move to Dunlap was counter to the will of the overall constituency. He further suggested that those who pushed for nomination by convention were not true Jacksonians, and that they were the same people who did not wholeheartedly support Jackson's proclamation concerning nullification. He said he would oppose and not support the nomination, and although he was in the minority, he must stand by his principles: "I must act for myself alone, and I will walk without fear, guided by the simple though feeble light of my own con-science." For Jonathan, it was just not right to push Governor Smith out of office, particularly when it was done not for the good of the people but for personal gain. Tensions were high in the room, particularly when Jonathan brought up the nullification issue. Speaker Clifford called Jona-than treasonous. One newspaper noted that Jonathan was "looking unut-terables at Mr. Clifford."

The Augusta *Kennebec Journal*, a Whig newspaper, and also the paper that reported in the most detail the proceedings of Maine government, saw itself as vindicated by the convention results. The paper reminded readers—over the denial of the Democratic press—that Dunlap had in fact been chosen to replace Governor Smith in a secret caucus. The Rug-gles/Smith faction was described as "a host of young lawyers who had little business to attend to," and it was said that they demanded all the offices and clamor even when there were no more to give.

Right after the convention, Jonathan planned to visit his family in Nottingham. On the way to New Hampshire, he intended to stop in Portland to meet with President Jackson, who was visiting New England. Unfortunately, Jackson became ill before he arrived in Portland and re-turned to Washington.

It was hard for Deborah to have Jonathan gone. At this time, she was seven months pregnant, and pregnancy was always difficult for her. She had been suffering from severe facial pain and told his mother that she wished he were home. She also lamented that she was cut off from the Ruggles family next door. She noted that "the Judge was bitter as ever." When Jonathan arrived in Nottingham he found that his brother Joseph was very sick, and there was concern that he might not live. Deborah reluctantly acknowledged that Jonathan's place was with his brother. She would persevere and would "try to do the best I can in his absence."

Another issue that likely came up while Jonathan was in Nottingham was the upcoming trial related to the will of his Uncle Bradbury, who had died in 1831. When General Joseph died in 1798, most of his estate went to Bradbury, his oldest son, and Bradbury had built his wealth to what was estimated at the time he died to be $125,000, a significant sum for that time. Upon his death he left his estate to his brothers and their children, and nothing to his three sisters and their children. Jonathan's cousin, Joseph Cilley, son of Uncle Jacob (who had died in January 1831), was named executor of the estate. Jonathan and his siblings had not been left out of the will; Joseph had received the most, but Jonathan and his sisters received a small tract of land. Also, the will excused Jonathan from paying back money he had borrowed from his uncle over the years.

When the will was initially filed with the court it was contested. The prime contester was Jonathan's aunt, Sarah Bartlett, the oldest of General Joseph Cilley's children. Also signing the court papers were Jonathan's four siblings, Joseph, Sarah, Susan, and Elizabeth. The objection was based on the supposition that when Uncle Bradbury drew up his will he "was of insane mind and laboring under mental delusions and wholly incompetent" to make a last will and testament. Given Jonathan's belief in doing the right thing, it is likely that he saw it as unjust that the sisters were excluded. The initial court decision upheld the will, but an appeal was filed, and the case was on the court docket for October.

While Jonathan was in Nottingham the pro-Dunlap press began a direct frontal assault on Jonathan and his character. They condemned his actions and comments at the convention as being guided more by his own self-interests than the interests of the party. He was characterized as "unquestionably a gentleman of talents, and if he would but follow the people, instead of endeavoring to lead them, he might render essential services to the cause which he professes to support." He was charged with political heresy. It was suggested that if he did not see the errors of his ways, he should look to the opposition party for support. Another Maine newspaper proclaimed those who opposed Dunlap to be "no friend of the State or National administration" and "rotten at the core and backbiters."

Soon after the Dunlap nomination, Jonathan wrote to Governor Smith to urge him to accept an irregular nomination; thus, in combination with the Whig candidate, there would not be enough votes cast for any one candidate to secure the election, and therefore the determination of who should be governor would be put into the hands of the state legislature. Here Jonathan held out a slight hope that Dunlap and his backers could be defeated. Governor Smith declined, however, and wrote to a friend that he appreciated the efforts of those who put his name before the convention. He would be happy to return to private life and not have to deal with the "abuse and ingratitude" of those in the party who opposed him. He wanted it known that he no longer wished his supporters to continue to pursue his reelection.

Most of the Democrats in the Thomaston area were supporters of Governor Smith. Part of their objection was a reaction against Ruggles, whom they saw as not serving their interests but aligning himself with those pushing the change for his own self-interest. Jonathan's father-in-law, Prince Sr., who had also served on Governor Smith's executive council, wrote a letter to the *Argus* under the pseudonym "Old Friend" that appeared on July 31. He began by saying, "I regret that I cannot, as in times past, approve of the general tone and spirit of the political department of the *Argus*. I have been a subscriber for this paper for nearly 30 years. We have supported the same men and the same principles through good report and evil: but in some cases of late I have found you varying, as I think, from the true old fashioned principles of Democracy." He chided the paper for its "unaccountable sympathy for the nullifiers" and its lack of full support for Jackson's Nullification Proclamation.

Prince Sr. then took the *Argus* to task for its role in casting aside Governor Smith for no good reason. He said that by his reading of the majority in the state, as well as Thomaston, that all were satisfied with Smith. He accused the paper of inappropriately working to influence the nominating process and the convention. Because there was no justifiable reason to replace Smith, he attributed the paper's underlying goal to be one of supporting "a restless few, who cannot have that influence with the present governor which they desire but do not merit, the unprincipled and selfish few who have been disappointed." While he had nothing against Dunlap, he believed Dunlap was unwittingly being used by the Ruggles/Smith faction. "The press may mislead the people for a time, but truth is mighty and justice in the end will prevail."

The *Argus* responded in the same issue by first naming Prince Sr. as Old Friend. They then suggested that he must be bitter because he was not reelected to the Executive Council, even though he had chosen not to seek reelection, and therefore he was turning his disappointment against the *Argus*. He was negated by being characterized "as a deceived man, rather than a principal in the work of disaffection and deception that is now going, and as a victim to an ambitious and domineering spirit which he does not yet comprehend. The chief managers are yet behind the curtain." The implication was that Prince Sr. was being manipulated by Jonathan.

By mid-August, with his brother recovering, Jonathan was back in Thomaston in time for the Lincoln County Democratic convention. At

that meeting Jonathan again voiced his strong opposition to the nomination of Dunlap and the disrespect it showed to Governor Smith. The
group resolved that they would support Smith. Jonathan's remarks were
supposed to have been published in the *Jeffersonian,* but they never appeared. The *Argus* described Jonathan's speech as a "long winded harangue," in which he verbally abused many of those it defined as the
most prominent members of the party.

After the Lincoln County convention, the *Argus* and Smith had had
enough of Jonathan and his threat to their agenda. In a frontal assault, the
August 23, 1833, edition of the *Argus* published an editorial headed with
the title "Jonathan Cilley":

> This is the name of an individual resident in Thomaston, Lincoln
> County, who is waging a ruthless war upon the gubernatorial nomina-
> tion of the republican party in this State, and also upon most of the
> prominent men of that party in this and other counties. He is the son-
> in-law of Hezekiah Prince, Esq., whose two communications we recent-
> ly spread before our readers, the better to expose the political delusions
> into which he had been betrayed by others. This Cilley has raised a
> spirit of disaffection among the republicans in Lincoln County, upon
> a foundation which he knows to be entirely wicked in itself. By his
> misrepresentations he has deceived not a few individuals around him,
> into a course towards the democratic party which they would utterly
> abhor, were they but undeceived and disabused of Cilley's imposi-
> tions. It is time, however, that the character of this Jonathan Cilley
> should be rightly appreciated and made known to those who are in the
> way of being duped by his artifices. Honest men will not rally around
> the standard of a knave, if they know it. But if the truth be kept from
> them, are they not less blameable than those who permit them to be
> kept uninformed.
>
> As an act of duty to the public, and of justice towards the individu-
> als whom Cilley is continually slandering, we will advert to an era in
> his life which developed the true character of the man, and will show
> the public to what extent he is to be relied on as the informant against
> any other man's reputation or claim to respect.

To substantiate its case against Jonathan, the paper reached back into
old court records and a case in which he was involved as a witness in the
latter part of the 1820s. The thrust of the accusations was that Jonathan
had lied on the witness stand to cover up his own guilt. The case involved a man named Cleland who was being prosecuted for stealing
money from the mail. At that time Jonathan, among other responsibil-

ities, was the assistant postmaster in Thomaston. The *Argus* claimed that Jonathan was overly zealous in pushing for Cleland's conviction in order to cover up his own guilt, and that the postmaster had been duped by Jonathan. At the first trial Cleland was found guilty. The *Argus* alleged that Jonathan spoke out against Cleland obtaining bail while the initial conviction was being appealed.

A second trial was granted to Cleland, and what the *Argus* presented as the crux of its argument against Jonathan was the supposed notes of a gentleman named Joseph Mitchell, who attended the trial. The paper quoted at length from what were alleged to be Mitchell's notes. The notes stated that the attorney for Cleland berated Jonathan as a man in whom one should have no confidence. It was stated that because Jonathan was about the same age as Cleland and also a lawyer, he should have shown more respect for Cleland. Instead, Jonathan was portrayed as going after Cleland with "the most bitter malignity, settled, wicked malignity . . . more so than that of any fiend from hell itself. Who but a fiend could so triumph over an agonizing and fallen brother?"

Jonathan was additionally accused of having an instructor in the Thomaston School fired after the instructor testified at the first trial. Also cited were the supposed comments of the judge regarding Jonathan's testimony. The judge reportedly said, "It is my duty to say gentlemen of the Jury, in respect to Cilley that he is not entitled to any credit—his conduct I need not comment upon—it has justly been commented upon by defendant's counsel." The *Argus* concluded with a challenge to Jonathan: "If he disputes any assertion which we have here made, we are prepared to substantiate it when and where he or his friends may choose to invite us. Truth is our guide, and public good our only aim." Not only did this editorial appear in the *Argus*, but it was also reprinted in a number of other Maine newspapers.

True to his character, Jonathan was quick to respond. He knew that what had been printed was not true, but he also believed that it crossed the threshold toward libel. This must have been a great blow to Jonathan—another malicious action against him from within his own party in response to faithfully representing his constituents and doing what was honorable and right. Accordingly, he sued. Every newspaper (not just the *Argus*) that printed the editorial was included in the suit.

*The Maine Enquirer* was surprised when Jonathan appeared at their office and demanded "to know by what authority" they reprinted the

*Argus* article. The *Enquirer*, in its printed response, wrote that when "aspiring politicians seek the destruction of the people's liberties," the paper had the obligation to expose "those who are playing a double game of deception upon the people and to expose the secret intrigues of public men, and if their actions merit it we will do our part to banish them forever from confidence."

When the *Argus* became aware that Jonathan was planning to sue the newspaper for slander and libel, it reassured readers that nothing had been said that could not be substantiated. The paper further suggested that if Jonathan was going to slander prominent members of the party, he could not really complain when attacks against him were made. It added that he should expect to have "his own character for truth, veracity, and honesty rigidly searched into and exposed." The *Argus* would stand by its assertions until they were proven wrong. Perhaps with some sense that it may have stepped over the line with regard to the facts, the paper acknowledged that "If they had set Mr. Cilley's character in a wrong light before the public they would suffer for our error, though our intentions had been honest."

After the *Argus*'s attempt to destroy Jonathan's reputation, the *Jeffersonian* stood by him, intimating that Ruggles was the one who wrote the *Argus* piece, and also accusing Ruggles of being behind the lies spread about Jonathan during the last session of the legislature. The paper concluded with regard to Ruggles that "this man will yet learn by dear experience, that the ways of private revenge are dangerous, and that those who wish to rise in society must do it by other means than that of privately assailing those who hold a more respectable rank in the estimation of the public, than themselves." Of Jonathan, the *Jeffersonian* wrote, "Mr. Cilley is as much his superior in moral as in intellectual endowments. He stands in the very first rank among the young men of his profession in the State. He is one of those whom the juntos of young lawyers have not been able to bend to their purpose, and as they cannot bring him into their own schemes they are determined to destroy him. But Mr. Cilley need not fear."

The *Jeffersonian* was not the only newspaper to assail Ruggles's behavior. The *Maine Workingmen's Advocate* placed Ruggles as the head of the Dunlap party. They also noted that Ruggles had originally encouraged Smith to run for election in 1831. After Smith was elected Ruggles replaced him as a judge in the Common Pleas Court. Now, by switching his support to Dunlap, Ruggles looked to be appointed chief justice of the Supreme Court.

The *Kennebec Journal,* an opposition newspaper, commented, "If the private character of Mr. Cilley of Thomaston is good, as we suppose it to be, he will make the *Argus* men repent in dust and ashes for their atrocious assault upon him. We are led to believe the Dunlap men will have to take back what they have said about him. It is of no light matter to accuse a man of perjury and theft, and such charges must have a prodigious reaction on those who make them."

Right from the beginning it was apparent that the accusations against Jonathan lacked any basis in fact. It was reported that neither Judge Weston nor Mitchell acknowledged the comments or written notes that were attributed to them. This new attack on Jonathan had to have been very painful for both him and Deborah. He had to defend his integrity and honor. Slander was to be challenged. With the help of Edward Nealley and Edwin Smith, he doggedly set out to collect the evidence to refute the *Argus*'s charges. It was not until 1835 that the suit got into court.

The election of the governor took place the first part of September, and Dunlap, as expected, was the winner. Interestingly, in the towns of Thomaston and Warren, Governor Smith, though not an official candidate, received more votes than either Dunlap or the Whig candidate. So Jonathan's contention that his continued support for Smith was in part based on the wishes of his constituents was right. In September Jonathan's third child, Bowdoin, was born. Right from the beginning Bowdoin's health was tenuous, putting additional strain on his anxious parents. Also in September came the election for Jonathan's seat in the 1834 Maine House. In spite of the bad press he had received and the opposition of Ruggles, the people of Thomaston reelected Jonathan for a third term in the House.

In October the appeal of Uncle Bradbury's will went to trial in Exeter, New Hampshire. There was no reference to the trial in the family letters—Jonathan was likely not there—but the trial received mention in the New Hampshire newspapers. What adds interest to this little trial, and to the lore of the Cilley family, were the two attorneys representing the parties. Daniel Webster, at the time a U.S. senator from Massachusetts, represented the will. Webster had served in the U.S. House of Representatives alongside Jonathan's Uncle Bradbury when Webster lived in New Hampshire. Webster had gained wide notoriety in 1828 for his impassioned speech to the Senate in defense of the Union, and in opposition to Calhoun's nullification proposal. Jeremiah Mason represented the family members who opposed the will. Mason's son Alfred had been a class-mate of Jonathan at Bowdoin. Mason had served in the U.S. Senate as well as other public offices.

So two of the most famous attorneys in New England opposed each other at this little New Hampshire trial—men who were good friends, and there are numerous letters between the two men to be found in the collection of Daniel Webster's correspondence. But there was no mention of the Cilley trial in the letters. The trial took place in a local church in front of an overflow crowd that attended to see the two stars in action. The trial lasted about one week. Mason's closing argument lasted nearly four hours, while Webster talked for about six hours. One of the news-papers that covered the trial commented that "Webster, by his unrivalled clearness of statement, great force of reasoning, and peculiar energy of manner," riveted the onlookers. Webster and the will won the day, and the family returned to their lives. The trial was profitable for both Mason and Webster, who were estimated to have been paid $1,000 each for their services. Sarah Bartlett, the one who had challenged the will, died in December at the age of seventy-six.

While Jonathan was scrambling to retain his seat in the Maine House, in Virginia, Henry Wise, the man who would forever be held responsible for Jonathan's untimely death, was seeking a seat in the U.S. House of Representatives. He was described as "a tall young man, about five feet eleven inches in height, and thin as a rail, of fair complexion, with light auburn hair, almost flaxen, worn long behind the ears, and deep-set piercing eyes, which at times appeared gray in color."

Born in Virginia, he attended Washington College in Pennsylvania, graduating in 1825. He studied law and then followed his new lady friend, soon to be his wife, to Nashville, Tennessee. In Tennessee he be-came acquainted with Jackson and spent time at Jackson's home, the Hermitage. He found that the legal community in Nashville was not very inclusive of outsiders and returned to Virginia in 1830. As a fervent sup-porter of Jackson, he was elected at age twenty-seven to his first term in Congress. He defeated the incumbent congressman, Richard Coke, who had supported Calhoun and South Carolina in the nullification debate. It was a bitter campaign and the animosity lingered. With the beginning of the 23rd Congress in December 1833, Wise wasted little time in asserting his confrontational style in the House, and for the next ten years he would be one of the men responsible for the lack of decorum and fractiousness that prevailed in the House.

Over time the issues between Henry Wise and Richard Coke festered, and in January 1835 the two of them ended up facing each other at ten paces. Wise got the better of the situation, and Coke was left with a bullet in his elbow. That was the only duel in which Wise participated as a combatant, but he was regularly involved in disputes of his friends and had a reputation for mediating settlements. He knew he inflamed tempers and never left home without a pistol.

# SEVEN

## Expelled

Jonathan started his third term in the Maine legislature on an optimistic note and wrote to Deborah that he believed they would "have a pleasant session." It was only a day or two, however, before Jonathan realized that this session would again test his hardiness and resolve to fight off attempts to crush his growing influence in the party and to punish him for his refusal to align with the Ruggles/Smith cabal. This faction had had enough of Jonathan, so at one of the first meetings of the Democratic caucus, during the first week of the session, they voted to expel him from the caucus. He wrote that at the time of the caucus no reason was given for the expulsion, and it came as a surprise to him and his friends. He was at the meeting and an attempt was made to prevent him from speaking. Jonathan, however, had his say, and the *Advertiser* later commented that "his enemies have not recovered from the severity of his lash." Hawthorne wrote that Jonathan told them "that they might undertake to expel him from their caucuses, but they could not expel him from the Democratic Party; they might stigmatize him with any appellation they might choose, but they could not reach the height on which he stood nor shake his position with the people." Jonathan told Deborah that many left the meeting wondering what had happened and what it meant. Some, he said, regretted their vote.

Jonathan was not the only Governor Smith supporter to be punished by the caucus. Colonel Seaver, from southern Maine's York County, was also put on probation. Smith, now in the U.S. House of Representatives, thought much harsher action should be taken with Seaver. He wrote to

91

G. W. Pierce that Seaver had no more integrity than Cilley and could not be trusted. He asserted that Seaver was a mere spy and should be discarded along with Cilley. He added that both Cilley and Seaver were aligned with the *Jeffersonian* and one could "effectively condemn any man before the public, by fixing upon him an allegiance with that establishment."

Ruggles was undoubtedly pleased with the action of the caucus. Jonathan's expulsion received approval in some newspapers in New England, which accused him of being a traitor to the party and of attempting to divide the party.

Ruggles was not done seeking revenge on those who opposed him. One of his business ventures was selling fire insurance. Edwin Smith was the brother of the former governor and assisted Jonathan with his suit against the *Argus*. In the spring of 1834, Ruggles denied Smith fire insurance on a home his family owned in Thomaston.

After Jonathan put an attachment on the *Argus*'s property, the newspaper acknowledged in early January that Jonathan had in fact sued them for $10,000 "for an alleged injury done to his good name." The paper stubbornly, in spite of developing evidence that its allegations lacked a factual basis, continued to justify its actions as designed to lower Jonathan's credibility with the people. It asserted that Jonathan had willfully attacked prominent members of the party and further disingenuously claimed that its actions were done "honestly and without one grain of personal malice toward the individual."

Despite what had happened, Jonathan assured Deborah that, despite being "persecuted by Ruggles and his tools with unrelenting malignity," he would remain true to his grit in the face of adversity and, at least through his public persona, turn adversity to his advantage. Deborah hoped that Jonathan would not be "drawn into any schemes." She was concerned that the opposition looked to destroy not only Jonathan but also her family. She hoped he had the "strength to resist and conquer temptation and when conscious whispers 'wrong,' listen, think and I know you will do right." He assured her, "My enemies have gone too far and they feel it. They have given me an advantage over them and I will improve it all in my power, by being prudent and discreet and doing nothing which is not right and submitting to nothing which is wrong."

He lamented, however, that "it does seem to me that no one who had endeavored in his whole political cause to do right was ever so malignantly burned." He told her though that he was not fighting all the battles alone. He had friends, and some of these friends were ones he did not expect. He had "no fear of the result, a better state of things was coming, and the day draws nigh when a blow will be given to some of the base intrigues in our party." He suggested to Deborah that they should be thankful to Ruggles, G. W. Pierce, and their cronies, because the whole affair (as he correctly predicted) would increase his standing within the party. He wrote that the actions of those he labeled his "enemies" would do him "more good than harm, and yet they have not the wisdom to perceive it." To again calm her worries, he said that he had "learned that my own interest as well as peace of mind are best controlled by keeping cool and acting with prudence." This last bit of personal wisdom, however, was something that escaped him three years later.

During the 1834 legislative session there were more letters between Jonathan and Deborah that survived than there were in any of the other years he served in the Maine House. In addition to his struggles in Augusta, Jonathan was confronted with a wife who had become more embroiled in inner turmoil. This year for Deborah was extremely stressful. Bowdoin, who was born in October, was in very ill health and demanded a lot of her time and energy. With Jonathan away through the winter, Deborah struggled with her own moods and religious beliefs. Again she was at home coping with the cold winter and three young children. She had never been physically strong, and bearing children took its toll. Bowdoin was only four months old when Jonathan left for Augusta. His constant need for care, even though she had help, sapped her energy. She experienced a lot of pain, which only exacerbated her brooding and worry. She was not able to do the things she believed she needed to do to properly care for Bowdoin. She was not producing enough milk. When one is immobilized, weak, and in pain, the natural tendency is toward negative thoughts, self-deprecation, and a focus on one's failings.

Maine winters are cold, and it was a constant struggle to keep the home warm. Given the lack of good insulation, it could take more than twenty cords of wood to get through the winter. Because of both Deborah's health and the need to keep the house warmer than usual in an attempt to prevent Bowdoin from getting sicker, the wood that Jonathan had secured for the winter was being depleted faster than anticipated. This was an added concern for Deborah, but he told her not to worry about it and just get what she needed. Her brother Hezekiah obtained extra wood for them.

Even before Jonathan left for Augusta, he was aware that Deborah was depressed, but he thought it was only from the strain of caring for Bowdoin. There was, however, something else on her mind that she was reluctant to bring up—religion. In one of the first letters to Jonathan during the 1834 legislative session, she profusely apologized for bringing up the subject and was concerned that he would be upset with her. She had always been sensitive to upsetting him and concerned that he would lose interest in her. She had apparently been holding in her concerns about religion, particularly his religious involvement, and was hesitant to bring this up to him. He apologized if he had given her any pain by being insensitive to her concerns. She responded, "You need not fear that you ever gave me pain. I alone ought to be punished that I concealed or kept a thought from you. I do not deserve so kind a friend, and I feel my utter unworthiness more and more every day."

In her January 3 letter, she wrote that "I feel that I can not let another take my place, although they might be more suitable for a wife and mother. I feel I could never bear that another should enjoy the same from you." She, however, knew that "'tis selfishness and I must conquer it." She was also overwhelmed by the difficulties he had encountered in Augusta, seeing them as an effort to destroy her family. She told him that "enemies, enemies is continually running in my mind."

Jonathan responded curtly to her fear for the marriage and that someone else might take her place when he wrote, "Why in the world do you try to bring your mind to such a point as that? Do you wish to torment yourself . . . why torment our feelings with borrowed trouble?" A typical response to her insecurities was to blame himself. But here, in one of his rare expressions of irritation with her, he reminded her that "I have real enough trouble from my enemies" without her adding stress to his life. He further commented, "How you could imagine that I know your mind was exercised on the weight of religion I know not." He said he had no idea that concerns about religion were affecting her mood.

In Thomaston in 1834, as in other communities throughout the country, there was an upsurge in religious interest and religious revival meetings were a very common occurrence. Deborah told Jonathan that in Thomaston there were as many as three meetings a day. She wrote that "there is quite a reformation here where numbers are converted." She was disappointed that she had only been to three meetings. Jonathan, however, because of her fragile health, encouraged her not to go out in the cold weather to attend a meeting. As an alternative, he suggested she have local clergy come to her. Prince, she said, was now serious about his religion, and there must have been pressure on her, particularly with Jonathan gone, to become actively involved. These meetings had to have been going on before Jonathan left, but, given his low interest in religion, he probably paid little attention to them.

It would only be natural for Deborah to look to religion as a way to bolster her inner strength and aid her with the weight of caring for a sick child whom she likely believed would not live long. She also had a deep sense of guilt because she did not have the strength to care for Bowdoin in the way she expected of herself. The prospect of losing Bowdoin was on her mind when she wrote to Ann, "How thankful we ought to be when we are blest with healthy and perfect children—it is very trying to mind as well as body to watch over and care for a sick babe for any length of time."

Jonathan responded to Deborah's concern about his religious convictions by agreeing with her that he was "not religious, yet I am firmly of the opinion that there is such a thing as true and undefiled religions, that influences the conduct of some at all times and under all circumstances. I am not religious, yet I am no stranger to its influence at times, I know well that I can not cherish that sentiment and yield to its dictates so much as I ought, nor can I just know, but the time may come when I shall be made stronger and able at all times to resist whatever of evil tendency is interwoven in my disposition."

Even into February Deborah continued to be concerned about Jonathan's commitment to his spiritual life. She wrote that while she knew his work in the legislature and the problems he had been having required a lot of his attention, he must not neglect his spiritual needs. She wanted him to "enquire and know whether you are on the right path, the straight and narrow one, as you have all the gifts of an upright and moral man, you ought to be more thankful to your heavenly father for such gifts and improve them for his glory, have you my dear that perfect reliance, in all your troubles his goodness? Do you find comfort and consolation in laying all your difficulties before him? I can tell you it will give you the greatest consolation, thus to address him, he is ever willing to assist and I hope and pray he will give you courage and prudence, and give you that peace of mind which the world cannot give nor take away." She reminded him that Hezekiah was active and had "risen to be prayed for." She said she prayed that Hezekiah would "be brought to see that he is a sinner, and that my husband, my dear, dear husband may also see and feel that he is one and that he may anxiously seek and obtain pure religion."

Jonathan responded that he always knew Hezekiah Prince was serious about religion, and that if Prince "feels happier in an open profession, it is his duty to make it." It is unlikely that Jonathan seriously put much thought into issues of religion, but, as a way of appeasing Deborah's concerns, he allowed that "it is possible I might see things in the same light you do and thereby increase your happiness." He added, "I am not without a religious belief, strong and fixed, though I am fully conscious I do not at all times act in accordance with it." He was sure those at home would set a good example for him to follow.

At one point, concerned about all she was dealing with at home, he told her that he thought of asking for a leave of absence from the legislature so he could come home. He reflected further, however, and concluded, "I am thought to be useful here." He said he owed the people of Thomaston his representation because they had elected him in spite of the lies that had been spread about him.

The Federal/Whig party in Maine in 1833–1834 must have relished the turmoil within the majority Democratic Party, hoping the internal conflict would open the door for them to surge back into power. After Jonathan was ousted from the party, a letter to the editor appeared in the January 13 issue of the *Advertiser* noting that Jonathan was "a much injured man and that his day of retribution must come." The letter writer also commented that the action taken against Jonathan was personal (implying Ruggles) in addition to being political. Jonathan was characterized as one of the strongest men in the legislature. The writer concluded, "I dislike his political principles, but I admire his manly independence."

The letter in the *Advertiser* spawned a response in the January 20 issue of the *Argus*, which the *Jeffersonian* reported was authored by Ruggles. Without directly mentioning Jonathan by name, but as the one that the Democrats in the legislature expelled, the writer in the *Argus* asserted that the Federal Party was always willing to take the castoffs of the Democratic Party, no matter how obnoxious, false, and treacherous that individual had been. Alluding to the recent comments in the *Advertiser* concerning Jonathan, the conclusion that was required was that Jonathan was in league with the Federalists and had always been. Jonathan was accused of serving the Federalists "by acting the part of a traitor, sowing the seed of discord among democrats, abusing and vilifying every prominent individual" in the party. Jonathan was characterized as a man who daily exerted a "deep rooted and bitter hostility to every man who possessed the confidence and respect of the Democratic Party." The writer concluded that the Federalists would soon discover that Jonathan would "prove as false and treacherous to them as he had been to others," and that it was not in Jonathan's "nature to be otherwise." The bitterness in this last statement certainly seems to point to Ruggles as the author.

On February 3, the *Jeffersonian*, as it had done the previous September, came to Jonathan's defense with a response to what it called a "most odious and malicious conspiracy against the character and reputation of Mr. Cilley." The paper informed readers that the supposed statements by Judge Weston and Mitchell, which were the basis of the *Argus*'s case against Jonathan, had been fabricated, and both men had denied the attributions. They accused Ruggles of being two-faced because, even though he had frequently spoken of his good feelings toward Jonathan and his regret for having to speak ill of him, he was the one who continued to circulate misinformation about Jonathan throughout the state.

The *Jeffersonian* asserted that Ruggles's charge that Jonathan was in league with the Federalists was without basis and correctly pointed out that Jonathan had won reelection in Thomaston to his seat in the House in both 1832 and 1833 despite the joint efforts of the Federalists and Ruggles to unseat him. The paper wrote that the primary reason Jonathan was being attacked was because he "refused to join that political combination whose object was to calumniate those who had justly earned the public confidence, and help each other into office—a combination, which is the shame of our State, and will, if not put down by the people, prove the disgrace and ruin of the democratic party." Jonathan's refusal to acquiesce to their agenda, the *Jeffersonian* concluded, and "his fine talents, which meritocracy, fear, and wishes to be rid of, constitute the damning moral political sins of Mr. Cilley."

The *Jeffersonian* also brought up what it labeled "one scandalous device resorted to, for the purpose of destroying the reputation of Mr. Cilley." There had been a story circulating that while at Bowdoin Jonathan had borrowed $10 from another student and claimed he had enclosed the

$10 as repayment in a letter. It was alleged that Jonathan knowingly did not put the money in the letter, implying that Jonathan had willfully attempted to cheat the student who had loaned him money, and thus earning another blotch on his character. In fact, someone else had borrowed the money and tried to deceive the loaner. The *Jeffersonian* strongly suggested that G. W. Pierce, also at Bowdoin at the time, had falsely attributed the incident to Jonathan. When confronted, the *Jeffersonian* claimed that G. W. Pierce justified his spreading of false rumors by saying that it had not been dishonorably done, but was done for the good of the party. This "anything goes for the good of the cabal" excuse was clearly consistent with the Ruggles/Smith strategy. G. W. Pierce was characterized as someone who had, only four or five years before, abandoned the Federalist Party in favor of the Democrats because he believed the switch would enhance his personal ambitions. The *Jeffersonian* also reminded its readers that G. W. Pierce had, for some time, been writing for the *Argus* under various names.

During the 1834 session, Jonathan had come into conflict with G. W. Pierce, his Pot-8-O-Club cohort from his Bowdoin years, on two occasions. One incident occurred when Pierce spoke in support of a bill that would allow the legislature to hire someone to draft bills for them, so the legislators themselves would not have to do it. Jonathan countered that it was not necessary to spend money on something the members were sent to Augusta to do. He then backhandedly added that "the gentleman from Portland will find it easy to draft his own bills and it will not prove such an intellectual effort as imagined."

The second confrontation came when a resolution was put before the House to authorize an investigation of the state prison and particularly the warden. The Democratic leadership opposed the investigation, and G. W. Pierce took the lead in arguing for the opposition. Jonathan was in favor of the investigation and pointed out that the warden's financial circumstances had recently dramatically improved. He reminded the House that it was always in order to inquire into the actions of public servants, and those who had done no wrong had nothing to fear, while those who had behaved badly would need to rely on the party to cover their actions. Clearly, what Jonathan was implying was that G. W. Pierce and other party insiders, particularly those from the Portland area, had something to hide.

Pierce then accused Jonathan of making disparaging remarks about the Portland delegation. Jonathan denied any intent to cast negative aspersions on those from Portland. Pierce shot back that at least the citizens of Portland would never send to the legislature "an individual who had been voted out of the confidence of the political party he was sent here to represent." At that point another House member questioned the appropriateness of Pierce's comment, but Speaker Clifford blew it off when he responded that Pierce had not named a specific individual. With regard to the party's attitude toward him, Jonathan at one point asserted that "he looked beyond anything they could do to him and should not hesitate to take the course which duty directed, regardless of consequences."

When the topic came up again the next day, Jonathan became the subject of "a virulent and unprovoked personal attack," which primarily came from G. W. Pierce. One newspaper reported that Jonathan's "retort upon him [Pierce] was electrical, and if he is not lost to the sensibilities of a man, he will rue the day he ever provoked the attack," and he "was indeed and in truth impaled on high, and lashed until his own blanched cheeks showed the working of a guilty conscience." Speaker Clifford took exception to Jonathan's attitude toward Pierce, as well as toward the chair. Jonathan replied that he had "always respected the dignity of the chair, because it was part of the dignity of the House." Then he bitingly added that "he would respect the dignity of the chair, when there was any dignity in the chair."

Regarding the war of words between Jonathan and Pierce, one observer wrote that Pierce was a poor choice to take a leadership position in the debate, "a station for which neither his age or capacity has fitted him." The *Thomaston Republican*, in comparing the two, stated, "In point of moral courage Mr. Cilley has the advantage over Mr. Pierce. Mr. Cilley is able to stand in the open field and alone; relying on his intrinsic resources." However, G. W. Pierce was "obliged to *shy and dodge* behind the stumps and stones and logs of the Democratic Party." The *Republican* suggested that Jonathan, given his exclusion from the party, was not obliged to adhere to a strict party agenda and was free "to speak and act and vote as justice and a regard for the interests of the State would require."

After all the discord and conflict around the process for nominating the party candidate for governor in 1833, when it came time to nominate Dunlap for a second term in 1834, the use of the convention so vigorously expounded the previous year went by the board. Dunlap was renominated unanimously in a caucus of Democratic legislators in February. At that time Jonathan was most likely excluded from the party caucus, but if he had been there, he likely would have voted for Dunlap anyway. He did not dislike Dunlap—he merely saw him as a tool of others.

Another interesting event occurred during the 1834 session that reflected Jonathan's growing influence in the party. Governor Dunlap, as a part of his obligation to those who put him in office, wanted to appoint Speaker of the House Clifford to the post of attorney general. The Ruggles/Smith faction had hoped to install one of their cohorts to fill Clifford's position for the rest of the term, and then have that individual in a prime position to take the Speaker's chair in 1835. They soon realized, however, that Clifford's position would likely go to Jonathan. In order to prevent this, Clifford was persuaded to delay his resignation until the end of the term. So, in spite of his ouster from the party caucus, Jonathan's status among his peers was on the rise, and his leadership potential was becoming apparent.

On June 25, as his parents had feared, little Bowdoin died. He was only nine months old and had never been healthy. His poor health had been an immense strain on Deborah, particularly during the cold winter when Jonathan was in Augusta. Her health had suffered over the winter, and she was frequently sick. She also worried that her own illnesses put Bowdoin at risk. Even though infant mortality in the early nineteenth century was common, for individual families the death of a child was still a devastating loss. To some degree, Deborah's religious beliefs helped her cope with the loss. In a letter to New Hampshire she wrote, "It is right that we should be afflicted occasionally, we can then see our own feebleness and our unworthiness and look for comfort to that blessed Being, who has said that if we place our trust in Him he will never desert us but kindly support and comfort us."

While there is no record concerning Jonathan's response to the death of his son, it had to have been a crushing loss. He had been forced as a child to cope with the deaths of his father and brothers, but losing one's own child cuts to the very core of one's being. In typical fashion, Jonathan focused his attention on Deborah and her guilt. He wanted her to be strong and endure, believing that the future would bring better days.

One thing that Jonathan focused on over the summer was his lawsuit against the *Argus* and the other newspapers that had printed the *Argus*'s attack the previous August. It was becoming increasingly apparent that the allegations printed in the *Argus* were a fabrication, and some of those who had hastily reprinted the attack against Jonathan looked for ways to get off the hook. Over the summer, for example, a lawyer representing Hamlett Bates, the young publisher of the *Maine Enquirer*, wrote to Jonathan and conceded that his young client had been hasty in reprinting the article, having naively taken bad advice from friends. Bates was looking for an amicable settlement, and his lawyer inquired of Jonathan what Bates needed to say in order to end the matter. Jonathan apparently replied and received a letter of apology from Bates in September that concluded, "I am satisfied I was wholly false, libelous without foundation in truth and I regret having published or given circulation to it as a deep injury to you."

The end of 1834 brought the start of the political jockeying to select a new U.S. senator. The current senator, Peleg Sprague, who had just been defeated as a Whig candidate for governor by Dunlap, resigned his seat, effective at the end of the year. A replacement was then needed to complete the last few months of Sprague's current term, followed by a new senator for a six-year term. Smith, Clifford, and Ruggles were all interested in the position. Ruggles was the front runner and had the support of the Portland-area Democrats. The Democrats retained a small majority in both the Maine House and Senate, and thus they were able to elect the man of their choosing.

Ruggles had been disappointed earlier when Dunlap did not appoint him as chief justice of the Maine Supreme Court. Deborah was elated that Ruggles did not get the seat. She wrote to Jonathan's sister that "Judge Ruggles is not chosen Supreme Judge as he anticipated—and great rejoicing there is—and truly we have reason to rejoice." One reason he was not appointed likely was that he had already been slated for the upcoming Senate vacancy.

Ruggles was lobbying for that seat. He wrote to Josiah Pierce, then president of the state Senate, in November to let him know he was very interested in the Senate seat. He reminded Pierce that he was told when he accepted his current judgeship in 1831 that he would not be in the position very long. At the time he had assumed he would get the 1833 Senate seat. Now he had waited another two years. He told Pierce that his present salary barely covered his expenses, and he was also concerned that the Common Pleas Court might be eliminated.

Jonathan, along with Charles Jarvis from Surrey, Maine, had moved into a leadership position within the party, particularly with those from "Downeast" Maine. While Ruggles was from their part of the state, he was not highly popular and was seen as too closely aligned with the Portland faction. In December, Jonathan looked for someone other than Ruggles to fill the last part of Sprague's term, hoping that if he could pull that off, then he and his friends would be in prime position to put someone other than Ruggles in the subsequent full term. With that in mind, toward the end of December, Jonathan wrote to Edward Kavanagh, who had just lost his U.S. House of Representatives seat in the fall election, and asked him to consider filling out the remainder of Sprague's term. Dissatisfaction with some Jackson policies in Washington had given the Whigs in Maine some hope of gaining ground on the Democrats. Kavanagh had been one casualty, and other races had been close.

Smith retained his seat in Washington by a narrow margin. Another close election was that of Leonard Jarvis, brother of Charles. During this period a feud between Leonard Jarvis and Smith was developing. Smith and Jarvis were serving in the House in Washington. Tension between the two had been mounting. Letters were exchanged back and forth, most of which were made public. In the fall Jarvis became particularly irked when Smith sent an open letter into Jarvis's district that alleged Jarvis was the most unpopular and despised representative in the Democratic Party. While Smith subsequently asserted that the letter was a private correspondence, it ended up in the local newspaper, whose editor was Bates—the same editor who had begged forgiveness from Jonathan.

Leonard Jarvis claimed that Smith and Bates conspired to put negative assertions about Jarvis before the public with the intention of sabotaging his election. While Smith denied any collusion with Bates, Jarvis wrote that, as was Smith's custom, he intended to cloud his actions: "The poison was intended to work secretly—the blow was to have been the blow of the assassin, aimed at the back and struck in the dark." This conflict was definitely one Jonathan was well aware of, and he undoubtedly sided with Jarvis. Their issues would carry over onto the floor of the 1835 session of Congress.

With the coming of September, the annual election to select the Thomaston-area representative to the Maine House was held. Jonathan was easily elected on the first ballot, even though two groups opposed him: the opposition Whig Party and again a small group within the local Democratic Party led by Ruggles, who persisted in his attempt to untrack Jonathan's political career. Early on in the local Democratic caucus, Ruggles had attempted to assert his own candidates, but failed. He then ran his own candidates in the general election, and again failed to garner much support. There was no suggestion that Ruggles opposed the local party candidate for any real political reason; instead, he was again driven by his uncompromising animosity toward Jonathan.

# EIGHT

## Mr. Speaker

One of the first things on the agenda of the new 1835 Maine House of Representatives was the selection of the Speaker. With Clifford now the state's attorney general, the position was open, and there were a number of people interested in the position, including Jonathan. The anti-Jonathan bloc was backing McCrates, who in 1832 had sided with Ruggles to oppose Jonathan's reelection. Not wanting to cause more internal party conflict, according to Hawthorne, Jonathan magnanimously stepped aside in order to allow Thomas Davee to obtain the position.

Next on the agenda was filling the U.S. Senate seat vacated by Sprague. Unfortunately for Jonathan and his friends, Kavanagh turned down the offer to assume the interim Senate seat. In his reply to Jonathan, Kavanagh cited his friendship with Ruggles, who he knew wanted the seat. He was more interested in a diplomatic post he had obtained in early 1835, when he was confirmed as the U.S. ambassador to Portugal. Kavanagh's biographer cited Jonathan's courage in offering Kavanagh the seat, because Kavanagh was Catholic and there were no New England Catholics in the Senate. Given Jonathan's limited interest in religion, it is unlikely that he was concerned about candidates' religious preferences. Jonathan and Jarvis believed that inasmuch as Ether Shepley, Maine's other senator, was from Portland, eastern Maine should have an active role in selecting the new senator, rather than having one they did not want forced upon them.

Smith had wanted the position, but many did not view his conflict with Leonard Jarvis favorably and saw his once shining star beginning to dim. In a letter from Charles Jarvis to Josiah Pierce, the Portland-area state Senate president, he wrote of Smith that it was "unfortunate for you in Cumberland that you have permitted a man as reckless of every honorable feeling to obtain such ascendency. I will not waste more words on the fellow but by what I have written you may judge of the terms I always use when his name is brought in question." With Smith out of the picture, Ruggles was the next choice. Jonathan and Jarvis were backing Reuel Williams from Augusta, but in the end they could not muster enough support, and Ruggles became Maine's new senator.

While the *Argus* mentioned the unbroken support for Ruggles by the Democratic members of the House, it is hard to imagine that Jonathan voted for Ruggles. He had, however, never been formally admitted back into the party after his ouster in 1834, so he may not have been included in the count of Democrats.

For reasons that are not clear, the *Argus* became friendlier and more supportive of Jonathan. Part of the reason may have been that Smith now had little influence with the paper, and it may not have wanted to aggravate its shaky case in regard to Jonathan's libel suit, since the case would soon be going to trial. Another reason could have been that the *Argus* saw that Jonathan was gaining a solid leadership position within the party.

At the end of January, an *Argus* correspondent commented positively about Jonathan's action in the House in response to speeches made by two Whig representatives. John Holmes, now a Whig representative, had been one of Maine's first U.S. senators after statehood in 1820 and had a controversial tenure in Washington. Holmes had given an afternoon-long speech initially related to an issue before the House, but the *Argus* correspondent reported that the speech, for the most part, was only aimed at "amusing the boys in the gallery by his ribald jokes and stale vulgar anecdotes."

The next day Jonathan rose to reply, "and for nearly two hours, commanded the undivided attention of the House, and crowded galleries. Messrs. Holmes and Vose (who had also made inappropriate comments the previous day), who descended to gross personalities in their remarks, were answered in a manner which made them literally wince and writhe in their seats. Mr. Cilley alluded to the meanness and cowardice" of Vose, because Vose had attacked one of Jonathan's constituents, who was not there to reply. Jonathan's performance, the *Argus* writer concluded, "was considered by all who heard it one of Mr. C's happiest and most powerful efforts." Apparently the next day Vose made an attempt to rebut Jonathan, but his effort was described by the *Argus* as "a weak and puerile effort which produced only a smile from his own friends. His gun which had been charged for the occasion went off without hitting an object whatever and only left the smell of the powder."

In Washington the conflict between Smith and Jarvis reached new heights in early February. One of the methods Smith commonly used to put his issues before the public was to print and circulate, at his own expense, a pamphlet. Pamphlets, frequently used in the first part of the nineteenth century, were usually not widely circulated but only issued to a limited audience—to men the author was attempting to influence or impress. When not writing newspaper editorials, Smith created pamphlets to attack those who disagreed with him or from whom he felt threatened. In February Jarvis wrote a lengthy letter to his constituents in which he compiled letters from influential politicians in Maine, including Kavanagh and Shepley, attesting to Jarvis's positive standing in the House. He also called Smith a liar, scoundrel, and coward. Smith responded by writing a new pamphlet that essentially blamed Jarvis for the feud. Smith placed his latest pamphlet on the desks of all the members of the House. This pushed Jarvis to his limit, and he sent fellow congressman Robert Lytle, of Ohio, to deliver a challenge that Smith refused to accept. This so irritated Lytle that he offered to stand in Jarvis's place. Again, Smith refused.

There is no documentation as to whether Jonathan commented on the controversy between Jarvis and Smith or offered any thoughts on the duel challenge. It had to have been a conflict discussed within Maine political circles. Given Jonathan's previous comments on dueling, one would assume that he would look upon the challenge negatively. In the back of his mind, he might have secretly hoped that Jarvis would rid him of a persistent thorn in his side. The challenge issued also must have provided Jonathan a sense of the negative attitude of Maine people about dueling. Smith, partly relying on his belief that the people of Maine would support his decision, did not accept the challenge and was willing to bear the charges of cowardice, enduring published comments such as "F.O.J. Smith, L.S.C. Mighty perpendicular and violent on paper, but when he comes to powder and balls then he squats." Another bit published in the *Advertiser* went:

I had a little editor, no bigger than my thumb,
I put him in an office, and there I bid him drum.
I sent him off to Congress, marked and labeled F.O.J.
But when he came back again, 'twas changed to L.S.C.

As the rumors circulated, a friend of Smith's wrote to him with some thoughtful advice—advice that might have influenced Jonathan's actions four years later had he received it. Smith's friend, Ira Berry, commented, "Your friends and constituents have some claim to your services, and your powers of usefulness are in some measure their property, and not to be rashly thrown away or put in jeopardy. The truth is you have much more need of reins than spurs in this and similar cases."

At the end of February, in Augusta, Speaker Davee gave up his seat in the House in order to become the sheriff in central Maine's Somerset County. Jonathan, owing to his growing influence, was rewarded by being elevated to the Speaker's chair. At the conclusion of the 1835 legislative session the *Advertiser* reflected, probably accurately, that "Mr. Cilley is a man of much more ability than Mr. Davee; but not so good a presiding officer. His talent is not adapted to such a station. He is too much interested in what is going on; whereas the more a Speaker can abstract himself, the better he will preside." It can be easily imagined that there were occasions when Jonathan had all he could do to keep from jumping into the debate.

Contrary to the *Advertiser*'s opinion, Jonathan had the knack of being able to work with people across the political spectrum. For the most part he was not someone who always held rigidly to the party line but was open to any opinion that he believed benefited the people of Maine. Jonathan never condemned a man for his political opinion, but he had contempt for those whose methods were belittling and personally insulting. In the comments he made to the House after a resolution had unanimously been passed in appreciation of his job as Speaker, he looked to allay hard feelings and any lingering bitterness and encouraged members to "let all minor causes of irritation and all differences and mutual faults be sunk into perpetual forgetfulness. Let kindness, respect and esteem for each other's good qualities, assert and maintain their predominance."

In a number of ways, 1835 was a turning point for Jonathan. The ascension to the Speaker's chair was an affirmation of his increasing prominence in government and his dedication to his personal and political principles. Over the course of his years in the House he had been unmercifully abused and defamed by others in his own party because he would not be driven by their agenda. In spite of this, he stuck to his core beliefs about right and wrong, and honor, and fought back. He ultimately found ways to turn crisis and adversity into opportunity.

Unfortunately, there are no surviving family letters from the 1835 legislative session, though they were undoubtedly written. It would have been interesting to read Jonathan's reactions to his selection as Speaker and how he thought he responded to his new office. The only letter we have is one written in March by Prince. Clearly, at this point in his life, Prince had immersed himself in his religious beliefs. Given that there was little mention of religion in the years he kept his diary, his immersion in religion was a notable change, which was also mirrored by others in the family, including Deborah. Prince's letter to Jonathan seemed to almost insist that Jonathan devote more attention and dedication to religion. He acknowledged that Jonathan was "probably destined, if you live, to be in the way of doing more good or more harm than any other man with whom I have ever or shall have so intimate connection." Prince wanted Jonathan to be guided by concern for his soul and afterlife. He urged Jonathan to "attend meetings, read your bible and go often to your closet and bow down the body if you cannot the soul before the Lord and ask his care and guidance." After Prince's lecture on religion and the importance of focusing one's daily life on the future, he did not forget his concern about the present, and he urged Jonathan to oppose a bill pending in the legislature that would affect the lime industry in Thomaston.

Given Jonathan's limited interest and concern for religious matters, he apparently played the middle ground by responding to the family's badgering about his religious life with just enough assurance that he would give it more attention while at the same time doing nothing. However, the family did not seem willing to let him deal with it in his own way, insisting that he follow their example.

Jonathan's libel suit trial against the *Argus* (and more specifically its editor, Thomas Todd) began in May. There were many witnesses, including Ruggles. The crux of the issue centered on whether the trial notes allegedly written by Mitchell and used to condemn Jonathan were in fact written by Mitchell and whether they were a true representation of what occurred at Cleland's trial. What came out in the libel suit trial was that the notes were not written by Mitchell but had been fabricated by a Thomaston bank cashier who was hard of hearing, so that even had he been at the trial, he would have been unable to hear what was going on. The notes later ended up in Ruggles's hands, and he subsequently passed on parts of them to Smith, who used them to substantiate the accusations against Jonathan. At trial Ruggles acknowledged that he had had the notes and that he gave them to Smith, but he never admitted that the notes were fabricated. Jonathan asserted that those involved knew the information was not true and published it anyway with the intent of doing harm to himself. After a brief deliberation, the jury found Todd and the *Argus* guilty of libel and awarded Jonathan $1,150, a sizeable amount at the time. Jonathan must have been very pleased with the result, and his vigorous pursuit of justice had to have added to his determination not to allow anyone to unjustifiably and maliciously attack his honor and reputation.

G. W. Pierce did not return to the House in 1835, instead putting his energy back into his law practice in Portland. He was also lobbying to have Dunlap appoint him reporter of decision in the Supreme Court of Maine. He believed he was still at odds with Jonathan and wrote to his brother in February that he had heard "Cilley is resolved to defeat my appointment." He expected Jonathan to recommend his own candidate at the last minute as a way of delaying the appointment. G. W. Pierce looked to his brother, who was again president of the state Senate, to run interference for him and aid him in getting the appointment.

By March Governor Dunlap had not yet made the appointment, and Pierce again wrote to his brother to inform him of the letters of recommendation he believed had been sent to Augusta. Interestingly, he had expected one from Ruggles that had not appeared. To some extent he was not surprised that Ruggles had not responded, and he told his brother that Ruggles had "always made strong professions of kindness toward me and there his kindness has generally ended." G. W. Pierce again brought up Jonathan, suggesting that "toward C. I am as willing as I can be to let bygones by bygones." Possibly he hoped to lessen any opposition Jonathan might have to his appointment as the Supreme Court's reporter of decision, or perhaps he sincerely wished to patch up his relationship with his college friend. He told his brother that "in the future I am willing to have the past forgotten and he [Jonathan] shall not find me among his enemies."

When October came, Pierce still had not been confirmed for the court position. By that time Franklin Pierce was actively involved in trying to mediate the dispute between G. W. and Jonathan. Pierce told G. W. that he had written to Jonathan, with whom he appeared to correspond on a regular basis, and reminded Jonathan of the generally good relationships that existed between Bowdoin graduates and that he had "deep regret that the same good understanding did not obtain between you and him." He told Jonathan that G. W. "apparently harbours no ill toward you and it strikes me that it would be much more pleasant for you both and probably to your mutual advantage."

On October 2, Pierce wrote to G. W. to tell him he had received a reply from Jonathan and that Jonathan had said that he had "no wish to retain the hardness I once felt; on the contrary I have much to induce me to be on good terms with him again. His brother Hon. Josiah Pierce is truly my friend." Josiah had told Jonathan during his last legislative session that G. W. was willing to let "bygones be bygones." Jonathan encouraged Pierce to let G. W. know of his willingness to patch things up. Sadly, the matter would never be resolved because, shortly after G. W. received news that he had in fact been confirmed for the court's reporter post, he contracted typhus and, after four weeks of suffering, died on November 15, at the age of thirty.

When Jonathan returned in 1836 for what would be his last term in the Maine House, he had to have been gratified when he was returned to the Speaker's chair with little opposition. It would be a rather uneventful session for him both personally and politically. On the agenda, though, was the issue of capital punishment, pushed into the 1836 session from the previous year. He also presided over a debate and passage of a resolution regarding the growing issue of slavery.

In October 1834, Joseph Sager was found guilty of poisoning his wife and sentenced to hang. In Augusta in early January 1835, just as the legislature was beginning, his execution was carried out. Even though it was a cold day, it was estimated that some ten thousand people—believed by one paper to be the biggest crowd for any event in Maine history—were on hand to view the hanging. Sager had, throughout his trial and right up to his death, maintained his innocence and hoped for a reprieve from Governor Dunlap and the Executive Council. It is not known whether Jonathan was at the execution, but given the very public nature of the hanging and lingering concern by a few that an innocent man may have been killed, the morality of capital punishment became a topic for public discussion.

One of the few newspapers to comment on the execution, the *America Advocate*, was concerned about the size of the crowd and the impact it would have on those attending. While apparently not opposed to executions, the writer believed a public execution defeated the deterrent purpose of the ultimate penalty. They commented that the death penalty was "calculated to strike dread, but its public infliction removes the dread, for the mind may become habituated to the fear of death by being accustomed to look often upon it. The execution which cannot be seen will be made the subject of reflection, and thought will be busy in imagining the situation and feeling of the criminal both before and at the time of the execution."

There was a push for the legislature to consider capital punishment. A joint committee was appointed to address the capital punishment concerns, and it issued a report recommending the abolishment of the death penalty. In explaining their reasoning the committee members first went to the Bible and noted that the scriptures forbid the infliction of any punishment that would be viewed as revenge. The members also said that the state had no right to end a person's life, and that the public's safety did not require executions, particularly during peacetime. The report was tabled and left to be dealt with by the next legislature. Throughout 1835 and 1836 there were numerous letters in the Maine newspapers concerning capital punishment, most of which supported the end of the death penalty. The Maine Supreme Court, however, came out in opposition to any change.

With Jonathan presiding in 1836, the question was taken up in the House. The initial bill recommended the abolishment of the death penalty, except for crimes of treason, with life imprisonment at hard labor to be the recommended punishment. One suggested change was that jurors be required to attend the executions. The thinking was that if they were forced to watch the death, they might be much more thoughtful before handing down a death sentence. Another recommendation was that executions no longer be public. At one point in the debate Jonathan stated that he would vote for in favor of abolition, but there must not have been enough support because the House let the issue drop, to be addressed again in 1837.

Slavery was allowed in the Constitution, and states with slaves were allowed to count them as three-fifths of a person for purposes of representation in Congress. This naturally resulted in the Southern states being overrepresented in the House, though they certainly did not see themselves as in any way representing the slaves. While many in the North were against the use of slaves, slavery was an issue that was not confronted head on, but it was always festering. In 1793 Washington signed a law requiring the return of runaway slaves to their owners. This was not always carried out in Maine, and the Southern states consistently wanted more done to get their slaves back. Importation of slaves was prohibited in 1808, so it was important for slaveholders to maintain an internal source of slaves.

Maine became part of the concern about the spread of slavery in 1820, when it was designated a non-slave state as part of the Missouri Compromise. Everyone, particularly the politicians, knew that slavery was an issue that was not going to go away, and the potential of civil war was always present. One of the underlying concerns on the part of Southerners during the nullification affair was that if the government could dictate to the states about tariffs, it might want to tackle the slave issue next. The hope by some in the North was that over time the need for slaves in the South would run its course and fade away on its own. For Northern politicians, particularly Democrats, the approach was not to rock the boat or interfere in the affairs of other states.

On the national scene things heated up in Congress when antislavery groups began to flood Congress with petitions pertaining to slavery and particularly demanding that Congress prohibit slavery in the District of Columbia as well as in the territories. Much to the chagrin of John Quincy Adams, who was now a member of the U.S. House of Representatives, the petitions were usually ignored, and by the end of 1835 Southern congressmen, hoping to gag Adams's insistence that all petitions be heard, proposed that all petitions related to slavery be permanently tabled. In March 1836, a resolution stating that Congress had no power to act on slavery passed by a vote of 182–9. In May the "gag resolution," which permitted all matters related to slavery to be permanently tabled, passed the House. All the Maine Democrats in the House voted in favor of the gag rule.

At the same time the American Antislavery Society, founded in 1833, was mailing its newspaper throughout the country, which infuriated the Southern states, and Southern postmasters refused to deliver it. The Jackson administration, consistent with Jackson's unwillingness to deal in any way with the slavery issue, supported their refusal—Jackson was, after all, a slaveholder.

A firsthand observer of the events in Washington throughout both the 24th and 25th Congresses was John Fairfield. He was a Democrat from southern Maine and served two terms as one of the eight members of the House of Representatives from Maine. Later he served two terms as Maine's governor and then represented Maine in the U.S. Senate from 1843 to 1847. During his years in Washington he corresponded regularly with his wife, and his surviving letters provide a wealth of information about the personalities and the issues of the day.

His opinion about the abolitionists was typical of most of the Democrats in Congress: "It appears to me if the abolitionists . . . knew what mischief they were doing, that they would abstain. The South will not have that question meddled with, and if we persist in attempting it, a dissolution of the Union must follow."

The abolition/slavery matter came to the Maine legislature with Governor Dunlap's message to the legislature in January 1836. South Carolina, along with other Southern states, forwarded seven resolutions to the Northern states, including Maine. They requested that their resolutions be passed by the state legislatures. Dunlap passed the request on to the Maine House and Senate. It was requested that the Northern states pledge to prohibit abolitionist activities and to also ban abolitionist literature from the mail. As Speaker of the House, Jonathan, along with Josiah Pierce, president of the Senate, appointed a joint committee to study and prepare a response to the southern governors. The majority of Mainers were opposed to slavery but disapproved of the abolitionists' methods, believing that they were creating more problems than the one they were looking to end.

The committee reported, "Slavery is a question in which we as a state have no interest, it is unknown in Maine, and those states who recognize its existence, have the exclusive control of the subject within their borders. As one of these United States, it is not for Maine, or the citizens of Maine to interfere with the internal regulations of any other independent state; no possible good can result from such an interference with affairs over which they can exercise no control." The report noted that many towns within Maine had held meetings and came to the same conclusions as the legislature.

The legislature skirted the South's demand concerning abolitionist literature by stating that, since there were no abolitionist publications in Maine, it was not something the state needed to deal with. With minimal debate, the Maine House overwhelmingly voted to adopt the resolutions offered by the committee, which were in line with Jonathan's position on the subject. He was a true Jacksonian Democrat and believed the issue of slavery was a matter that should be left to the individual states. He was clearly aware of how the slavery matter was playing out in Washington and of the tensions and conflict within the national House.

After the Maine legislature passed its resolutions, Ruggles informed the U.S. Senate of Maine's action, noting that Maine had no abolitionist newspapers, and that many Maine communities supported the legislature's stand. Senator Calhoun of South Carolina was not satisfied with Ruggles's remarks. He was disappointed that Maine had not come out more vigorously against the tactics of the abolitionists. He said he had information that there in fact was an abolition society in Maine, and he wanted Ruggles's assurance that he would vote to reject consideration of any abolitionist petitions. Calhoun was tired of Southerners being denounced as pirates, murderers, and robbers.

The Maine *Oxford Democrat* saw Calhoun's treatment of Ruggles and Maine's response to the increasingly contentious abolition/slavery debate as inflammatory. The paper wrote about the Southerners, "The truth is, they are determined not to be satisfied with anything on the subject; for it is against the political interest of the demagogues and agitators to be satisfied with any assurance of sacrifice that can be made for them. It is time and labor lost, to make any attempt at reconciliation."

As early as January, the Democratic newspapers in Maine reported that Jonathan would be a candidate for a seat in the U.S. House of Representatives. There are no references in any of the surviving family letters that suggest Jonathan had planned to move to the national scene, but it would certainly have been discussed within the family. Without a doubt, he was well aware of not only the issues that were the focus of the national legislature but also the raucous, confrontational, and hostile atmosphere in the House of Representatives and the men such as Adams and Wise who were at the center of the turmoil. Wise and his cohorts, the *Argus* charged, "thrive only in commotion, violence, and warfare. . . . The most insignificant proposition must run the gauntlet of these political malcontents." As appears to be the history of Congress then, before, and since, "The object of these noisy declaimers, is undoubted, to delay the business of the House, and, if possible, defeat the most important measures before it, and then gravely charge on the administration majority — whatever evils may result from their own misconduct."

Jonathan, however, was ambitious, so it is not surprising that he desired to follow the example of his Uncle Bradbury and looked to a seat in the national legislature. While he was popular in Thomaston, to win he would need to garner support from the other communities in his congressional district, and this would not be accomplished easily. When Kavanagh, a Democrat, gave up his seat in order to become ambassador to Portugal, Jeremiah Bailey, a Whig, took it. Bailey would be Jonathan's opposition during the election, which came in September.

As Jonathan prepared to run for the House, he had a surprising silent supporter. Ever since he had lost out to Ruggles for the U.S. Senate seat in 1835, Smith had plotted to be in position for the next Senate opening. The seat he was looking for was the one held by Shepley. Smith knew that Shepley had become disillusioned with Washington politics, and he also knew that Shepley would be open to a seat on the Maine Supreme Court. To move his plan along, he helped secure Shepley a place on the court, and Shepley jumped at the chance to return to Maine, resigning his Senate seat. Governor Dunlap appointed a replacement in September 1836, leaving the door open for a confident Smith when the Maine legislature convened in January 1837.

Smith partly blamed his failure to secure the 1835 Senate seat on Jonathan, and he was aware of Jonathan's growing power in state political circles. He believed, as one friend suggested, that the best way to negate Jonathan's influence would be to get him out of town and into the House of Representatives. When Jonathan announced his plan to run for Congress, Smith must have thought his chances had improved. Nor did it hurt Jonathan's election campaign when Smith's newspaper, the *Argus*, after years of bitter criticism, became friendly and supportive of Jonathan.

In April 1836, a freshman congressman in the U.S. House of Representatives named William J. Graves, from Kentucky, who had been quite silent during the early weeks of the new 24th Congress, made his presence known in the House. Graves was born in 1805 in Newcastle, Kentucky, to a slaveholding family. There is little information available about his early life. He was educated locally and studied law. In 1833, at age twenty-eight, he was elected to the Kentucky House of Representatives, and in 1834 he won election, as an anti-Jackson Whig, to the U.S. House of Representatives, where he would serve for three terms.

The issue that prompted Graves to assert himself in the House was a debate concerning a disputed House election in North Carolina. The representative currently serving in Washington was a Whig who was not supportive of Van Buren's pending candidacy to replace Jackson as president in 1836. The House was getting ready to vote on the disputed seat, and with a Democratic majority in the House, it was expected that the sitting Whig would lose his seat to one who would be supportive of Van Buren. The pending vote was scheduled for Saturday, March 25, and the House had a tradition of not meeting on Sunday, so the Whigs' plan was to delay the vote by filibustering—talking until midnight, when the House would then adjourn—in the hope that by Monday the Democrats would have more pressing business to deal with, and the North Carolina seat question would be delayed until the close of the session.

In order to delay the vote, Graves took the floor and talked, with occasional breaks, until nearly midnight, causing the *Eastern Argus* to call him a man "who in his first appearance in the House has signaled himself as one willing to thwart its proceedings by the very extraordinary course" he chose to follow. In the newspapers he was characterized as one of "the enemies of order in the House of Representatives." The *Argus* commented that "the recent debate which was pressed into the Sabbath, by the eloquence-against-time of the minority factionists of the House of Representatives, is a standing monument of their impious perversity—an assault on the reputation of the country, and an outrage, perpetrated without a shadow of justification, on the well-disposed, serious, and intelligent people of this union."

Graves's colleagues moved to adjourn, which was denied, and debate continued into Sunday. Tempers escalated. John Quincy Adams refused to vote. Henry Wise and Jesse Bynum exchanged hostile words. Bynum accused Wise of bullying him, to which Wise replied that he would sooner bully a fly. Bynum told Wise that if he was going to insult him, he should do it outside of the House—if he dared. Bynum was getting increasingly agitated; he jumped from his seat and, shaking his fist, called Wise a "damned little rascal." Wise shot back, "You are a scoundrel." Other House members had to step between them to prevent a physical altercation. On Monday the House passed a resolution urging them both to act more appropriately, but at the same time it excused their behavior as being the result of the heat of the moment and not intended to cause personal insult. The resolution excusing the two men short-circuited the need for either gentleman to regard the exchange as an honor issue, which would then require a duel challenge.

Bynum, who would later be directly involved in Jonathan's duel, was from North Carolina. He was a Democrat and came to the U.S. House in 1833, after serving six terms in the North Carolina House. In the U.S. House he had the reputation of being a staunch and combative supporter of President Jackson. Because of Bynum's ardent support of slavery, Adams labeled him in his diary as "drunk on slavery." John Fairfield called Bynum "a real fighter and duelist." Before the session was over, Bynum was on the dueling grounds himself.

In June, Bynum became embroiled in a dispute with Daniel Jenifer, a Whig from Maryland. As was typical in the House, commotion, noise, and confusion elevated tempers. Attempting to obtain the floor, Jenifer commented on the ungentlemanly behavior of some of the members of the House. Bynum responded, implying that Jenifer's own ungentlemanly behavior had caused the problems. Jenifer demanded an explanation of Bynum's words, questioning whether he was specifically calling Jenifer ungentlemanly. As was common when someone's honor was called into question, notes were exchanged after the session. Jenifer did not get the response he desired and demanded satisfaction.

Bynum's second was Congressman Francis Pickens from South Carolina, and Jenifer's was Senator Ambrose Sevier from Arkansas. The seconds were not able to mediate the dispute and the two men ended up facing each other with pistols at ten paces. They exchanged six shots, but neither man was injured. Of the affair, one newspaper sarcastically wrote that "Mr. Bynum comes off with very little credit, as all were inclined to consider him, from his braggadocio style, a crack shot—able to hit a dollar every fire. We would not be astonished if the party should discard him because he could not kill a Whig in six shots."

In his role as the Washington district attorney, Francis Scott Key (author of the song that eventually became the national anthem) attempted, without success, to prevent the Bynum/Jenifer duel. Sadly for Key, about a week later, his seventeen-year-old son Daniel, a navy midshipman, died in a duel with another midshipman. The dispute concerned a petty disagreement over the speed of two steamboats.

Fairfield, after the Bynum/Jennifer duel, wrote to his wife, "What a farce! to give it no harsher name. Nothing is more contemptible and but few things more wicked in my eyes than this practice of dueling." He added, however, that, given the behavior of Wise and his friends, "if a few of the opposition should get peppered a little, it would mend their manners very much in the House."

Later in the session, Graves drew the ire of members of his own party when he would not support a censure resolution against Adams. The slavery supporters were tired of Adams's never-ending attempts to present anti-slavery petitions in the House. The resolution aimed directly at Adams said that the petitions were "derogatory to the rights of the slave-holding states, and dangerous to the Union," and that anyone who would present the petition "shall be considered as an enemy to the Union, and as guilty of an outrage upon this House." Although he said he disagreed with nearly everything Adams favored, Graves believed that Adams, as a member of the House, had the right to speak his mind. He saw the censure as an attempt to stifle debate in the House, but "the gentleman had violated no rule of the House, however much he had embarrassed it."

Premature death again struck Jonathan and Deborah in May, when five-year-old Jane died, likely from an illness. Unlike with Bowdoin, who had always been frail and sickly, Jane's death was very unexpected. She was a vibrant young child closely attached to Jonathan. He was in the habit of writing little short letters to his children while he was away from home, and he had written to Jane in February while in Augusta.

Getting elected to the U.S. House of Representatives was not a sure bet for Jonathan. In Maine at that time, in order to be elected, the winner had to garner not just the most votes but more than 50 percent of the votes cast. While no reference can be found regarding Jonathan's campaign, it is likely that he traveled around his district making stump speeches and periodically engaging in debates with Jeremiah Bailey. The first election was in September and Bailey received the most votes, but not quite enough (49.66 percent). Therefore another election was required. That one was scheduled for November, at the same time as the presidential election, in which Van Buren was running against William

Henry Harrison. Van Buren won, easily carrying Maine. At the time Jonathan outpolled Bailey but was still fifty-eight votes short of a majority. However, what kept Jonathan from winning was the same issue that had so often haunted him over the course of his political life—opposition from within his own party. This time it came from McCrates, who had worked with Ruggles in 1832 to oppose Jonathan's reelection to the Maine House. McCrates was now tax collector—a party patronage post—in the coastal town of Wiscasset and had been successful in getting men in Wiscasset and a few neighboring town to vote for him, thus taking 195 votes away from Jonathan. *The Age* chided McCrates for what they saw as selfish opposition, suggesting that he was angry over not getting the party's nomination. The paper also thought that he had gotten his present job because of the Democratic Party and so should show more appreciation. It was believed that he might not retain his position. Another election was needed, which would not occur until February 1837.

On November 15, a few days after Jonathan's second unsuccessful attempt to get elected to Congress, Horatio Bridge opened the packet given to him by Jonathan and Hawthorne back in 1824 concerning the marriage bet. As of November 15, 1836, Hawthorne was not married, and therefore Jonathan had lost the bet. Bridge immediately wrote to Jonathan to inform him that he had lost, and reminded him that he owed Hawthorne a barrel of Madeira and that, according to the terms of the bet, payment was due within a month.

Bridge and Hawthorne had maintained a regular correspondence over the years, in which Bridge provided constant encouragement and support for Hawthorne's literary endeavors. Bridge also wrote to Hawthorne to report that Jonathan had lost the bet. Bridge indicated that he believed Jonathan would respond and pay quickly, as "He is running for Congress and would not like his Democratic friends at the seat of government to think him dishonorable." He told Hawthorne that Jonathan could certainly afford to pay the bet, writing that if the bet had turned out the other way, Jonathan would be quick to look for his Madeira. Knowing Hawthorne well, Bridge added that he was not surprised that Jonathan had lost because he also didn't think Hawthorne would have been married.

Upon graduating from Bowdoin Bridge studied law and returned home to Augusta to practice. He was in Augusta the entire time Jonathan served in the legislature and, having the same party affiliation, undoubtedly had contact with Jonathan from time to time. It is not known where Bridge fell in the interparty wrangling that had so adversely affected Jonathan and his political career.

Jonathan was quick to reply to Bridge's letter, writing to both Bridge and Hawthorne. His handling of his obligation was not viewed positively by some of Hawthorne's biographers, one of whom wrote that Jonathan "behaved in this matter in the style of a tricky Van Buren politician, making a great bluster of words, and privately intending to do nothing." Jonathan acknowledged to Hawthorne that he had in fact lost the bet and was more than willing to pay his debt. Jonathan's sense of humor at times was somewhat peculiar, as was often the case in his adolescent letters to his sister. In his letter to Hawthorne, he attempted a little humor by asking Hawthorne to be specific and verify that he was in fact not married. Bridge was put off by Jonathan's response. In his reply to Bridge, Jonathan again attempted to put some humor into the matter and told Bridge that he had given Hawthorne interrogatories to which he needed to respond; if Hawthorne provided satisfactory responses, Jonathan would be forthcoming with the barrel of wine. Bridge interpreted the jest as an indication that Jonathan might not pay his debt and wrote to Hawthorne, "I doubt whether you will ever get your wine from Cilley. His inquiring of you whether he had really lost the bet is suspicious, and he has written me in a manner inconsistent with an intention of paying promptly, and if a bet grows old it grows cold."

In fact, Jonathan was not looking to get out of his obligation. He did suggest to both Bridge and Hawthorne that the bet be paid off at the next Bowdoin commencement that was to be held in September 1837, so others from their class could also share the Madeira, "where we would have a regular drunk, as my chum in college used to call it, on that same barrel of wine." Jonathan was in the habit of returning to Bowdoin for commencement, frequently to give a talk to the Athenaen Society. There was no further mention of the bet or the barrel of Madeira until Bridge noted that Jonathan, who was in Washington at the time of the 1837 Bowdoin commencement, had actually been planning for the 1838 commencement.

Regrettably, for two men who had been close during their time in college, it appears that there had been no contact between Jonathan and Hawthorne over the years, but he likely got updates from Bridge. In his letter about the bet, he also mentioned the upcoming publication of Hawthorne's *Twice Told Tales*, his first major publication, and Jonathan requested a copy to review. He wittily suggested to Hawthorne that, given his political and persuasive reputation, any review he might write would certainly improve sales. Jonathan also commented, "You are a writer of great repute," and added that while he had been wrong about Hawthorne's marital prospects, he was always certain Hawthorne would receive notoriety as an author. He reminded Hawthorne that, as with politicians, authors could receive fame and honor, as well as immortality.

In his letter to Hawthorne, Jonathan revealed some of his thoughts about marriage and family when he suggested what Hawthorne had missed by not being married, with "no wife, no children, to soothe your care, make you happy, and call you blessed." He also lamented the loss of Bowdoin and Jane: "I mourn that some of them are not. Peace be with them."

# NINE

## U.S. House of Representatives

Jonathan had to wait until February 7 to win election to the U.S. House of Representatives. He bested Bailey by 228 votes (51.49 percent). *The Age* rejoiced that "the Democracy of the County have done nobly—the contest has been a severe one—and they have triumphed. The ability, political experience, and stern attachment to democratic principles of the gentleman elected need no eulogisms from us." Cyrus Eaton, in his history of the Thomaston area, commented that "in spite of the common opposition, then powerful in the district, and that of a remnant of the opposing faction led on by J. D. McCrates of Wiscasset . . . the latter had the satisfaction to see himself triumphant over them all, and placed in a position where his talents, energy, and independence might find a more extended field of action." Even though his district had a decidedly Whig leaning, and would elect a Whig to replace him, Jonathan, particularly in the Thomaston area, was seen as someone who represented all his constituents, and not as one to be led by party politics.

While he would not go to Washington until September, his term as a member of the House of Representatives began on March 4. Today, members of Congress have offices and staff in Washington as well as in their respective districts, but Jonathan had none. He was undoubtedly overwhelmed by correspondence from people wanting him to address their personal issues. Patronage jobs were in great abundance, and there were numerous requests for his support and recommendations.

Deborah was pleased that Jonathan had been home over the winter, believing that he would be there until December, but Van Buren called a special session of Congress in September. In addition to his new duties as a congressman, Jonathan also had to maintain his law practice.

One of the more notable occurrences of the year was a visit from his old friend Hawthorne. The two men had not seen each other since leaving Bowdoin in 1825, and other than the correspondence concerning the marriage bet the previous November, there is no record of other contacts. Hawthorne had come to Maine to visit Bridge, and on July 28, 1837, he paid a visit to Jonathan's home in Thomaston. Hawthorne's remembrances of this visit were recorded in his *American Notebooks*:

> Saw my classmate, and formerly intimate associate, Cilley, for the first time since we graduated. He has met with good success in life, and that in spite of circumstances, having struggled upward against bitter opposition, by the force of his own abilities, to be a member of Congress, after having been some time the leader of his party in the state legislature. We met like old friends, and conversed almost as freely as we used to do in College days, twelve years ago and more. He is a singular man, shrewd, crafty, insinuating, with wonderful tact, seizing on each man by his manageable point, and using him for his own purposes, often without the man's suspecting that he is made a tool of; and yet, artificial as his character would seem to be, his conversation, at least to myself, was full of natural feeling, the expression of which can hardly be mistaken; and his revelations with regard to himself had really a great deal of frankness. He spoke of his ambition; of the obstacles which he had encountered; of the means by which he had overcome them, imputing great efficacy to his personal intercourse with people, and study of their characters; then of his course as a member of the legislature and speaker, and his style of speaking, and its effects; of the dishonorable things which had been imputed to him, and in what manner he had repelled the charges; in short, he would have seemed to have opened himself very freely as to his public life. Then, as to private affairs, he spoke of his marriage, of his wife, his children, and told me with tears in his eyes, of the death of a dear little girl, and how it had affected him, and how impossible it had been for him to believe that she was really to die. A man of the most open nature might well have been more reserved to a friend, after twelve years separation, than Cilley was to me. Nevertheless, he is really a crafty man, concealing like a murder-secret, anything that it is not good for him to have known. He by no means feigns the good feeling that he professes, nor is there anything affected in the frankness of his conversation; and it is this that makes him so very fascinating. There is such a quantity of truth, and kindliness, and warm affection, that a man's heart opens to

him in spite of himself; he deceives by truth. And not only is he crafty, but, when occasion demands, bold and fierce as a tiger, determined, and even straightforward and undisguised in his measures—a daring fellow as well as a sly one. Yet, notwithstanding his consummate art, the general estimate of his character seems to be pretty just; hardly anybody, thinks him better than he is, and many think him worse. Nevertheless unless he should fall into some great and overwhelming discovery of rascality, he will always possess influence; though I should hardly think that he could take any prominent part in Congress. As to any rascality, I rather believe that he has thought out for himself a much higher system of morality than any natural integrity would have prompted him to adopt; that he has seen the thorough advantage of morality and honesty; and the sentiment of these qualities has now got into his mind and spirit, and pretty well impregnated them. I believe him to be about as honest, now as the great run of the world—with something even approaching to high mindedness. His person in some degree accords with his character—thin, and a thin face, sharp features, sallow, a projecting brow, not very high, deep-set eyes; an insinuating smile and look, when he meets you, or is about to address you. I should think he would do away with this peculiar expression; for it lets out more of himself than can be detected in any other way, in personal intercourse with him. Upon the whole, I have quite a good liking for him; and mean to go to Thomaston to see him.

Shortly after his visit with Hawthorne, Jonathan was on his way to Washington for the special session of Congress, with great anticipation and possibly some anxiety. The trip would take a number of days, part by land and part by sea, and he connected with other members of the new Congress in Boston for the trip. He was well aware of the issues he would confront, the personalities with whom he would have to deal, and he certainly expected that he would be an active participant. He had honed his debating and oratorical skills in the Maine House and in the courts, and he looked forward to making his mark in Congress, relishing the opportunity to challenge men like Henry Wise and John Quincy Adams. He was headed, however, into an environment where a duel challenge or an affair of honor had moved away from being a personal matter to becoming a form of political manipulation, in which the actions of Wise and other Southern House members were intended to provoke an opposition member and to challenge their honor and character.

The Washington to which Jonathan headed had served as the nation's capital for only thirty-seven years, and it had been carved out of the marshes on the Maryland-Virginia border. In 1800, John Adams, in the last year of his presidency, moved into the new, but not yet completed, Presidential Mansion, later known as the White House. George Washington had laid the cornerstone of the Capitol in 1793, but it was not until November 1800 that the first sessions of Congress were held in that still unfinished building. By the time Jonathan arrived in 1837, the Capitol was still a work in progress. Both the White House and the Capitol were damaged during the British invasion in 1814. Over the years, the focus of development in the new city was along Pennsylvania Avenue, between the Capitol and the White House.

One of the first things Jonathan had to do when he arrived in Washington was arrange for a place to live. In considering his living arrangements in Washington, he likely talked with those who had been there. Ruggles, who lived next door to Jonathan in Thomaston, was returning to Washington, but given the animosity between the two men, it is unlikely that they discussed this or any other topic. Pierce, who had been in the House, was going back to Washington as the new senator from New Hampshire, and he was probably Jonathan's primary contact.

Given that the members of Congress were only in Washington for limited periods of time and typically did not have family with them, they relied on one of the many boarding houses that had developed around the Capitol. They were typically within walking distance of the Capitol and varied in size. The accommodations were rather spartan, and the cost ranged from $8 to $12 per week, with smaller rooms or upper-floor rooms being cheaper. Meals were served in a common dining area. Members from the same region of the country and same political party tended to board together. For his first session, Jonathan roomed on Third Street with Pierce and Reuel Williams from Maine, as well as Garret Wall, a senator from New Jersey.

In one of his early letters home Jonathan commented that Washington was not like the North. It was too flat and too hot. He was, however, impressed by the great buildings, but at the same time he voiced the negative comment that "I cannot help the reflection that a greater portion of them are the fruits of avariciousness, meanness, and selfish pride secured from wealth dishonestly wrung from the hands of honest labour and ministering to narrow selfishness, inflated pride, and servile vanity and to false and factitious religion and worship, rather than real heartfelt and active benevolence, mutual simplicity, unaffected humility, manly strength of mind and everlasting truth."

When Jonathan left, Deborah was six months pregnant and at home with two young boys. She had live-in help but always felt overwhelmed by her responsibilities. At the same time, her insecurities about her marriage became more intense when Jonathan was away. She always feared that he would lose interest in her and find someone to replace her, so Jonathan had to regularly reassure her that he would forever be faithful. Her uneasiness was intensified now that Jonathan was so far away in Washington. It was a big city; he would be attending parties and other social events, and coming into contact with many intelligent and attractive women. Though it must have frustrated him, Jonathan diligently (and without much emotion) gave her the reassurance she requested. But he occasionally showed his frustration with her all too frequent requests, as he did in an early letter from Washington when he wrote that "you make me say over again and again what you made me say a long time ago, that you were my love and only love."

Still smarting from the troubles Jonathan had in Maine politics, she was concerned that he would be too outspoken and confrontational in Washington and urged him to be cautious. He responded that he was not going to sit back and do nothing: "It will not do for one who is sustained by the democracy to shrink from responsibility, or to be driven from his principles. They shall hear from me. I will avow the sentiments I have ever entertained and acted upon. I know my duty and shall do it." He clearly defined himself as a man guided by his principles, whose obligation was to represent the needs of his constituents, and if they did not like his representation, they could vote him out of office. He saw himself as someone "who never tires in the cause of equal rights and who never despairs of the success of a good cause and who by having courage himself arouses the same feelings and determination in others."

Records from this brief session, which only lasted from September 4 to October 16, do not list Jonathan as participating in any of the debates. He did serve on the District of Columbia Committee. One vote that Jonathan made during early in this session changed the House rules and banned the wearing of hats in the House chambers. This rule, right up to 2011, resisted repeal despite the urging of female members of the House.

Davee, also now a first-term congressman from Maine, was quick to size up the tenor of the House. In a letter to Josiah Pierce just two weeks into the session, he wrote little else had been done "but organize and quarrel. The opposition are desperate and, some of them, very vindictive. They seem, at the threshold, to be prepared to contest every thing that comes up, however unimportant."

One of the first issues before the House was the awarding of the government printing contract. It was always a political issue because the contract typically went to publishers who supported the party in power; thus it was grounds for debate even though the minority party had no power over the issue, and it gave men like Wise an opportunity to assail the administration. During the debate, Wise accused the administration party "of an utter destitution of all manly independence and alleged that the press of the country was corrupted and bribed." Samuel Gholson of Mississippi did not let Wise's remarks go by without a response. He reminded Wise that the opposition party was not immune to bribery charges, pointing out that James Watson Webb, publisher of the New York *Courier and Enquirer*, after receiving a $52,000 loan from the U.S. Bank, had switched the paper's political support from Jacksonian to Anti-Jacksonian. The charge of changing his political leaning because of the loan was not new to Webb. There had been a congressional hearing concerning it, and in 1833 Thomas Hart Benton made the same insinuation on the floor of the Senate.

Webb, who was born in New York in 1802, the same year as Jonathan, had the well-earned reputation of being brash, impulsive, and confrontational. At age seventeen, he received an officer's commission in the army, resigning in 1827. While in the army, he had frequent conflicts with others and fought two duels. He returned to New York to work as a journalist and had his first newspaper in 1829. As a publisher and editor, he had numerous conflicts with the editors of other newspapers. His most notorious conflict was with James Gordon Bennett of the New York *Herald*. The issues carried over into the streets of New York, with Webb assaulting Bennett with his cane on at least three different occasions. Caning was considered an insult and an accepted way to confront someone believed to be of lesser social standing. If one were your equal, a duel challenge would be warranted.

The often-repeated bribery accusation was not something Webb typically let pass without a challenge. Jonathan was in the House when Gholson brought up Webb and was certainly aware of Webb's response either through rumors among colleagues or from the newspapers. Webb, who was in Washington at the time, immediately wrote to Gholson, stating, "I cannot resist the conviction that (your remarks) were intended to be personally offensive as you know them to be without the shadow of foundation in truth." Webb went on, "In the section of the country where I reside, sir, any man who should avail himself of his position in society, or public life, basely to manufacture and extensively circulate a falsehood, would be looked upon as a craven wretch, and beneath the notice of a gentleman, were it not for the adventitious circumstances connected with his public and private standing: and I deem it my duty to remark that, in my estimation, your conduct is but the more cowardly because it is your 'privilege' not to be responsible for words spoken in debate." He concluded by saying, "I deem it my duty to apprize you, that your attack on me yesterday was false, cowardly, and unbecoming of one who lays claim to the character of a gentleman."

Article 1, section 6, of the Constitution provides members of Congress with protection from any repercussions for what is said in the course of debate, and members are not to be held accountable in any fashion by those inside or outside of Congress. The purpose of this section was to ensure that members were free to speak their minds without fearing civil actions by others. In the early part of the nineteenth century, individual honor and perceived attacks on one's honor were sensitive issues, particularly to Southerners. Men like Wise played on both honor and privilege, turning them into a form of badgering and political manipulation: intentionally provoking members through insults and insinuation, baiting those challenged to respond, thus giving Wise and his cohorts an excuse to turn the comments into an affair of honor. Wise would suggest that if the member's honor was affronted, he should be man enough to do something about it. Being a sly and cagey politician, Wise knew which members of the opposition he could easily draw into conflict.

An accompanying tactic was to accuse the man of cowardice and a lack of honor if he used the privilege to avoid taking personal responsibility for his words in the House. Wise correctly assumed that most men, particularly those he knew were vulnerable to his provocations, would not resort to privilege as a way to avoid a challenge. The issue of privilege became a more complex one when an individual such as Webb was offended by something said in the House by a member.

In the conflict between Gholson and Webb, someone outside of Congress took offense to the comments that a member of the House made in the course of debate. In his letter to Gholson, Webb challenged him not to avoid responsibility for his words by invoking his congressional privilege. Gholson replied to Webb, writing, "I claim no privilege from my situation as a member of the House of Representatives, and any gentleman who feels himself injured or offended by anything falling from me, in debate, will at all times find me perfectly disposed to afford him the most prompt and adequate satisfaction." Webb was not satisfied with Gholson's reply and informed Gholson's second John Claiborne, the other representative from Mississippi, that the only response he looked for was a challenge. It appears that Webb was not inclined to issue a challenge directly to a member of Congress, so he hoped to provoke Gholson into doing so. The matter ultimately faded away; Gholson did not issue a challenge, and Webb had to return to New York. Jonathan, however, was fully cognizant of the whole affair and aware that Webb was extremely sensitive to remarks that concerned the $52,000 loan, and that Webb would not hesitate to call out anyone who brought the loan up.

Also in 1837, the growing sectional hostilities regarding slavery tragically ended in the death of a young man from Maine. In November, while Jonathan was back in Maine, Elijah Lovejoy became what some have called the first casualty of the Civil War. Born in 1802 in Albion, Lovejoy graduated first in his class from what is now called Colby College in Waterville in 1826. He subsequently attended Princeton Theological Seminary and then settled in St. Louis. He became the editor of the *St. Louis Observer* and was soon the center of controversy when the paper took a decidedly abolitionist stance. After he published an article about the killing of a free black man, a mob destroyed his printing press. Then Lovejoy moved across the Mississippi River to Alton, Illinois; he believed that since Illinois was a free state, he would have fewer problems. He was mistaken, because the antislavery position of the newly christened *Alton Observer* continued to breed violence. His press was thrown into the river twice. On November 7, even though he had the support of some friends, a mob attacked the warehouse where his new press was stored. Lovejoy was killed instantly in a hail of gunfire.

Just as Jonathan would soon thereafter be called a martyr, Lovejoy was hailed as a martyr for the cause of free speech and freedom of the press. So, as Jonathan headed back to Washington, the abolitionist cause had a new hero. The majority of Democrats, however, including Jonathan, did not feel tremendous sadness over Lovejoy's death. They wholeheartedly believed that the hurried push to abolish slavery was destined to destroy the Union.

As Jonathan headed back to Washington for the December 4 opening of Congress, an unfortunate family tragedy occurred: his last surviving uncle, fifty-nine-year-old Horatio Gates Cilley, met an untimely death. New Hampshire newspapers reported that he had awoken in the middle of the night and, unbeknownst to his wife, went to the well to get some water. His wife found him dead at the bottom of the thirty-foot well in the morning. His death marked the end of a generation of Cilley men who had all served their country in both war and peacetime. The Cilley legacy would, however, continue with the many sons and grandsons of these men.

# TEN
## Confrontation

After his brief stay at home with his family, Jonathan headed back to Washington for what would be the last three months of his life. On the trip back Fairfield, Williams and his wife, as well as Thomas Davee, accompanied Jonathan on the trip from Boston. He returned to the same boarding house on Third Street, again rooming with Pierce, Williams, and Wall, as well as Timothy Carter, another congressman from Maine. Jonathan's letters to Deborah mentioned women who resided in the same house and who ate meals with the men. The thought that Jonathan was socializing with women rekindled Deborah's own insecurities and required more reassurances from him that he was not interested in other women and would be true to her.

At home, Deborah was just weeks away from the end of her final pregnancy. In addition to not having Jonathan with her these last few weeks (he had always been with her previously), she had grave concerns about her mother's health, who was believed to be near death. Given that Deborah was now in bed most of the time for the confinement period before delivery, she had ample time to think and brood. She wrote to Jonathan that she was afraid she might die during childbirth. He replied, "Death to me has no errors and never had, except the thought of being separate from those I love and cherish." Her fears were unfounded, however. On December 20, she gave birth to a healthy baby girl, who, after a few weeks of indecision, was named Julia. Deborah was slow to get her strength back, and by the end of the month two-year-old Prinny's health became a concern. Deborah saw in him some of the same symptoms that were seen in Jane before she died, which only magnified her worry. Fortunately, Prinny recovered.

Jonathan clearly missed his family—at one time he wrote that he missed Leo the cat, the cow, the bird, and the hen. He told Deborah that it was easier for him to cope with the concerns at home because he was so busy he had no time to worry. Jonathan was also a man who believed that misfortune was unavoidable and you just had to put it behind you and move forward.

It was also clear from his letters home that he missed his children. He regularly wrote little letters to them, and Greenleaf, now eight, would write back. As Jonathan attempted to visualize his new daughter Julia, he kept coming to his memory of Jane; as he wrote to Deborah, "The looks of dear Janey are often before my mind, nor can I even yet bear to think she is no more. May God spare this one to us and may she be as lovely and dear to us as was little Jane."

Jonathan was indeed busy. In addition to House sessions that frequently went late into the evening, he also served on the Judiciary Committee. While he was not much for nightlife, he did attend one party at which he met sixty-nine-year-old Dolley Madison. Her mental faculties and her ability to remember names and faces impressed him. He also had occasion to have dinner with President Van Buren. Whenever he told Deborah about his social life, he always made a point of telling her how little contact he had with any of the women in attendance. At some point Hawthorne was in Washington, undoubtedly to garner support and recommendations from his political friends for a federal position.

Early in the session, Democrats reveled in a speech by Congressman Alexander Duncan from Ohio. Duncan, a physician, who was also in his first term in the House, took aim at Wise and other Whigs for their constant disruptions of the administration and its agenda. He specifically called Wise to task for his continuous bashing of the president. The Democratic press took great pleasure in Duncan's speech and his willingness to condemn Wise for his inflammatory behavior. Duncan would later be one of Jonathan's advisors in his conflict with Graves.

One of the issues before the House early in the second session of the 25th Congress was the dispute over Mississippi's representatives in the House. Unlike most states, Mississippi held elections for the House of Representatives in odd years. In the 24th Congress and the first session of the 25th, Mississippi was represented by Democrats Gholson and Claiborne, but when the members of the House returned in December 1837, Sergeant Prentiss, originally from Maine, and Thomas Word, both Whigs, were in Washington to assert that they were the newly elected representatives from Mississippi.

Prentiss was born and raised in Maine in the Portland area, and he graduated from Bowdoin College at age seventeen a year after Jonathan in 1826. He was someone Jonathan certainly would have known and someone he may even have debated against, as Prentiss was a member of the opposing debating society, the Peucinians. After studying law for a brief period in Portland, Prentiss left Maine for Mississippi, where he initially worked as a teacher. He resumed his law studies and was admitted to the Mississippi bar in 1829. He quickly developed a reputation for verbal persuasiveness and was well known for his argumentative powers. In later years Prentiss was often mentioned as one of the greatest orators in American history. He was particularly noted for his ability to think on his feet and to make the most brilliant observations, even when he did not have time to prepare. It was a skill he'd begun to develop at Bowdoin when he and a few of his friends formed a group called the Spouteroi Society, whose purpose was to develop extemporaneous speaking skills.

Though Prentiss served in the Mississippi legislature in 1835, he never lost his connection to Maine, corresponding regularly with family there. He visited Maine in the summer of 1837 and gave a speech at the Whig Fourth of July celebration in Portland. The Portland *Advertiser* gave Prentiss's speech rave reviews not only for its content but also for his eloquence. Jonathan must have been envious of the praise and desirous that he might someday be recognized for his public speaking. Jonathan soon had the opportunity to observe Prentiss in action when he addressed the House for two or three days in support of his right to the Mississippi seat. It was reported that at one point the Senate adjourned so its members could hear Prentiss speak.

Being from the North and raised in a society that disapproved of dueling, Prentiss quickly became aware that things were different in Mississippi. In 1833, General Henry Foote, later governor of Mississippi, took offense with some comments Prentiss made. When the matter was not resolved amicably, Foote issued a challenge and Prentiss accepted. Their first meeting took place in Louisiana, across the river from Vicksburg at sunrise on October 5. Prentiss chose pistols at ten paces. Both men missed their marks. For his whole life, Prentiss had problems with his legs and walked with a cane. Foote's second complained that the cane and the way Prentiss stood gave him an unfair advantage. Foote was still not satisfied, so a second duel took place. Foote's second again objected to the cane, based on the notion that as Prentiss leaned on the cane and stood sideways, and the cane was between him and his opponent, it might turn the ball from the pistol. This time Prentiss threw down his cane and faced his opponent standing on one foot. Despite all the complaints from Foote's second, it was Foote who was injured when Prentiss's shot struck him in the arm.

Later, when Prentiss was seeking the contested House seat in 1838, he was portrayed as a duelist. Yet his two encounters with Foote were his only dueling experiences, and he was not particularly proud of them. In a letter to his elder brother in Maine he explained his rationale for accepting the challenge, while pleading for his brother not to tell their mother because he knew she would strongly disapprove:

> I regretted the occurrence as much as any one. I neither sought the difficulty nor sent the challenge, but having received it under the circumstances that existed, I could not have acted differently from what I did. If I had, I should have lost my own self-respect, and life itself would have had no further objects for me. I know that with your principles, no excuse will be sufficient in such a case. I am no advocate of dueling, and always shall from principle avoid such a thing, as much as possible: but when a man is placed in a situation where if he does not fight, life will be rendered valueless to him, both in his own eyes and those of the community, and existence will become a burden to him then I say he will fight and by doing so will select the least of two evils. I know you will say that such a case as I have supposed, cannot occur: but brother, I think you are mistaken, and such cases may occur, but not often.

Prentiss's brother later wrote that he believed his brother had accepted the challenge to protect the reputation of New England and that Prentiss had believed one of the reasons Foote issued the challenge was because he believed a Yankee would not fight (a sentiment later attributed to Jonathan). In this case, however, Prentiss lived in an area of the South where the code of honor and dueling formed an integral part of male culture. In that environment the repercussions of not responding to a challenge would have been detrimental to Prentiss's standing in his community. He had chosen to live in Mississippi and hoped to be successful in Southern male society, so by necessity, and in spite of his personal ethics, he would be required to play by their rules if he wanted to maintain his standing.

In a January letter to Deborah, Jonathan wrote that in the House Wise and Gholson had called each other bad names, and he believed they were headed for a duel. "Wise is an impudent and fancy fellow," he said. "I do not like him at all." The dispute between the two took place during the debate concerning the Mississippi election when Gholson questioned an insinuating remark by Wise. Wise responded by calling Gholson ignorant and impudent; Gholson came back saying that Wise was a scoundrel and a coward. To men from the South, these were fighting words. James Polk, the Speaker of the House, attempted to call the House to order and a representative from Georgia proposed a resolution requesting that the two men behave, at which point both men apologized to the House for their improper language. Another resolution was put forth asking both men to pledge not to carry their dispute outside the House, but that resolution never came to a vote.

Wise subsequently wrote a challenge and asked Prentiss to serve as his second and deliver the note to Gholson. Prentiss, however, refused to deliver the challenge, telling Wise that Gholson was the one who should issue the challenge. Fortunately, Prentiss, as others had done before for Wise, mediated the dispute and kept the parties off the dueling ground. There were some in the House who secretly hoped Wise would end up in a duel and get himself killed so they would be rid of him.

In the end, Prentiss, in spite of his persuasive arguments, did not gain the House seat. The vote ended in a tie, with Jonathan voting against Prentiss. Then Polk, as Speaker of the House, cast the deciding vote against Prentiss and Word. The election was sent back to the people of Mississippi. Prentiss and Word conclusively won the next election and returned to Washington for the third session of the 25th Congress. Prentiss did not seek reelection.

Jonathan's first comments in the House that brought him into conflict with Wise came on January 25 in a debate regarding the continued funding for military actions against the Seminole Indians in Florida. This was a long-standing conflict and had brought notoriety to Andrew Jackson after his victory in New Orleans. The administration was looking for additional funding to pursue the campaign more vigorously. Wise spoke in opposition to the funding, stating that the administration had not demonstrated sufficient reason to warrant additional funding and he was concerned about the treatment of the Indians. Jonathan responded in a typical fashion, wholeheartedly supporting the administration. His comments, however, were extremely disparaging of both Indians and blacks.

This was Jonathan's only impressive speech during his short career in the House, and by most reports he spoke eloquently and took Wise to task for being overly sympathetic to the plight of the Indians. He said that he "was impelled to say something when he heard the American citizen held up to the world in the light of a savage, and barbarous and cruel Indians of the south-west described as heroes and martyrs." The focus of the debate, he said, should be on the white men who had suffered at the hands of the Seminoles and other Indian tribes. Jonathan went on to emphasize that he "knew something of the Indian character, from a perusal of the history of those who formerly inhabited the North. When the cattle of his people had been driven off, their houses burnt to the ground, and their wives and children slaughtered, his fathers and the fathers of his people had hunted them to the wilderness, and pursued them even to extermination." He was most likely referring to the Indians who had harassed early Nottingham as well as the Indians of upstate New York, who were essentially wiped out by his grandfather and the Continental Army during the Revolutionary War. Jonathan also spoke very unflatteringly of slaves, declaring that any sympathy for the Indian was as misplaced as "that expressed in some quarters for the man of a yet darker hue."

Jonathan went on to criticize the general in charge of the Florida campaign for being too humane with the Indians and wasting the government's money. If he had been in charge, he said, "and had got his hands upon those Seminole chiefs, he would have hanged them all, and never have permitted them to escape to their swamps again." With regard to the nation's Indians in general, he said:

> It would still be as it had been for centuries past, that they must disappear before the face of the whites. He hoped the gentleman would read the early history of their own states before they too warmly interested their sensibilities in the condition of the other states. They had better peruse the early history of Maine, and Massachusetts, and Vermont; and they would find that in order to carry out their own doctrine with consistency, they would there read the policy of their fathers towards the red man; and how they tracked him through the winter snows to his wigwam among the hills and slaughtered him on his threshold.

They will see that it has been a principle of this country's history that these two currents could not run together, but that the weaker must give way to the strong.

When he finished, he received praise for his comments from Waddy Thompson of South Carolina, who characterized Jonathan as one of the few Northerners who understood the South. In a letter home, Jonathan commented that the Whig newspapers were critical of him, even before they had an opportunity to actually read what he had said. He was clearly proud of his comments. John O'Sullivan, publisher of the *Democratic Review*, later pointed to Jonathan's confrontation with Wise over the Seminole funding as the point at which Wise began to plot revenge against Jonathan. According to O'Sullivan, Wise had been "utterly annihilated before the face of a moral power of reason and patriotism nobly represented in the person of Cilley." Whig newspapers, however, took Jonathan to task for his inhumanity. The Belfast, Maine, *Waldo Patriot* labeled him an "Indian hater." Adams, in a letter to his son, described Jonathan as having "no sympathies for Indians or for human beings of a darker hue, and this declaration had already brought him golden opinions from the carnation colour of the South."

All in all, Jonathan was happy with his work in the House and of the way he handled himself in this new and regularly conflicted and belligerent environment. On February 9 he suggested to Deborah that "If you could see me now you would find me the same as I have ever been, neither puffed up or cut down, not truly above or below anyone, and making my way among men, acting myself and reflecting my own sentiments freely and without fear. All is going well here. I am as happy as I could well be so far from you and children, no other drawbacks. Some worries I have, but no worse." What these worries may have been is unknown. Perhaps he was beginning to get negative comments from his friends about what appeared to be, as Adams had suggested, Jonathan's perceived alliance with the pro-slavery Democrats.

At some point in early February, Hawthorne was in Washington. He had become involved in a matter of honor involving Mary Silsbee of Salem, Massachusetts—the daughter of former U.S. senator Nathaniel Silsbee of Massachusetts—and O'Sullivan, a friend of Hawthorne. Mary told Hawthorne that O'Sullivan, whom she likely met when she was visiting her father in Washington, had acted inappropriately toward her, and she urged Hawthorne to defend her honor. So off to Washington he went, having already sent a challenge to O'Sullivan. Fortunately for all involved, Hawthorne consulted with his college friends Jonathan and Pierce, who talked him out of the duel and convinced him that Mary had duped him. It was later suggested by Hawthorne's son Julian that Hawthorne always felt some guilt for Jonathan's death. He suggested that his father believed that, had he not been so quick to duel, Jonathan might not have acted as he did. Bridge, however, likely Hawthorne's closest friend, always insisted that Hawthorne never felt any guilt.

On February 12, Wise came to the House to recommend a resolution authorizing the formation of a select committee to investigate a charge of corruption by an as yet unnamed member of Congress and, when they identified the member, to question him. The basis for his assertion was a letter that appeared in Webb's *Courier and Enquirer.* The paper regularly published news and opinion from Washington provided by a correspondent who wrote under the name "the Spy in Washington." This spy, as most at the time knew, was Matthew Davis—the same Davis who had been a confidante of Aaron Burr at the time of Burr's duel with Alexander Hamilton in 1804. Davis also later wrote a memoir of Burr.

Wise asserted that the spy's letter made "a direct and unequivocal charge against a member of the United States Congress, of corruption; a charge which is openly made by the editors of two responsible papers in this country, who vouch that the charges can be proved by a responsible witness or witnesses." The day after Davis's allegations appeared in his paper, Webb demanded that Congress conduct an investigation "as an act of justice to itself and to the country." Webb also promised that "the Spy" would be available to answer any questions from the committee. The charge against the unnamed congressman was that he offered to assist a gentleman desiring a government contract. The congressman had suggested that while the man's proposed venture was important, "things do not go here by merit, but by pulling the right strings. Make it in my interest, and I will pull the strings for you." Wise claimed to know which congressman it was and that he was not a member of Wise's party. He obviously brought up the matter as a way of aggravating the Democrats and stalling any agenda the Democrats had in mind.

At the conclusion of Wise's demand for an investigation, Jonathan took the floor. His comments, as reported in the *Congressional Globe*, were as follows:

That as the course proposed to be pursued on this occasion was novel and extraordinary, he hoped the House would pause before it embarked in this business, on such authority as was produced. The charges come from an editor of a newspaper, and we all know that in a country where the press is free, few men can expect to escape abuse and charges of a similar description. Ordinarily, when we are about to enter upon a business of this kind before a magistrate, a conservator of the peace, the charges submitted are obliged to be made distinctly, clearly, and under the solemnity of an oath: and why should we now depart from this well known and well settled rule. He knew nothing of the editor; but that if it was the same editor who had once made grave charges against an institution of this country, and afterwards was said to have received facilities to the amount of some $52,000 from the same institution, and gave it his hearty support, he did not think that his charges were entitled to much credit in an American Congress. If he has charges to make let him make then distinctly, and not vaguely. Let him make them under the solemnity of an oath, and then it will be quite time enough to act. He trusted the House would not go into an investigation of this kind, on a mere newspaper statement, without any proof.

If we look, we will see what had been said by the public press against Washington, Jefferson, Madison, and the two Adams, Jackson, and Van Buren, yet the people passed upon the merits of all these men, and afterwards the press retracted much that it had said against them. If the House thought differently from him, it could pursue a different course; but it seemed to him that some more definite charge than this ought to be made out before we acted. It was giving too much importance, in his opinion to this newspaper editor for this House to institute an investigation upon his mere statement, without any proof whatever. He considered that all public men were liable to have charges of this kind made against them; and if their character were not sufficient to bear it without an investigation into the matter before a committee of the House, they were not fit to be the representative of the people. If a man was slandered in this way, the people would do him justice, and afterwards the press would do him justice, because "truth is mighty and will prevail." He was in favor of the utmost freedom of the press; but this was an inconvenience attending its freedom, which every man ought to be prepared to bear. He thought the gentleman from Virginia himself, upon reflection, would come to the conclusion that this charge was too vague and undefined to warrant the action of the House upon it.

Wise rebutted, accusing Jonathan of merely holding to the party line. He then questioned Jonathan's honor, saying that "he trusted that no man who was jealous of his own honor, of the honor of the House, and Purity of the Government" would quibble over the specifics of a charge. He said Jonathan was only objecting because he knew the likely guilty member was a Democrat and therefore would not want the truth to come out.

An exchange followed in which Wise attempted to bait Jonathan by insinuating that Jonathan had made comments that could be interpreted as insulting. Jonathan countered that it had not been his intent to insult Wise, but that he would stand by his words. Jonathan had heard Wise tell another member that he knew the name of the accused, and he requested that Wise reveal the name. Wise took offense at Jonathan's request, accusing him of ungentlemanly behavior for divulging what Wise had said to another member. Jonathan calmly replied that Wise's comment had been loud enough for many to hear, so he could not see how he had violated any kind of confidential conversation. Wise would not reveal the name, and in the end the matter faded. A few moments later, in a further attempt to provoke Jonathan, Wise commented, loudly enough for others to hear, "But what's the use on bandying words with a man who won't hold himself personally accountable for his words?"

While Jonathan had alluded to Webb's credibility, both Bynum and Duncan, who had previously taken on Wise, attacked the source of the accusations. Bynum said Davis was nothing more than a spokesman for the banking corporations. He characterized Davis and others of his ilk as being "employed for the purpose of defaming the representatives of the people" and "a set of individuals which would disgrace any man who comes in contact with them. They are a set of men who batten and fatten upon the slang and slander of barrooms and tippling shops and no honorable and honest man can come in contact with them." These were certainly words that Wise could have taken as a personal offense, but he let them slide.

Duncan complained that these continued feeble calls for investigations were wasting the people's time. He referred to Davis, who was sitting silently in the gallery, as "black, base, and foul." He questioned whether Wise, and any others who would speak to Davis's respectability, would not do so if they "Knew the general character of the 'Washington Spy.'" Duncan said that "he would not defame and blacken the term 'respectable' designedly by applying it to a wretch so base and degraded as the Washington Spy." He went on to state "that the author of this base slander, is a scoundrel, a liar, and a coward."

Both Bynum's and Duncan's comments, which were directed at Davis, were also indirect and pointed rebukes of Wise for bringing up the matter, and of Webb for publishing Davis's correspondence. Wise's request never came to a vote, but the next day Davis appeared before the House and said the individual he had accused of corruption was not a member of the House.

After Jonathan left the House at the conclusion of the session on February 12, there was nothing to suggest he had given any thought to the possible implications of his comments about Webb and the $52,000. Had he forgotten the recent incident between Webb and Gholson? In his letter to Deborah the day after his speech pertaining to the corruption charges, he did not mention his comments or his clash with Wise. By then it had come out that Ruggles was the one charged with corruption. Jonathan reveled in Ruggles's quandary, and he did not see any way that Ruggles could extricate himself from this predicament. He wrote, "Ruggles gets deeper into the mire the more he struggles to get out of his scrape. Public resentment here, any honourable man of our parties is against him. He must take the consequences of his loose and mercenary conduct." Jonathan had also heard rumors that there might be another case that would implicate Ruggles in further misdeeds. "He is a disgrace to our state." He urged Deborah to "tell your father that Ruggles is caught short in his base conduct and where he will have had work for succor in the smoke and dust of his own wishing. He is known here now and will give us no great trouble hereafter." A few days later he wrote, "Ruggles's character is gone here, he cannot retain it. The act under the most favorable construction is so little and mean that gentlemen have but one opinion of the Senator who would have stooped to it."

It appears that in Jonathan's exhilaration over Ruggles's predicament, he lost sight of the source of the accusations—accusations that the previous day he had urged the House to ignore because the source was not credible.

On February 16, Webb wrote in the *Enquirer* that, as was already known in Washington, the accused member of Congress was a senator. Webb wrote that he had seen all the evidence against Ruggles and was certain that, after an inquiry by the Senate, Ruggles would be expelled.

He went on to rebuke those who had spoken against Davis and Wise, referring back to the time Wise had accused Gholson of being impudent and ignorant. Webb said those words also applied to Duncan and Bynum for their attacks on Davis and the press in general. He claimed their language would even "disgrace the lowest brothel" in New York. He suggested that they would not take public responsibility for their words, instead hiding behind their congressional privilege.

Then Webb singled Jonathan out for his comments about the credibility of Webb's newspaper, but he did not at this point mention the $52,000 issue. He believed Jonathan had planned his words in advance because of "the force and character of his personal attack." He dared Jonathan to screen himself from personal responsibility for his comments by claiming privilege. The previous day, Webb had intimated that those who attacked his paper were whiskey-guzzling men whose life before coming to Washington was limited to the county courthouse, and who, when they arrived in Washington, would then "abuse and vilify those immeasurably above them in education, intelligence, and manners."

The crux of the charge against Ruggles was that he had agreed to help Henry Jones from New Jersey obtain a patent if Jones signed an agreement drawn up by Ruggles that was interpreted by some as giving Ruggles a financial interest in the profits. Ruggles prided himself on being an inventor and was instrumental in the founding of the U.S. Patent Office. He received the first patent issued for a device that provided locomotives with more traction on hills and in inclement weather. Given this background, he had been contacted by Jones, who was looking for help getting a lock he had developed for postal pouches patented and adopted by the Post Office.

Initially, Jones said that Ruggles wanted the money to be assigned to his brother in Massachusetts so that it would not appear that Ruggles was involved. Jones claimed that he balked at this arrangement, at which point Ruggles backed off, requesting instead a one-quarter share in the profits. When Jones again objected to signing the agreement, Ruggles reportedly replied, "Things do not go down here by their own merit, but by pulling the right string, and if you will make me interested I will pull the right string, otherwise I will have nothing to do about it."

Ruggles was quick to discover that he was the member of Congress accused of misconduct by Davis, and on February 13 he prepared a letter defending himself that was published in the newspapers over the next few days. He wrote that while he had made a financial arrangement with Jones for his help, he argued that it was an appropriate consultation fee and in no way related to any influence he could exert as a U.S. senator. Ruggles urged the Senate to conduct a full inquiry, certain that he would be exonerated.

An annual February event in Washington was a ball on the 22nd — George Washington's birthday. It was a bipartisan affair and select members of Congress took responsibility for the organization and arrangements. Starting with the senior ball at Bowdoin's graduation in 1825, and continuing during his years in Thomaston, Jonathan had regularly served as a manager of local dances. Now that he was in Washington, it is not surprising that he was appointed one of the managers of the Washington ball. Apparently, he did not tell Deborah about his involvement, likely hoping to avoid her reaction. She found out, however, when an announcement for the ball, as well as the names of the managers, was printed in the newspaper. In her next letter to Jonathan she lamented, "I see in the *Globe* you are chosen as member to attend the ball on the 22nd—I feel sorry for this and cannot help it. I did hope you would not dance again—*never again*— I feel sorry from my heart—it will be next Thursday I believe—I fear I shall not sleep much that night. *O dear* often says my heart. How I *hate that* Washington, as Green says. I wish there was no Washington. But I must not allow myself to think much of these things, and I do not, for I should not be able to do anything properly."

# ELEVEN

## The Note

When Jonathan left his boarding house on the morning of Wednesday, February 21, and headed to the Capitol, he had no idea what was going to occur that day, or that the choices he would make would set in motion events that would end his life three days later.

What actually transpired over the next four days can be sorted out mainly from the written responses that many of those involved prepared for a congressional committee established to investigate the circumstances surrounding Jonathan's death. Newspaper accounts tended to distort the facts in favor of the paper's political leanings. All the correspondence between the parties was widely published. In subsequent years, Graves, Wise, George Jones, and Henry Clay also wrote about their involvement in the affair, sometimes giving versions of their respective roles that were slightly different from their original statements. Naturally, looking to present themselves in a positive light so as not to suggest they had done anything improper or outside the dueling code, all those involved were somewhat biased in their recollections. Having survived, Graves could speak for himself. For Jonathan, however, we only have the recollections of his friends to reveal what he was thinking and what he did over those four days.

Webb had arrived in Washington the previous day and was looking for someone to deliver a note to Jonathan. He had come at the invitation of Daniel Webster to attend a dinner for New York Whigs on February 22, but because the Washington Birthday Ball was scheduled for that day, the dinner was moved to the 21st. On the morning of February 21, Webb penned the following note:

Gadsby's Hotel, Washington, Feb. 21, 1838

To the Hon. Jonathan Cilley,
   Sir: In the Washington Globe on the 12th inst. You are reported as having said in the course of the debate which took place in the House of Representatives of that day, growing out of a publication in the New York Courier and Enquirer: "He (you) knew nothing about this editor; but if it was the same editor who had once made grave charges against an institution of this country, and afterwards was said to have received facilities to the amount of $52,000 from the same institution, and gave it hearty support, he did not think his charges were entitled to much credit in an American Congress." I deem it my duty to apprise you, Sir, that I am the editor of the paper in which the letter from "The Spy in Washington," charging a Member of Congress with corruption, was first published; and the object of this communication is to enquire of you whether I am the editor to whom you allude, and if so, to ask the explanation which the character of your remarks renders necessary.

Very respectfully, your ob't serv't
J. Watson Webb

Note in hand, Webb went to the Capitol to find someone to deliver it to Jonathan. He encountered Graves early on but did not mention the note. He had met Graves before at Whig dinners in New York the previous November, and later they had both attended other Whig functions. But when the first two congressmen Webb asked to deliver the note turned him down, he returned to Graves. When Graves explained his initial involvement, he said that the second time he'd met Webb that morning they'd initially had a pleasant conversation, after which Webb asked Graves for a favor. He showed Graves the note and asked him to deliver it to Jonathan. Graves, certainly aware of what Jonathan had said concerning Webb, initially thought the note was a challenge. He told Webb that if it were a challenge, he would not deliver it because, in principle, he was against dueling, and he was unfamiliar with the etiquette of dueling. After Webb assured him it was not a challenge, but "merely a note of inquiry to which a definite answer was required," Graves reluctantly agreed to deliver it, not imagining that he was embarking on an unfamiliar and tragic course. When he arrived at the

House he asked a page to get Jonathan for him. Jonathan came immediately.

According to Graves's version of their conversation, when he told Jonathan he had a note from Webb, Jonathan thought the note was a duel challenge. Graves told Jonathan that it was not a challenge, and if it had been, he would not have delivered it because he bore no ill feelings toward Jonathan and was opposed to dueling. Without looking at the note, Jonathan said he would not accept it. He informed Graves "that he had learned that morning from a friend, that Colonel Webb had been making an attack upon him in his paper, and that he did not wish to get into collision with him." Graves responded that he had read the note and thought it was "respectable" and only asked Jonathan whether he had been accurately quoted in the *Globe*. Graves never mentioned that Webb required a definite response.

At this point, Graves, with some awareness of the code of honor, began to sense that Jonathan's refusal to accept the note might put him in an awkward position. Graves encouraged Jonathan to simply take it, claiming that he did not care what Jonathan did with it. He suggested that if Jonathan did not take the note, it would place Graves in "an embarrassing situation," which at that point he had no idea of how to handle. He told Jonathan that he "was ignorant of the etiquette in such cases and had never contemplated or thought of such an event as his refusal to take the communication." Both men admitted having no experience in this type of situation or knowledge about how to proceed. They agreed they would consult with others more knowledgeable about these matters and arranged to meet later in the day.

Throughout his brief time in Washington there had been no suggestion that Jonathan perceived himself as threatened, challenged, or targeted by the political opposition as someone who was a threat to them, needed to be reined in, or attacked. After his death, he was portrayed as a rising star, whose growing influence the Southern Whigs feared. He had come to Washington with a history of being targeted, so his sensitivity to and suspicion of plots by those who opposed his politics always lingered in the back of his mind.

Immediately after his conversation with Graves, Jonathan went to the Senate chambers to find Pierce for advice. Jonathan told Pierce that Graves had called him out of the House and had a note for him. As Jonathan reached out to take the note, Graves said the note was from

Webb, so Jonathan pulled back. Even though Graves reassured him the note was not a duel challenge, it made no difference to Jonathan. He told Pierce he had no intention of engaging in any way with Webb.

After hearing Jonathan's version of events, Pierce said he wanted to consult with a friend who had more experience in these matters. He left Jonathan standing in the hall and headed back toward the Senate. It is not known with whom Pierce spoke, but when he returned a short time later he told Jonathan that the gentleman agreed with Jonathan's course. Pierce suggested that when he met with Graves again, Jonathan should continue to decline to take the note. He should be sure, however, to tell Graves that in declining the note he meant no disrespect to Graves. Pierce recommended that Jonathan should avoid any insult to Graves's character and thus relieve Graves of any responsibility to defend his own honor. While both Jonathan and Pierce were from a part of the country where dueling over points of honor was not a recognized protocol for settling issues that could be viewed as offending a gentleman, they chose to proceed from a Southern affair of honor framework in which they had no experience, rather than sticking to their New England values.

Before the two men separated, Pierce intimated that Jonathan might be in immediate physical danger and recommended that he arm himself. While Webb had a reputation of being combative with other newspaper editors, he had no history of physically assaulting members of Congress, so it is unclear why Pierce would believe that Webb might directly attack Jonathan. Jonathan was certainly not the only member of Congress to have attacked Webb on the floors of Congress.

In the past, in Maine, attacks against Jonathan had targeted only his political influence and personal honor. There was never any hint that he feared for his personal or family's safety. Pierce's ill-advised warning likely heightened Jonathan's sense of danger and raised his suspicion of a repeat of the schemes that had threatened his political career in Maine. Taking Pierce's suggestion seriously, Jonathan sought out Duncan. He related what had transpired with Graves and asked if Duncan could provide him with a weapon to defend himself from Webb. Duncan told Jonathan he could get what was needed.

When Graves left Jonathan, the first person he sought out was Wise. Wise later said he told Graves he should not have agreed to deliver the note because his relationship with Webb was only marginal, so Webb should not have imposed on Graves in that manner. Wise then told

Graves that "there was no necessity to get into a difficulty with Mr. Cilley, as he had not placed his refusal to receive the communication of Col. Webb on objection to him as a gentlemen." Had that been the case, then, by the Southern code that governed these matters, Graves would have been required to defend Webb's honor, for the underlying inference would have been that Graves himself was not a gentleman because he had agreed to deliver a message from a man not considered a gentleman.

Early in the afternoon, Jonathan and Graves met again. What Jonathan said and what Graves believed Jonathan said during this brief exchange was at the center of what followed. Jonathan insisted that he had decided not to accept Webb's note. He told friends that he specifically told Graves his reason was only that he was not going to get involved in any controversy with Webb, but that he had the utmost respect for Graves. Jonathan later said that Graves had asked him why he did not consider Webb a gentleman, to which Jonathan replied that he would not express any opinion of Webb.

Graves, however, believed Jonathan had said "that he hoped I would not consider his refusal disrespectful to me; that he declined to receive the communication solely upon the grounds that he could not allow himself to be drawn into personal difficulties with the conductor of public journals." This would be what Jonathan reported he had said. However, Graves added that Jonathan said, "for what he might consider it his duty to say in debate as a representative of the people" and "that he said nothing against Webb as a gentleman." At another point, Graves wrote that Jonathan said "that his friends had advised him not to accept any communication from Col. Webb; but that he had no objection to saying to me, that he had no personal disrespect for Col. Webb, and only had spoken of him in debate according to the privileges of the House, without intending anything of a personal or private nature."

At this point Graves believed that what Jonathan had said was sufficient to absolve himself of further responsibility to Webb; consequently, he would extricate him from any responsibility to defend Webb's honor. After consulting with Wise and possibly Menefee, Graves suggested to Jonathan that since their conversations had taken place in private, it would be a good idea for Jonathan to put his reasons for refusing the note in writing. Jonathan agreed to do this.

Later in the afternoon Graves sought out Jonathan and asked whether he had written his response, to which Jonathan replied that he first wanted Graves to put his request in writing. Without consulting anyone, Graves promptly wrote the following:

House of Representatives, February 21, 1838.

> In the interview which I had with you this morning, when you declined receiving from me the note of Colonel J. W. Webb, asking whether you were correctly reported in the Globe in what you are there represented to have said of him in this House upon the 12th instant, you will please say whether you did not remark, in substance, that in declining to receive the note, you hoped I would not consider it in any respect disrespectful to me, and that the ground on which you rested your declining to receive the note was distinctly this: that you could not consent to get yourself into personal difficulties with the conductors of public journals for what you might think proper to say in debate upon this floor, in discharge of your duties as a representative of the people, and that you did not rest your objection in our interview upon any personal objection to Colonel Webb as a gentleman. Very respectfully your obedient servant,
>
>                                                        W. J. Graves

After Jonathan received Graves's note, he first went to Duncan and together they went to Pierce. The three of them met in the Clerk of the House's office. Jonathan was incensed with the content of Graves's note because he believed it implied that he had said things to Graves that he insisted he had not said. He reiterated that he had told Graves he would not accept Webb's note only because he did not wish to be drawn into a conflict with Webb. He claimed that he had never mentioned privilege or said anything about Webb's status as a gentleman. Jonathan stressed that he saw Graves as wanting to dictate to him how he should reply, and "that he should not be forced to place his refusal on the grounds of privilege or that James W. Webb was or was not a gentleman." After the duel no one remembered having heard Jonathan say that he mentioned privilege to Graves, and he was not the type of person to back off from an issue on the basis of a procedural excuse. Never would Jonathan ever make a statement to Graves regarding Webb's status as a gentleman. Jonathan had no personal acquaintance with Webb, but he certainly knew of Webb's reputation, so if he were to say anything about Webb, it would not be favorable. But when put in a position where he believed he would be required to give an opinion about Webb's character, he insisted he would not do it.

Both Pierce and Duncan later commented that at this early stage Jonathan strongly believed Graves was only the front man in an attempt to disgrace and humiliate him for his efforts in the House. Duncan, being the most outspoken of the trio, remarked that, though unfamiliar with the formal requirements of this situation, he was one to simply say what he thought. His response to Graves would be that he "could not accept a communication from any man because he thought Webb an unprincipled scoundrel, a degraded coward, and a bought vassal." Pierce replied that Duncan's brash approach might be acceptable from someone from the Southwest, but Jonathan needed a more subtle approach because of the North's opposition to dueling. Pierce urged caution in responding to Graves and believed Jonathan "should only act in the defensive, and be clearly in the right; should it so turn out that Mr. Cilley should be obliged to put his life in jeopardy, it must clearly appear that he is forced to do so in defence of his honor and his rights."

So, in the presence of Duncan and Pierce, Jonathan penned his reply to Graves. Since the House had adjourned for the day, Jonathan gave his note to a House page, who then delivered it to Graves's boarding house.

House of Representatives, February 21, 1838.

The note which you just placed in my hands has been received. In reply I have to state that in your interview with me this morning, when you proposed to deliver a communication from Colonel Webb, of the New York Courier and Enquirer, I declined to receive it because I chose to be drawn into no controversy with him. I neither affirmed nor denied anything in regard to his character, but when you remarked that this course on my part might place you in an unpleasant situation, I stated to you, and now repeat, that I intended by the refusal no disrespect to you. Very respectfully, your obedient servant,

Jona. Cilley

Following through on Pierce's concern about the threat Webb might pose to him, Jonathan went with Duncan to meet John Claiborne, an acquaintance of Duncan's. Claiborne produced two pistols, which Duncan took outside to test fire. While Duncan was gone, Jonathan related to Claiborne what had transpired. He said that Graves asked him why he did not consider Webb a gentleman. Jonathan said that he would not express any opinion about Webb.

By the end of a day that had started typically enough for both Jonathan and Graves, a series of exchanges had occurred that would culminate in tragedy three days later. The note from Webb, which had sparked the whole affair, was lost in the developing events. Jonathan never even saw the note. He was determined, however, that he was not going to deal with Webb. By not doing so, he unintentionally opened the door to a conflict with Graves. His friends also nudged him toward conflict by upholding the rituals of the Southern code of honor as the only way to navigate the dispute with Graves. It did not help matters, and only served to strengthen Jonathan's misplaced resolve, when they reinforced his belief that the controversy was part of some conspiracy—something for which they had no evidence, and that never would be found to be true.

Graves spent his evening at Webster's Whig dinner along with Webb, Wise, and John Crittenden. Wise was one of the featured speakers. None of the principals involved in Graves's controversy with Jonathan later mentioned any discussion about Webb's note, what had transpired during the day, or what Graves should do next. Webb, if he did not already know, would have wanted to know what had happened when Graves gave the note to Jonathan. Webb would have been unhappy to hear that Jonathan would not accept his note. It is hard to believe the matter was not discussed with Graves, particularly by Webb and Wise, and suggestions given for how to push the matter further. Graves had anticipated that Jonathan's reply would be in line with what he believed Jonathan had said to him earlier in the day, and that he would be able to then extricate himself from further responsibility to Webb. Unfortunately for both men, Graves believed he had heard Jonathan say things that in all likelihood Jonathan had not said.

Graves did not receive Jonathan's reply until late in the evening, after he returned to his boarding house. It was not the response he anticipated, and his approach the next day was highly confrontational, elevating the conflict to a new level.

# TWELVE

## Rifle Practice

Graves took the note he had received from Jonathan Wednesday evening to Wise on Thursday morning. Wise described Graves as "highly incensed" with the tenor of Jonathan's reply, and also saw it as disrespectful and insulting to Webb. Graves continued to maintain, and Wise accepted as fact, that Jonathan, in their conversation the previous day, told Graves that he declined Webb's note because of privilege and also that his refusal was not related to any negative personal opinions of Webb. From Graves's point of view, Jonathan had not put in writing what he had said earlier. This was awkward for Graves because he had told others what he believed Jonathan had said and now he thought Jonathan was intentionally denying it. Graves was then concerned that his friends would question his credibility and thus his integrity.

After talking with Wise, and with his agreement, Graves wrote his next note to Jonathan.

House of Representatives, February 22, 1838

Sir, Your note of yesterday, in reply to mine of that date, is inexplicit, unsatisfactory, and insufficient; among other things is this, that in your declining to receive Colonel Webb's communication, it does not disclaim any exception to him personally as a gentleman. I have therefore to inquire whether you declined to receive his communication on the ground of any personal exception to him as a gentleman or a man of honor? A categorical answer is expected. Very respectfully,

William J. Graves

With this note, Graves was telling Jonathan that the conflict was now between the two of them, and Webb and his note were out of the picture. By insisting on a categorical answer, Graves was using language typical of a pre-challenge inquiry. It was a throwing down of the gauntlet and demanded that Jonathan explain why he had not confirmed what Graves insisted Jonathan had told him the day before.

Graves then took the note to Congressman Menefee, a fellow Kentuckian, who resided with him at Mrs. Hill's boarding house, and asked him to take the note to Jonathan. When he found Jonathan, Menefee told Jonathan he wished that Jonathan "would perceive the propriety of relieving Mr. Graves from a position from which he was sure was very painful."

At this point Graves, along with all those with whom he had consulted, believed that Jonathan had willfully refused to put in writing what Graves insisted Jonathan had said. By refusing to acknowledge Webb as a gentleman, they all believed it forced, according to the dueling code, Graves to take the insult personally, therefore obliging Graves to issue a challenge in defense of his own honor.

As soon as he received the note from Menefee, Jonathan went to Pierce, and they agreed to meet later in the afternoon to discuss a response. When they did meet at the end of the afternoon Duncan was there, and Jonathan had asked Bynum, a Southerner, to join them. After Bynum had been filled in on what had already transpired, he thought that nothing serious was likely to result (i.e., no duel challenge), and it would only happen if Graves was urged on by others. But once he had seen the tone of Graves's latest note, he voiced concern that the situation was becoming more serious; since Graves was insisting on a categorical response, something more sinister appeared to be in the works.

Jonathan believed Graves's note showed a lack of respect. He insisted that in his note to Graves he had affirmed what he had said to him previously—that he would not comment either way as to Webb's character. He believed Graves had no right to insist on a categorical response, and he would not give him one. By categorical, Jonathan (and apparently his friends) meant that he had no other choice but to acknowledge Webb as a gentleman, and he said he would never do so. He told them that he saw no reason for Graves to have any animosity toward him and continued to assert that Graves was being pushed into this by others. Even before he knew Graves had been consulting with Wise, he suspected that

Wise was somehow involved. As a group they also saw that Graves and those they believed to be his co-conspirators were planning to put Jonathan in a position where he would be required to accede to terms that, staying in line with his own principles, he could not honorably do. Jonathan further stated that "he saw in the note a determination to disgrace him and destroy his standing and force him into a personal rencounter."

Duncan also recalled that Jonathan expressed his belief that others were behind Graves's actions and that there was a "determination to force him into personal combat or disgrace him." And that he "was selected for this attack because he was from the New England region, where they knew that the moral feeling was against dueling, but if they thought to break him down by frightening him, they were mistaken. He was opposed to dueling, but was determined at all times to defend his person and his honor."

At this point the discussions shifted to a possible duel challenge. It was clear to all that Jonathan was determined, even at this early point, and had made up his mind to fight. Jonathan told the group that if it could not be avoided, the only weapon he had ever used was a rifle, although he had not shot one in years. When he was young he had used them to shoot squirrels. There was, however, no talk or noted advice from those Jonathan had consulted about not engaging in the Southern dueling culture or advice about how Jonathan could disengage himself from this situation without compromising his principles. Then Jonathan penned his response:

> House of Representatives, February 22, 1838.
>
> Sir, Your note of this date has just been placed in my hands. I regret that mine of yesterday was not satisfactory to you, but I cannot admit the right on your part to propound the question to which you ask a categorical answer, and therefore decline any further response to it. Very respectfully
>
> Jonathan Cilley

Jonathan asked Bynum to take his response to Graves and also asked him to be his second if a challenge ensued. Bynum declined, citing past friendships between his family and Graves's, but added that should Jonathan decide to accept a challenge from Graves, he would be available to Jonathan to consult on the details of a duel. Duncan was the one to deliver the note to Graves.

After leaving Jonathan, Pierce sought another opinion. He went to Representative Francis Pickens. After giving Pickens a synopsis of what had already occurred, Pierce asked Pickens if he thought a challenge would be likely. Pickens said no, not believing the matter, as it stood, was serious enough to provoke a challenge. Pickens than asked Pierce what he thought Jonathan would do if he were challenged. To this Pierce replied he believed Jonathan would fight. He based this on what he saw as Jonathan's "determined character, his strong impression that his rights were wantonly invaded, and that there was a settled purpose to disgrace him."

Pierce then turned his conversation with Pickens toward the importance of having someone experienced on the field with Jonathan if a challenge was issued. Pierce at this point appeared to be assuming that Jonathan would accept the challenge. Pickens apparently thought Pierce was asking him to be Jonathan's second and said he had been involved in duels in the past that he wished he had avoided, and he saw involvement in this type of affair as being damaging to one's reputation. If he ever agreed to be involved again, he said, it would have to be for a very close friend.

Graves went to Wise in the House after he received Jonathan's "decline any further response" note. Jonathan's response so angered him that he came with a draft of a duel challenge already written. That original challenge and its exact wording did not survive. He was not interested in further discussions, and he wanted Wise to deliver the challenge to Jonathan. Wise later wrote that he was initially reluctant to deliver the challenge and wanted to think about it. The two men, after the House adjourned for the day, left together and walked to Wise's boarding house. Wise told Graves that he was still hesitant to deliver the challenge, and, in any case, he would not do it that evening. The issue was then left to the next morning.

Those who boarded with Jonathan, other than Pierce, were not aware of the developing issue with Graves. Reuel Williams, in a letter to his son following the duel, wrote that he first sensed that something was going on when, after the Senate adjourned on February 22, he saw Jonathan talking with Pierce, Duncan, and Bynum in the coatroom. That evening Jonathan was late for dinner, and after the ladies had left the table,

Williams asked Jonathan if there was a problem, to which Jonathan replied "not much."

The reason Jonathan was late for dinner was that he had gone with Duncan to practice shooting a rifle. The rifle he practiced with, and subsequently used in the duel, belonged to Duncan. He was rusty, but after a couple of shots his aim improved. In spite of what had occurred over the last two days, after shooting practice he returned to his room to dress for the Washington Birthday Ball.

Before leaving for the ball he wrote to Deborah:

> I did not write you yesterday, if any letter of the day before was wrong in temper or word you will pardon all, there was no foundation, my dear, not the least in the world for your fears, I wished to assure you of this, nothing more; my labors here are arduous, & the opposition is as relentless & persecuting as can be, a man, if he think free & boldly must take his life in his hand. I am not one to flinch in the service of my country & my own constituents but I do covet confidence & confiding love at home. & I know I shall in the end receive it at your hands, I fully pardon your fears Debby, proceeding as I believe they do from a pure attachment to me, none of us are perfect, nor can we expect it. I have been constant to you Debby, & my other failings you will pass over. I know for you took me for better or worse. But it is true that I love you as I could love not another woman. That strong, all absorbing attachment, which women so frequently possess, may not be in my disposition, but all there is you have. Is not this enough?

In this letter, he hinted that he was having problems, framing it in the notion that his problems were part of a "relentless and persecuting" plan by those he defined as the opposition. He also hinted that any course of action he might take could put his life in danger. Somewhere in the back of his mind, he believed, naively, that his constituents would approve of the direction he was resolute in following.

When he was leaving to go to ball he talked briefly again with Williams and gave him a quick rundown of what had transpired. What Jonathan told Williams was consistent with Pierce's account of what had happened and what had been said over Wednesday and Thursday. Jonathan told Williams that since he was one of the managers of the ball he needed to attend, but he was concerned that Webb or some of his friends might either insult or attack him. With this concern in his mind he went to the ball with one of the pistols he had obtained from Claiborne under his coat.

# THIRTEEN

## The Challenge

At the ball the previous evening Jonathan had no conflicts and no need for the pistol he had tucked under his coat. The first thing Friday morning, Jonathan and Pierce had breakfast with Williams. After breakfast, still anticipating a duel challenge, Jonathan asked Pierce to go with him for more rifle practice. On the way they picked up Duncan, and the three of them found a wooded area on the outskirts of Washington. At that time Duncan told Jonathan he didn't believe a challenge would be forthcoming, but Jonathan still wanted to practice. He was convinced by the tone of Graves's last note that "they" were determined to pursue him. He would not to allow himself to be disgraced.

Pierce remembered that they practiced from about sixty yards, and he was concerned that at that distance there was a good possibility Jonathan would be shot. So Pierce suggested the distance be moved back to eighty yards. Jonathan revealed to Pierce that his vision was not very good, and he needed glasses (which he had) to shoot at any distance. At both sixty and eighty yards Jonathan usually hit his target, and his last shot from eighty yards hit a four-inch square. Jonathan told Pierce that he had "confidence in the weapon, confidence in himself, and reliance upon the motives upon which he was acting."

Jonathan believed he had the best chance of not getting killed if rifles were used, but he suspected that since Graves was from Kentucky, he would be experienced with a rifle. He did not know that Graves had little rifle experience. At this point, both Jonathan and Pierce supposed only one shot would be needed. Given the apparently trivial basis for this

161

potential duel, if both men fired and were unhurt, it was not uncommon for them to conclude that they had each willingly faced fire and would therefore agree their honor had been defended, thereby settling the matter so everyone could go home.

When Williams saw Jonathan and Pierce leave in a carriage after breakfast, he feared a duel was in the works; he later wrote that the situation "caused me so much anxiety that instead of going to the Capitol I went upon the avenue and back to my lodging repeatedly to find their carriage or ascertain where they had gone." When Jonathan returned around 11 a.m., and Williams asked him what had occurred, Jonathan replied, "Nothing," adding that there had as yet been no challenge, but he was expecting one soon.

Also early Friday morning, Graves spoke with Menefee and told him that Jonathan persisted in not acknowledging what Graves understood him to have said. Because of that, and because he found Jonathan's response offensive to him personally, he had written the challenge and given it to Wise to deliver. After talking with Menefee, Graves left their boarding house to find out what Wise had decided to do with the challenge note. He told Wise he was still determined to have Wise deliver the challenge to Jonathan. In his later report Wise said that when they met Graves changed some of the wording. He did not mention what changes Graves made or whether he had made any suggestions for the wording. Wise also claimed that he no longer remembered what the initial challenge had said.

There is no record at this point of what needed to occur or be said by Jonathan that would absolve Graves of what he believed to be his honor responsibility. Graves said that he firmly believed there was a concerted effort by Jonathan and his "friends" to force him into a position that would require him to issue a challenge. So, like Jonathan, Graves was operating under the belief that there was some sort of conspiracy against him. And, as with Jonathan, when Graves perceived himself as the target of a scheme by a group versus an individual, it was significantly more difficult for him to see alternatives or solutions, and therefore more likely to dig in his heels.

The revised challenge note read,

Washington City, February 23, 1838

As you have declined accepting a communication which I bore to you from Colonel Webb, and as, by your note of yesterday, you have refused to decline on grounds which would exonerate me from all responsibility growing out of the affair, I am left no other alternative but to ask that satisfaction which is recognized among gentlemen. My friend, Honorable Henry A. Wise, is authorized by me to make the arrangements suitable for the occasion. Your obedient servant,

W. J. Graves

With the changes, Wise, who now had agreed to serve as Graves's second, left to find Jonathan. He went directly to Jonathan's boarding house, where the first person he encountered was Williams, who then got Jonathan for Wise. After Wise left, Jonathan told Williams he had received a challenge, and "that his mind was made up and it could be of no use to attempt to change it, he could not have the affair hanging over his head and he must have the meeting as soon as possible." He also told Williams that he was aware of "the Northern feeling on the subject and the deep interest that I, in common with others felt, but which he could not permit to influence him." He further said that, given the circumstances, he needed to "look to friends from other sections than New England for assistance."

After his conversation with Williams, Jonathan took the challenge to Pierce and reiterated his determination to go ahead in order to avoid disgrace. He repeated his belief that Graves was the pawn of others and that he could not see how Graves could have animosity toward him. He was not surprised, however, to see Wise, for he had assumed all along that Wise was one of those urging Graves on. He told Pierce that he wanted to get the matter settled quickly. There was no explanation of why he was in such a hurry to get the duel over with, other than a comment that the whole issue was interfering with his congressional responsibilities. Pierce later wrote that since Jonathan believed he was being forced into this confrontation, Jonathan thought "he should go out with as much patriotism as ever his grandfather or his brother went to the battlefield; that not only his own rights were invaded by this pursuit of him, but the rights and interests of others."

Jonathan needed Pierce's help getting the arrangements made. He knew he required a second, but he told Pierce that he did not want any of his Northern colleagues to serve in that regard. His reason for this was that Northerners would certainly attempt to talk him out of his course of action. He also could probably not find a Northerner willing to serve as his second. Friday was still a workday, and Congress was in session, but as the two men headed toward the Capitol, Jonathan told Pierce that he did not want him at the duel. Pierce never did state Jonathan's reasons. At some level Jonathan knew that what he was doing might reflect poorly on Pierce, so keeping Pierce away from the actual duel would shield him from later scorn.

While Pierce was searching for a second, Jonathan was in the House. He told Bynum that he had received a challenge and intended to accept. Bynum later related that on Friday he saw Webb in the lobby of the House talking with a group of men, one of whom was Graves. This was the only report of any contact between Graves and Webb after their initial meeting on Wednesday. Neither Graves nor Webb ever mentioned that they'd had any contact after Webb had asked Graves to deliver the note. Bynum was furious that Webb was in the House, particularly given the trouble that was brewing, and he complained to Speaker Polk. Polk told Bynum that he had not given permission to Webb, and that ended the matter.

The first person Pierce approached to be Jonathan's second was Dr. Lewis Linn, a senator from Missouri. As with his fellow Missouri senator, Benton, Linn was no stranger to affairs of honor and duels. Back in 1816, his brother-in-law William McArthur had killed Auguste de Mun. After a political row McArthur had challenged de Mun to a duel, but de Mun refused, stating that McArthur was not his social equal. This ended in a shootout on a Missouri street, during which de Mun was killed.

Linn was also involved in one of the more notorious duels in Missouri history. In August 1831, a dispute erupted between Thomas Biddle and Spencer Pettis. Biddle was the brother of Nicholas Biddle, head of the U.S. Bank and the archenemy of Andrew Jackson and the Democrats. Pettis, a Democratic U.S. congressman from Missouri, had made negative comments about Nicholas in the Missouri newspapers during his reelection campaign, and Biddle took offense. He went to Pettis's hotel room and beat the sleeping Pettis with a horsewhip, only to be pulled off by other hotel guests who had heard the commotion. Pettis wanted to immediately issue a challenge, but his fellow Missouri Democrat, Senator Benton, urged him to wait until after the election, not wanting to risk the Democratic seat in the House.

After Pettis easily won reelection, he sent Biddle a challenge. Biddle accepted and, as the one challenged, he chose pistols. However, because of his significant vision problems, he set the distance at a suicidal five feet. Pettis and his friends thought the short distance was meant to intimidate him into backing down. However, Pettis was determined to press the matter, so the two men met on Bloody Island, the same place where Benton had killed Lucas in 1817. Linn was there to serve as Pettis's surgeon. As expected, at five feet both men were mortally wounded. There was nothing Linn could do to save his friend.

When Pierce located Linn at his boarding house, he was sick in bed, and in no position to be of any help to Jonathan. He did, however, recommend that Pierce talk to George W. Jones, the representative from the Wisconsin Territory in the House, who resided in the same house with Linn. Jones was not in his room, so Pierce waited until he returned. He gave Jones a summary of what had occurred and asked Jones to serve as Jonathan's second. Jones's first inclination was to decline, and he told Pierce that he did not really know Jonathan well enough to take on such a delicate responsibility. Pierce pressed Jones to reconsider, and he asked Jones to accompany him to the Senate chamber. Leaving Jones in the Vice President's Room, Pierce went into the Senate chamber and returned shortly with an unnamed "friend." This "friend" had asked Representative John Miller of Missouri to be Jonathan's second, but Miller had declined, saying that he did not know Jonathan well enough. Jones was then left as the last alternative, but before Jones would agree he first wanted to talk to Jonathan.

Jones and Pierce left the Capitol in a hack and headed toward the boarding house where Duncan stayed and where Pierce had planned to connect with Jonathan. On the way down Pennsylvania Avenue, Jones spotted Colonel James Schaumburg, who had been a classmate of Jones's at Transylvania University in Lexington, Kentucky. For some reason Jones suggested they bring Schaumburg along, and Pierce agreed. Also in Washington at this time was Jefferson Davis, who had attended Transylvania University with Jones. He was staying in Jones's boarding house. Jones later said Davis was at the duel, but none of the others present mentioned Davis.

At Duncan's were Jonathan, Pierce, Jones, and Schaumburg. Pierce again requested that Jones serve as Jonathan's second. After a discussion with Jonathan, Jones agreed. At this point Pierce left and, as Jonathan desired, divorced himself from planning the duel. Bynum was not present at this meeting and later said he was disappointed that he had not been there because he believed he could have been effective in preventing the duel. It was clear to everyone present that Jonathan was fixed in his determination to accept the challenge and get it over with as soon as possible. He was not open to anyone who might offer an alternative to his determined plan for resolving this conflict. He had already decided that a rifle would be his weapon of choice, because he had no experience with a pistol, and that the distance would be eighty yards. He also wanted to shoot between the words *fire* and *four*.

In discussing the conflict with Schaumburg, Jonathan said that he believed Graves was demanding he say "that James Watson Webb is a gentleman and a man of honor." Jonathan would not disgrace himself by saying that, partly because he didn't see Webb as a gentleman and partly because he was not going to bow to intimidation by others. Graves, Jonathan said, had made a mistake of attempting to deliver a note on "behalf of a man who had been disgraced, and for whom the public had no respect." He believed Graves was allowing himself to be used by Webb and his associates: "I see the whole affair. Webb has come on here to challenge me because he, and perhaps others think that, as I am from New England, I am to be bluffed; and Mr. Webb will then proclaim himself a brave man, having obtained for himself acknowledgement, on my part, that he is 'a gentleman and a man of honor.'"

Jonathan told Schaumburg that Webb and his cohorts had miscalculated. He believed that while those in New England were opposed to dueling, he was sure people at home would be pleased if he stood his ground rather than "disgrace myself by humiliating concessions—the name I bear will never permit me to cower beneath the frown of mortal man; it is an attempt made on the part of certain individuals to browbeat us; because they think that I am from the East, I will tamely submit."

He buttressed his belief that he was being singled out by telling Schaumburg that men such as Duncan, Bynum, and Gholson had said much worse things about Webb and had not been challenged. Duncan and Bynum, however, had not brought up the $52,000. While Webb would forever be a man who seemed to delight in confrontation, he was particularly sensitive to the charge that he had accepted a $52,000 loan in exchange for switching the political allegiance of his newspaper. When Gholson mentioned the $52,000 in the House in 1837, Webb reacted with a note that was significantly more inflammatory, slanderous, and confrontational than the note he had addressed to Jonathan, but Jonathan never saw Webb's note.

Schaumburg, not being involved in politics, asked about Wise. Jonathan told him about his previous dealings with Wise: "Mr. Wise and myself had, not long since, some very severe words on the debate on the Florida war: in fact, sir, he is my enemy." *Enemy* would seem like a very strong word, but it was one that Jonathan had used frequently over the years to describe those adversaries whom he believed were knowingly attempting to humiliate him and to subvert his influence, integrity, and honor.

Schaumburg believed that Jonathan should protest Wise's involvement because of their past conflicts and because Wise would be biased against Jonathan, which would cloud Wise's objectivity throughout the upcoming proceedings. Jonathan agreed that he should have objected, but he did not want to slow down the arrangements. He told Schaumburg he was determined to push forward as quickly as possible. Speeding the whole process up negated the chances for any amicable resolution that might have prevented a duel.

At about 5 p.m., Jones left to find Wise with Jonathan's acceptance note:

Washington City, February 23, 1838

Honorable W. J. Graves:
Your note of this morning has been received. My friend, General Jones, will make the arrangements suitable to the occasion.
Your obedient servant,

Jona. Cilley

A short time later, Jones returned to Wise's room with their proposed terms and procedures for the duel.

Washington City,
February 23, 1838

Sir. Mr. Cilley proposes to meet Mr. Graves at such place as may be agreed upon between us tomorrow at twelve o'clock.
The weapons to be used on the occasion shall be rifles, the parties placed side to side at eighty yards distance from each other, to hold the rifles horizontally at arm's length downward: the rifles to be cocked and triggers set; the word to be, "Gentlemen, are you ready?" After which, neither answering "no," the words shall be in regular succession, "Fire, one, two, three, four." Neither party shall fire before the word "fire," nor after the word "four." The positions of the parties at the end of the line to be determined by lot. The second of the party

losing the position shall have the giving of the word. The dress to be ordinary winter clothing and subject to the examination of both parties. Both parties may have on the ground, besides his second, a surgeon and two other friends. The seconds, for the execution of their respective trusts are allowed to have a pair of pistols each on the ground, but no other persons shall have any weapon. The rifles to be loaded in the presence of the seconds. Should Mr. Graves not to be able to procure a rifle in the time prescribed, time shall be allowed for that purpose. Your very obedient servant,

George W. Jones

Wise was initially stunned that rifles would be the weapons of choice. Graves and Wise had all along assumed pistols would be used. Graves had no experience with a pistol and they had made arrangements to practice. Wise informed Jones that before he would agree to the conditions and the time of the duel he needed to find a rifle for Graves to use. As Jones was leaving Wise's room, Menefee arrived. He had come at Graves's request to find out what had happened with his challenge. He found Wise infuriated by the proposal to use rifles. When the two men brought the terms to Graves, Wise told him the proposed terms were barbarous and could be rejected. The consensus of those present was that the terms had been structured to be intimidating. Although rifles were potentially more lethal than pistols, Wise thought the eighty-yard distance might reduce some of the risk. He believed the intent behind the proposal "was either to make the duel fatal, or to deter Graves from accepting," similar to Biddle's five-foot distance in 1831.

An immediate problem for Wise and Graves, however, was they had no rifle. Wise spent several hours attempting to locate a rifle without success. Around 9 p.m., he delivered the following note to Jones:

Washington City, February 23, 1838

Sir: The terms arranging the meeting between Mr. Graves and Mr. Cilley, which you presented to me this evening, though unusual and objectionable, are accepted with the understanding that the rifles are to be loaded with a single ball, and that neither party is to raise his weapon from the downward horizontal position until the word "fire." I will inform you, sir, by the hour of eleven o'clock tomorrow whether Mr. Graves has been able to procure a rifle, and, consequently, whether he will require a postponement of the time of meeting. Your very obedient servant,

Henry A. Wise

Wise also told Jones that he did not believe he would be able to find a suitable rifle in Washington and thought he might need to send to Philadelphia for one, which would require a postponement of the duel. Jones did not want a postponement, and he was sure there was a good rifle in Washington. He gave Wise the names of some men who possibly had rifles. He also suggested that Wise go to the local arsenal. Jones even offered help in finding a rifle, to which Wise agreed; he asked Jones to let him know by 11 a.m. Saturday if he found one.

Wise then returned to Graves to update him. By midnight, Menefee and Crittenden had procured a rifle from John Rives, a local newspaper editor. It was not in good condition, and Menefee reconditioned it. He got help from Kentucky congressmen Richard Hawes and John C. Calhoun, and the rifle was in working order by 2 a.m.

Earlier in the evening Jonathan was again out practicing. When he returned to his room he told Williams that he had accepted the challenge. Williams later wrote that he implored Jonathan to think of his family and friends. Jonathan was resolute, saying "that he must fight or be ruined, that he believed that there was a determined purpose to disgrace or silence him, and that while holding a seat in the House he could not and would not be restrained from speaking his sentiments on all questions freely and fully." Acknowledging that he was putting his life at risk, he was going to meet Graves the next morning, "in defense of freedom of debate and the rights of his constituents which were dearer to him than life itself." If he should be killed, he asked Williams to be responsible for his possessions and to send them to his family.

Late in the evening, Jonathan wrote his last, brief letter to Deborah. He began with the innocuous comment that "I have had an exciting day of it . . . and hardly found time to write you a single line." This, on the day that he had been challenged to a duel and had accepted. He had spent time that day practicing with a rifle, and the next day he would be putting his life on the line. He closed his letter with the words:

> I cannot say more now, though there is much on my mind. I feel the need of a wife's love and consolation this very night, and my children too. God bless, how much I would give to see them and you. May a merciful God preserve us all and keep us all in the path of duty. You have my love, I feel that I enjoy yours wholly, would that I were now present with you.
>
> Love and kisses to yourself and the dear children.

Jonathan went to bed that night with his resolve fixed and inflexible. He believed himself to be the target, as had happened to him before, of a calculated plot to destroy his political usefulness and aspirations. Had Deborah been there, she would most assuredly have protested with all her energy. She made her opinion clear in her last letter to him, but it arrived too late and he never saw it. She wrote:

> But what is it I hear, Ruggles writes you have been challenged by Webber of New York. I will not believe it, as it is only come through him. I also hear Webber is a villainous fellow and not worth your notice or the notice of a man of honour. From the first second I felt uneasy, then came the assurance that my husband would not do wrong, would never accept a challenge. I trust you have a letter this eve informing me of the whole, as everyone has Ruggles' story I wish to know the whole truth. I will never believe you will accept a challenge—is it not the same as suicide & murder, horrible, I will not think of it a moment. I cannot speak or write about it.

# FOURTEEN

## The Duel

Saturday, February 24, 1838, in Washington, D.C., was an unusually chilly day with strong gusty winds. The House of Representatives was in session, but attendance was meager. Rumors were circulating about a possible duel between the congressmen from Maine and Kentucky, but not many actually knew the details. It was noted by most that Jonathan and Graves were not there. When John Quincy Adams arrived that morning, he had not heard the rumors, but he quickly discovered that a duel between Jonathan and Graves was likely occurring. Adams wrote of that day:

> There was an agitation in the house different from that which is occasioned by an irritated debate; a restless uneasy whispering disposition, clustering into little groups with inquisitive looks, listening ears, and varying reports as one member or another went out of, or came into the Hall. At one time it was rumoured that the parties had been separated by interposition of a magistrate. At another that they had adjusted their differences on the field and returned to their quarters.

The start of Graves's day came with the pressing need to learn how to fire a rifle, the one that had only been put in working order at two in the morning. He left around 8 a.m. with Menefee and Calhoun to practice. Graves had very little experience with a rifle, and his friends were very concerned about how vulnerable he would be when the two men met. Menefee had to adjust the trigger to compensate for Graves's inexperience, and he took some practice shots to be sure the rifle worked properly. He then had Graves shoot at a plank from sixty-five to eighty yards, and he hit it only about half the time. He also practiced using the commands established for the duel.

Wise went to Graves's room before breakfast, but Graves had already left with Menefee. Wise then returned to his room, where he found a note left by Jones, who had wanted to find out if Wise had found a rifle:

Washington City, February 24, 1838.

Sir: I will receive at Dr. Reilly's, on F Street, any communication you may see proper to make me until eleven o'clock a.m. today.
Respectfully, your obedient servant,

George W. Jones

Wise took his reply to Duncan's room, the designated meeting place for Jonathan and his friends. Finding no one, he left his note and went to find Graves and Menefee.

Dr. Reilly's, F. Street, February 24, 1838, 10 a. m.

Sir: I have called at this place in conformity to your note of this morning, to inform you that Mr. Graves has not as yet been able to procure a rifle and put it in order, and cannot be ready by twelve o'clock today. He is desirous, however, to have the meeting today, if possible, and I will inform you by half-past twelve o'clock today what time he will require to procure and prepare a weapon. Very respectfully, etc.,

Henry A. Wise

Wise knew that Graves had in fact found a rifle, but he was not certain that it worked. Looking for a way to stall the duel, Wise was not completely truthful in his note. When he found Graves and watched him shoot, it only reinforced his desire to delay the duel.

After Jones left his early morning note for Wise, he went to see Jonathan. Jonathan had written three pages of a letter to Deborah, and Jones encouraged him to finish it before they left for Duncan's. Jonathan told him that he had not mentioned anything in the letter about his conflict with Graves or the impending duel. He said that he would write to her when he came back and tossed the unfinished letter into the fire. While Jones was with Jonathan, Pierce came in, but he promptly left on seeing Jones. Jonathan told Jones that Pierce wanted to accompany him to his meeting with Graves, but Jonathan, concerned that Pierce's involvement might reflect poorly on Pierce and possibly affect the upcoming New Hampshire elections, didn't want Pierce there. So at some level Jonathan knew that his actions would not go over well in New England. Jonathan also saw Mrs. Pierce as fragile and believed Pierce's presence at the duel would be too upsetting for her.

Before they left Jonathan again strongly expressed his belief that those at home would approve of his course of action. This was something that he regularly asserted, but if he had allowed himself to truly think critically about it, he would know that those at home, even within his family, would disapprove of his choices. Throughout the whole affair he (in some sense delusionally) assured himself that family and friends at home would support his decision.

That morning Jones had also found a rifle for Graves and wrote another note to Wise:

Washington, 10.30 a. m. a. in., February 24, 1838.

Sir: Your note, dated at ten o'clock today, is received. In reply I have the pleasure to inform you that I have in my possession an excellent rifle, in good order, which is at the service of Mr. Graves. Very respectfully, etc.,

George W. Jones

Not hearing from Wise, Jones sent Duncan with a follow-up note, along with the rifle and ammunition, which he left in Wise's room.

Washington, February 24, 1838, 11 a.m.

Sir: Through the politeness of my friend Dr. Duncan, I now tender to you, for the use of Mr. Graves, the rifle referred to in my note of 10 o'clock this morning. Respectfully, your obedient servant,

George W. Jones

With this rifle now in Wise's hands, there was no longer any way to postpone the duel, and Wise thought that if they did not proceed, Graves would be open to charges of cowardice. Wise had already decided that if they had not had a rifle, he would not let Graves use the one Jones had acquired because, as he reasoned, Jonathan would have kept the better of the two rifles, so therefore he would have the advantage. With no room left for delay, Wise let Jones know they would meet at 3 p.m.

Around 11 a.m., Jonathan, Jones, Bynum, and Schaumburg met in Duncan's room to "prepare." That morning Jonathan had read a letter in a Baltimore newspaper that reported the rumor that Webb had come to Washington to challenge Jonathan. The letter writer also said that it was believed Jonathan would not accept Webb's challenge because he was a "pious man" and would skirt danger, and therefore he would shield himself behind his privilege. Jones believed the letter was calculated to paint a picture of Jonathan as not being brave or a gentleman.

This letter only reinforced Jonathan's determination not to back down. Jonathan reiterated to those present that he was certain Graves and his advisors were attempting to put him into one of three impossible positions: either to recognize Webb as a gentleman, shield himself behind congressional privilege, or force him to disgrace himself. He would not do any of these things. He would "never dishonor the name he bore by making such concessions as were demanded of him." Again he repeated his belief that his choices would meet with the approval of those at home, just as they had with those who knew what was happening in Washington. Unfortunately for Jonathan, the men he brought into his circle, other than Pierce, were not representative of people from the Northeast. He had only aligned himself with men who agreed with his thinking.

Around noon the five men left Duncan's room, got into the omnibus procured by Schaumburg, and headed out of town for the rendezvous point. On the way they stopped at Jones's residence. Jones said he needed to pick up some things he had forgotten, but Duncan wrote the reason for stopping was to get advice from Benton, who resided in the same house, about what should happen after an inconclusive first shot. Leaving Jonathan and Schaumburg in the omnibus, Jones, Duncan, and Bynum went to Linn's room and someone went to get Benton. Benton was later accused of being Jonathan's primary advisor and pushing him into the duel. Benton had heard the rumors of a duel, but he had no involvement other than the comments he offered on the day of the duel. Benton told them that in the early days of dueling men exchanged shots until the challenger was satisfied or until one of the parties was shot. But in this instance, especially since neither Jonathan nor Graves had any personal animosity toward the other, and the matter was over a minor point of honor, only one shot should be demanded by the challenging party. He reminded them that both men had families, and every effort should be made to stop it after the first exchange, if not before.

When Graves returned from shooting practice he and his friends met at the rooming house of Hawes and Calhoun. He decided that he wanted Menefee and Crittenden to act as his friends. Wise had encouraged Graves to have Crittenden as a friend instead of Hawes. He believed that because of Crittenden's age and seniority in Congress, his presence would assure others that anything that might occur would be handled appropriately.

Graves still did not have a doctor to accompany him, so he sent a note to Jonathan Foltz, a twenty-seven-year-old naval surgeon, and asked him to come see him. Why Graves choose Foltz is unknown, but Foltz came immediately. He, too, had heard rumors about a possible duel between Graves and Jonathan, and he surely had some idea of why Graves had asked to see him. When he arrived, Wise was quick to press him into service and sent him back to his office to get any equipment he might need.

After Foltz left, Graves told those present that since they all knew his position, he "desired them to conduct the affair upon their deliberate judgment, entirely without reference to consideration connected with my safety; and to avoid doing anything on the ground precipitately or unadvisedly from an over-anxiety to adjust the affair." Graves insisted that Jonathan must affirm what Graves had repeatedly claimed Jonathan had said to him during their last conversation on Wednesday. He then left the room, leaving Wise, Menefee, and Crittenden to talk among themselves and agree on the course they would take and what would be expected from Jonathan to satisfy Graves's needs.

The discussion between the three men centered on what they would require Jonathan to say in order to end the affair if, after the first exchange, no one was injured. Wise asked Menefee and Crittenden to put their stipulations in writing. Menefee wrote, "That, in declining to receive from Mr. Graves the note from Colonel Webb, Mr. Cilley was not influenced by considerations affecting the honor of Colonel Webb." Crittenden wrote, "Mr. Cilley states that he did not decline to receive Colonel Webb's communication from Mr. Graves in consequence of any personal exception to Colonel Webb as a gentleman or a man of honor." Wise added his own: "Mr. Cilley declined to receive the communication from Colonel Webb, at the hand of Mr. Graves, upon the ground that he, Mr. Cilley, did not hold himself answerable to Colonel Webb for words spoken in debate, on the floor of the House of Representatives." When they departed, Wise had all three written conditions in his pocket. For him, any of "these, or any admissions approaching in substance to these, were to be considered satisfactory. Mr. Graves would not be satisfied with anything short of these because he alleged that Cilley had made both these admissions to him verbally."

When Graves left for his meeting with Jonathan, he left his wife, who had accompanied him to Washington, back at their room. There is nothing to suggest that he had confided with her about his dispute (and the subsequent duel) with Jonathan. It appears that at this time in American society men did not confide in their wives about matters of honor; they would put their lives on the line and leave their wives in the dark regarding the risks and potentially fatal consequences of their actions. There is no record that Graves left any letter for her.

Somehow, after Graves left, Mrs. Graves learned about the impending duel late in the morning, and, in spite of the cold and her fragile health, she went to the local magistrate to obtain bench warrants for the arrest of all those involved. She hired a carriage and, with a court representative, left Washington for Maryland, the frequent location for these affairs of honor, in an attempt to find the combatants and put a stop to the duel. However, she was unable to find them, because they had kept their destination a secret and avoided the customary dueling grounds.

After the stop at Jones's room, Jonathan and his party proceeded out of the city, over the Anacostia Bridge, and into Maryland. Once over the bridge they stopped and waited for Graves. After a wait of thirty-five minutes, Graves arrived, accompanied by Wise and Menefee. Jones and Wise talked briefly, but there is no record of the content of their conversation. They were still waiting for Crittenden and Foltz. The pair had initially headed in the wrong direction, and they had also stopped at the Naval Hospital so Foltz could get more bandages.

Duels were typically private affairs where spectators were not encouraged; occasionally, however, others appeared on the scene. Grafton Powell, a government clerk, had heard the rumors of an impending duel and it sparked his interest. He had never witnessed a duel and was determined to see this one. He at first assumed that the duel involved two other men, but when he saw a carriage headed out of town he decided to follow. Attempting to go unnoticed when the carriage stopped over the bridge, he rode past the waiting parties. He got off his horse and paced, trying to stay warm. Fuller, the owner of Jonathan's carriage, spotted Powell, and he sent his coach driver to tell Powell to stay out of sight. Powell requested that the messenger "give my compliments to the gentlemen, and tell them that I am determined to see the duel, if I had to take a shot for it." Hawes and Calhoun also lingered in the rear. Hawes later said he was asked to come help Graves if he were hurt, and to transport quick information back to Mrs. Graves.

When everyone had arrived they proceeded into Maryland, wanting to be sure they had left the District of Columbia. It appears they did not head for a specific location, instead simply looking for a site that would serve their purpose. About two miles down the road they stopped at a field, and Jones and Wise left their carriages to inspect the area. After half an hour or so, they decided that this cow pasture would be adequate and directed the carriages to move into the field. A few pieces of the fence had to be removed to get into what would now be the dueling grounds. After they all had moved into the field, everyone except Jonathan and Graves and Foltz exited their coaches and gathered in the center of the field. They agreed that the distance between Jonathan and Graves would be eighty yards, so Jones and Wise walked arm in arm to measure out the distance.

While Jones and Wise paced off the distance, Jonathan remained alone in his carriage with his thoughts. Graves sat with Foltz. Unfortunately, there are no records of what either man was thinking. They were putting their lives at serious, if not deadly, risk. Did they reflect upon the implications of their actions on their families? Were there second thoughts? Neither man had participated in a duel before. Neither had ever shot at another man. Neither even had any real animosity toward the other. This was merely an issue of honor. Did they truly believe that one of them might be seriously injured or killed? While frowned upon in dueling etiquette, it was not uncommon for one party to intentionally miss their opponent. Did either of them have that intent? The mere act of facing an adversary with weapon in hand would be enough in some cases to settle a matter of honor. Both men were at the mercy of their seconds, both of whom had some experience with dueling, and according to the rules of dueling, these two young men's lives were in the hands of Jones and Wise, who were responsible for the honor of the man they represented.

With the preliminaries settled, and apparently no discussion between Wise and Jones about how to reconcile the differences, Jonathan and Graves were summoned from their carriages and escorted to their positions. Graves was placed at the top of a slight rise in front of a fence and with trees in the background. Jonathan was positioned in the open field with a slight elevation at his back. A cold and gusty wind blew diagonally in Jonathan's direction from his left to right. The rifles were brought out. Duncan loaded Jonathan's rifle, and Menefee loaded the rifle that had been borrowed for Graves's use. At three in the afternoon both men were directed to prepare to fire. Jones and Wise were stationed in the middle of the field of fire. One of their responsibilities was to be sure that neither Jonathan nor Graves shot outside of the agreed-upon time frame. They each carried a pistol, and if their opponent fired after the count was over, they could then shoot the offender of the rules.

With all set, Jones ordered the men to prepare to fire. They could not fire before the fire command and must not fire after the count of four. Both men were required to stand still and not move until the count was completed. If one fired first, he had to hold his position until the other man had fired. Both men, when shooting their rifles, would be standing sideways, which would make them a more difficult target to hit.

Jones said loudly and clearly, "Gentlemen, are you ready?" Each man raised his rifle to his shoulder. Then came "Fire," after which he began the count. Jonathan was the first to fire, right at the count of one. He pulled the trigger too quickly and his bullet went into the ground about forty yards out. Graves fired at two; the bullet whizzed past Jonathan harmlessly

After the first shot, Jonathan and Graves remained in their positions, while the other men met in the center. Jones asked Wise if Graves was satisfied, likely thinking Wise would say yes and they could all return to Washington with no one hurt and honor defended. For his part, Wise was also anxious to end the affair, but rather than use his own best judgment, as a second typically had the prerogative to do, he felt duty bound to adhere to Graves's determined stance that he would only be satisfied when Jonathan had, in some fashion, acquiesced. Wise responded to Jones's inquiry by asking if Jonathan could not "assign some reasons for not receiving Colonel Webb's communication, or make some disclaimer which would relieve Mr. Graves from his position."

Knowing exactly what Wise was asking for, Jones went back to Jonathan, but there is no record of the specifics of their conversation, other than Jonathan's remark that the hair trigger on the rifle had caused him to fire early, and he would be more deliberate the next time.

When Jones returned with Jonathan's reply, both men remembered what Jones said to Wise differently. According to Jones, he said, "I am authorized by my friend Mr. Cilley to say, that in declining to receive the note from Mr. Graves, purporting to be from Colonel Webb, he meant no disrespect to Mr. Graves, because he entertained for him then, as he now does, the highest respect and the most kind feeling; but that he declined to receive the note, because he chose not to be drawn into any controversy with Colonel Webb." What Wise heard Jones say was this: "I am authorized by Mr. Cilley to say that in declining to receive the note from Mr. Graves, purporting to be from Colonel Webb, he meant no disrespect to Mr. Graves, because he entertained for him then, as he does now, the highest respect and the most kind feelings; but my friend refuses to disclaim disrespect for Colonel Webb, because he does not choose to be drawn into an expression of opinion as to him."

For Wise, the failure on Jonathan's part to specifically acknowledge respect for Webb was unacceptable. Saying nothing about Webb was also unacceptable. While Wise and Menefee later asserted that it was not necessary for Jonathan to recognize Webb as a gentleman, it is clear that it was in fact required, unless Jonathan stated that he did not take Webb's note because of congressional privilege.

In the ensuing discussion, those with Jonathan believed, given the minor point of honor being disputed, that the matter should be terminated. Crittenden and Foltz agreed. Crittenden later said he did not see it as his place to assert his opinion. After about a half hour of discussion with both Jonathan and Graves standing alone in the cold, Wise concluded that nothing had changed and that Jonathan was still not willing to admit what Graves believed he had said to him in private. Therefore a second exchange of fire would be needed. Wise could have ended the affair at this point by agreeing that Graves's honor had been satisfied, but he chose not to.

Duncan and Menefee then reloaded the rifles, and Jonathan and Graves took their positions. Jones again gave the command and proceeded with the count. Graves fired first, but being unaccustomed to firing a rifle, particularly one with a hair trigger, he discharged his rifle before he had it in the firing position. Jonathan fired next and his bullet passed by Graves, striking the fence behind him. Many of those present saw Graves flinch after Jonathan fired and thought he had been hit. Wise and Menefee went to Graves to check on him. He assured them he was uninjured, but he was agitated that his misfire had startled him. He told Wise that he had to have another shot, because Jonathan had taken deliberate aim at him.

Again the parties met in the middle of the field to deliberate and try to agree on a resolution. Jones started the discussion, telling Wise that "my friend, in coming to the ground and exchanging shots with Mr. Graves, has shown to the world that, in declining to receive the note of Colonel Webb, he did not do so because he dreaded a controversy. He has shown himself a brave man, and disposed to render satisfaction to Mr. Graves. I do think that he has done so, and that the matter should end here." Duncan, Schaumburg, and Foltz also supported ending the duel. Bynum then articulated very adroitly his perspective on what had transpired up to this point:

> Gentlemen, we have come here this day as men of honor, as prescribed among gentlemen. Both the principles of civilization and humanity, in my judgment, when all the purposes of honor have been complied with, should induce the parties to arrest the prosecution of a matter that may terminate fatally if persevered in; this I observed, we are bound to do, as men imbued with the feelings of humanity, as founded upon every principle of civilization. Each of those gentlemen has now hazarded their lives in defence of their honor, showing most incontestably that they appreciate their honor more highly than life it self; and what man can go further, or do more, than to hazard and sacrifice his life for his honor? There is nothing in the code of honor that could require more. To prosecute this affair, then further, after all the requisitions of honor have been complied with, would be savage barbarity; showing that we were in thirst of blood and revenge—a thing that should be recognized to belong only to savage life, and not to that of civilized man, in refined society.
>
> I here declare, if this matter is persisted in further, and if one or both of those gentlemen shall fall, their blood will rest upon the heads of those who alone have it in their power to prevent it now.

Bynum then concluded with a very insightful and perceptive observation of the whole conflict:

> [T]he whole was founded on an abstraction . . . the challenge it self had been predicated upon a mere implication that the refusal to receive Webb's note through Graves, on the part of Mr. Cilley, was on the ground of Webb's not being a gentleman; this had never been asserted by Mr. Cilley to Mr. Graves, either verbally or by letter, but that Mr. Graves had only inferred it, by the refusal of Mr. Cilley to receive the note of Webb; let whatever might be the private opinions of Mr. Cilley of any person, he could not acknowledge the right, in a third person, to extract from him an expression of that opinion, without basely degrad-

ing himself in the eyes of the world. There was no malice between the parties; no injury complained of by either of them; nor wrong done, as far as had come within my knowledge; nor did I think public opinion would justify the prosecution of this affair beyond the extent to which it had been carried.

Ignoring the opinions of all the others, Wise and Menefee were not ready to end the affair, still looking for Jonathan to give ground and either recognize Webb as a gentleman or assert congressional privilege. He told Jones that Graves "does not require of Mr. Cilley a certificate of character for Colonel Webb, he considers himself bound not only to preserve the respect due himself, but to defend the honor of his friend Colonel Webb." With that said, Wise appeared to contradict himself, telling Jones that "Mr. Graves only insists that he has not borne the note of a man who is not a man of honor, and not a gentleman." Wise knew, however, that Jonathan would not make any statement about Webb.

With the debate between the parties no closer to a resolution, Wise and Jones moved away from the group. Wise then urged Jones to have Jonathan say he refused the note because he could not be held accountable for what he said in the House. Jones told Wise that Jonathan would not say that. Jonathan was not going to say anything different from what he had said before. Trying a new approach, Wise asked Jones if Jonathan would say that he refused the note because he meant no disrespect to Graves "either directly or indirectly." Jones never discussed this with Jonathan. Wise insisted on a third shot. Wise also suggested to Jones that if the matter was not settled after this round, and a fourth round was needed, the distance should be shortened. Jones replied that he would consider that.

After Wise and Menefee had left Graves to resume the discussion between the parties, Fuller and Powell wandered up to Graves to inquire whether he had been struck by the previous shot. Graves stated again that he had not been hit; he had only moved when his rifle had fired before he had it up to his shoulder. Fuller then asked Graves if the ball had come close, to which Graves responded that it had not. Fuller proceeded to talk with Graves about the distance and believed it was more like one hundred yards instead of eighty. Fuller said Graves responded that it would be "a chance shot to hit a man at that distance, as the wind was blowing."

Just after Graves had his rifle readied for the third exchange, James Brown, the owner of the land, appeared and asked Graves what was happening. Graves told him "that they were merely taking a little sport." Brown pushed for more detail, and after answering a few questions, Graves told Brown that he did not want to talk about it anymore. Then Brown told Graves that he would not allow a duel on his property, to which Graves responded, "You do not allow it. My friend, come and stand by my side, or take my place, if you wish to be shot." At this suggestion, Brown moved aside.

After the meeting in which the third exchange was ordered, Bynum went to Jonathan and told him that his friends had done all they could to reach an agreement that would leave both men's honor intact, but it had proved fruitless. To this Jonathan replied, "They must thirst for my blood mightily." He also said to Schaumburg, "They better give up the consideration of Webb."

With the rifles again ready and the command given, both men took aim and fired at about the same time. Again Jonathan's ball passed by Graves and caught the fence again. Graves, however, hit his mark. Jonathan dropped his rifle, threw up his right hand toward Schaumburg, and said, "I am shot." Schaumburg rushed to him and caught him before he hit the ground. Jonathan's other friends were quickly at his side. Dr. Foltz, after finding that Graves was unhurt, also rushed to Jonathan, but it was too late. The bullet had entered just under Jonathan's left ribs, passing through his body. On the way through it punctured either his descending aorta or the inferior vena cava, causing him to bleed to death in one or two minutes. There was nothing that could be done. He had no last words.

Wise and Graves approached, and Wise asked Jones about Jonathan's condition, to which Jones replied, "My friend is dead." Fuller was requested to bring his carriage up as close as possible to Jonathan's corpse. Hawes and Calhoun left immediately to let Mrs. Graves know that her husband was unhurt. Wise asked Powell to take a note to Henry Clay. The note simply said, "Mr. Cilley is killed—Mr. Graves is unhurt." Wise also asked Powell to find Pierce and inform him of what had happened. After Powell had given Wise's message to Clay, he headed toward the Capitol to find Pierce. He stopped to ask where he might find Pierce's boarding house, and one of the men he asked was Pierce, so Powell gave him the tragic news.

Jonathan's body was placed in Fuller's carriage, and along with those who accompanied him to this fatal affair, they headed back into the city. The living were left at Jones's boarding house while Fuller continued on to Jonathan's boarding house, where his blood-covered body was placed on the floor of his room.

Hawthorne wrote, "A challenge was never given on a more shadowy pretext: a duel was never pressed to a fatal close in the face of such open kindness as was expressed by Mr. Cilley; and the conclusion is inevitable that Mr. Graves and his principal second, Mr. Wise, have gone further than their own dreadful code will warrant them, and overstepped the imaginary distinction which, on their own principle, separates manslaughter from murder."

# FIFTEEN
## Blame and Investigation

News of the fatal duel quickly spread through Washington. On Sunday the *Journal of Commerce* wrote, "Mr. Cilley has a wife and three young children in Maine. In her quiet New England village, perhaps preparing herself and her children for Church or the Sabbath School, she little dreams that he lies here, the helpless victim of a foul conspiracy and assassination." It would be another week before Deborah would learn of the death of her husband.

With Jonathan's body still on the floor of his room, Washington was abuzz. Everyone looked for information and details. The rumors and misinformation flourished. One rumor was that both Duncan and Bynum were armed and looking to challenge Webb. Webb, always ready for a fight, was said to have walked up and down Pennsylvania Avenue most of Sunday waiting for Duncan to confront him, but Duncan never appeared. Another rumor had it that if Webb did not leave town soon, he would be lynched. Phillip Hone, a prominent New York Whig and once mayor of New York City, was in Washington at the time and noted in his diary that he had received word from a friend that "Webb is truly and deeply distressed, and will remain here till Tuesday, rather so as to appear not to avoid any consequences, than because there are any consequences to be apprehended."

Early Sunday morning, Jones and Wise met to write a synopsis of the events surrounding the duel and explain their actions, which were already being questioned. Their brief report appeared in the local newspapers the next day, and then slowly circulated around the country. They were hopeful that it would put the matter to rest. Their report concluded by saying:

> Such is the naked statement of all the material facts and circumstances attending this unfortunate affair, which we make in justice to our friends, to ourselves, to all concerned, to the living, and to the dead; and it is made for the only purpose of allaying excitement in the public mind, and to prevent any and all further controversy upon a subject which already is full enough of woe. We have fully and substantially stated wherein we agree and disagree. We cordially agree, at all events, in bearing unqualified testimony to the fair and honorable manner in which this duel was conducted. We endeavored to discharge our duties according to that code under which the parties met, regulated by magnanimous principles, and the laws of humanity. Neither of us has taken the least exception to the course of the other; and we sincerely hope that here all controversy whatever may cease. We especially desire our respective friends to make no publication on the subject. None can regret the termination of the affair more than ourselves; and we hope, again, that the last of it will be the signatures of our names to this paper, which we now affix.

Unfortunately for them, their actions throughout the affair, particularly during the duel itself, would come under intense scrutiny and dog them both for the rest of their lives.

In Congress on Monday, John Fairfield addressed the House. Initially it was George Evans, also a Maine representative, who was to announce Jonathan's death. Although Evans was well respected in Maine, he was a Whig, and the majority of those in the Maine delegation believed someone from Jonathan's party would be more appropriate, so they turned to Fairfield. Fairfield wrote to his wife that he believed Evans's feelings were hurt by the change. In the House Fairfield began his speech by expressing what everyone at that point already knew: "An event has occurred since our last adjournment, which has spread a deep gloom over this community, and deprived this body of one of its most valuable members." He continued with highlights of Jonathan's life and his distinguished political career, and then he offered three resolutions, which passed unanimously. A committee was appointed to manage Jonathan's funeral, scheduled for noon on Tuesday. The only member of the committee from Maine was Evans, possibly as a gesture to compensate for being replaced earlier by Fairfield. The members of the House also agreed to wear black crepe armbands for thirty days in memory of Jonathan. It is not known how it was decided, and by whom, to have Jonathan's funeral before his family even knew of his death. While not mentioned in the discussion about Fairfield's resolutions, concern was voiced outside the House about the propriety of having a funeral conducted in the House chambers, given the circumstances surrounding Jonathan's death.

In the Senate on Monday afternoon, Williams announced Jonathan's death and paid tribute to his short life and career. He informed the senators of the funeral taking place the next day, and they, too, voted to wear black armbands for thirty days. There is no record of Ruggles making any public comment about Jonathan's death, nor is it known whether he wore the armband. But his own actions were then under investigation by a Senate committee. Before the term was over, the committee found that his accuser's allegations were not credible and concluded that Ruggles had done nothing wrong.

On Tuesday morning Evans and the funeral committee escorted Jonathan's body from his boarding house to Capitol Hill, where it was placed for a brief time in the Capitol rotunda, below the painting of Burgoyne's surrender; it then moved into the House chamber. John Quincy Adams commented in a letter to his son Charles that "the ceremonies were performed with great and more than usual Solemnity. The attendance of members of both Houses of Congress was more numerous than I have witnessed on any similar occasion. All the galleries of the House were crowded with spectators of both sexes." In attendance, along with members of the House, were the members of the Senate, cabinet members, the vice president, and President Van Buren. The justices of the Supreme Court voted not to attend because Jonathan had died in a duel. After a short prayer, House chaplain Levi Reese spoke, not about Jonathan, but about the practice of dueling. He told those assembled that his remarks were not meant to speak to those involved in the recent duel, but rather to implore those present to work to change the public's attitude toward dueling.

Reese said that a duel resolved nothing related to honor, only that "the parties who engage in them possess sufficient courage to expose their lives in combat, but not enough to meet and virtuously oppose the demands which a corrupt and heartless world make upon them . . . the despotism of public opinion fastens its chain upon the bodies and souls of men, and leads some of the most talented and promising of the nation to offer themselves willing victims on the altar of sacrifice; it binds them to the observance of a custom which, in all its features, finds a parallel only in the barbarous custom of heathenism." He said public servants must be held to higher, more honorable standards, and the public standard should make it dishonorable to issue or accept a challenge. Adams wrote that "some of the Gentlemen of the South were offended by the severity of the preacher upon the practice of dueling."

After the funeral those present accompanied Jonathan to the Congressional Cemetery on Capitol Hill, where he was placed in a public vault. Because the ground was still frozen in Maine, it would be April before his body would be transported back for a funeral and burial there.

The day after the Washington funeral, the House went back to work. Fairfield noted, "Graves I have not seen, though I believe he is in the House. It is said he looks solemn and oppressed; Wise looks haggard, and feels, I apprehend, that the weight of public indignation is too heavy for him. The others being more remotely implicated in the affair look sorrowful." Fairfield requested the House approve the establishment of a committee to investigate the causes and circumstances surrounding Jonathan's death. He said the House owed it to the Cilley family, so they might fully understand what had happened. He also hoped that opening the practice of dueling to congressional inquiry would result in laws that prohibited it.

As would be expected, the Whigs protested. They claimed that the facts had all been published in the newspapers and that nobody was asserting the code of honor had not been followed. It was said that Congress and the public were still in an agitated state and time should be allowed for things to settle down. Pushing forward now, they asserted, would only inflame partisan bickering. Given the Democrats' majority in the House, the Whigs could not see any investigation being impartial. The Whigs also said that Congress had no right to meddle in private issues between men and no authority to legislate state issues. They were advised, however, that Congress did have the authority to pass laws related specifically to dueling in Washington.

The members were reminded that a congressional committee only had the power to investigate whether the House privilege had been breached. The final resolution put to the House for a vote read, "That a committee consisting of seven members be appointed to investigate the causes which led to the death of the honorable Jonathan Cilley, late member of this house, and the circumstances connected therewith, and further to inquire whether, in the case alluded to, there was not a breach of the privilege of this House." None of the House members involved in the duel, if they were even present, voted. The vote was 152 in favor and 50 against.

Adams had been asked by friends to offer a resolution urging the expulsion of those members of Congress involved in the duel. He declined, saying that after "giving to Mr. Cilley the burial of a Saint, he did not perceive the Justice, Humanity or Piety of expelling all his accomplices as felons." Adams, along with other Whigs, hoped the investigating committee would address ways to stop dueling. A resolution was presented "to inquire into the means more effectually to suppress the practice of dueling and report a Bill for this purpose as early as is practicable." The majority of Democrats rejected this resolution.

Adams saw the motivation behind the call for an investigating committee as a means of turning the whole affair "into a conspiracy to murder Cilley, and if possible to expel Wise and Graves from the House, to destroy the printing Establishment of the New York Courier and Enquirer, and to bury the charge of corruption against Ruggles in Cilley's grave."

It did not take long for the duel and its tragic result to morph into party politics. Each party was quick to frame the whole affair as a conspiracy between opposing party leaders aimed at lessening the influence of the other party. Whigs accused Jonathan and the Democrats of intentionally provoking Graves to challenge Jonathan because it was an opportunity for Jonathan to establish himself as someone to be feared by the insolent Whigs. After all, it was the Democrats who were the party of the duelist, and they pointed to Democratic Party leader Andrew Jackson and his bloody dueling history.

Hone commented on the Democrats' politcalization of Jonathan's death as follows: "Some of the vile supporters of the administration attempt to give it political bearing. These, who have always supported Jackson and made him the standard of their religion, morals, and politics, are now loud in their condemnation of the practice of dueling, although the wooden god of their idolatry was known as one of the most notorious duelists in the United States, and even had a rencontre of the most savage and sanguinary character with another of their oracles, Mr. Benton of the Senate."

The Democrats likewise accused Webb, Wise, and the Whigs of targeting Jonathan for personal reasons and as a way to assert their own power by going after a young Northern first-term representative. It would show others who dared speak up against Wise and his ilk that they did so at the risk of their personal well-being. Jonathan was presented as one who had no choice but to fight.

Webb quickly added fuel to the Democrats' charges when accounts of his actions on the day of the duel were made known. It was reported that early on the day of the duel, Webb, still in Washington, had gone to the room of Major William Morrell, one of his henchmen. While Webb was aware of the duel challenge, he believed it was not going to occur for a few days. When he discovered it was to occur that day, he was determined to find the parties and force Jonathan to fight him first. He wanted Morrell to go with him to Jonathan's room, where Webb said he would insist that Jonathan meet him first. He told Morrell that if Jonathan refused, they were to break his right arm.

When another henchman, Daniel Jackson, discovered that Jonathan was not in his room, they assumed he was headed off to the duel. The three men left Washington and proceeded into Maryland in search of Jonathan and Graves. On the way, Webb told his companions that if they found Jonathan, he would tell Jonathan that the quarrel was between the two of them and that Jonathan would have to fight him first. If Jonathan raised his rifle in Graves's direction, Webb would shoot Jonathan. Webb also told his companions that they should be prepared to deal with anyone who objected to their intrusion, even Wise and Graves. They all were well armed and ready for a shootout if need be, but they never found Jonathan and Graves. Like the rest of Washington, they only found out the results when the parties returned to the city. The accounts of Webb's plan only reinforced the notion that the whole affair was planned to destroy Jonathan.

The Democratic press was quick to portray Jonathan as a victim, a martyr who fell in defense of his family name and the values of New England. In early March, "The Martyrdom of Cilley" was published in O'Sullivan's *Democratic Review*. "A great crime has been committed," O'Sullivan wrote. "Fierce demons of human passions have been abroad, in the light of the sun and before the eyes of men, and have lapped from the ground the innocent blood which they have nerved human hands to shed."

. The major focus of the article was to lay the entire blame for Jonathan's death on Henry Wise, "the one individual upon whose head centres the general responsibility of the bloody results, and was no other than the same wretched man now on his trial before the bar of Public Opinion, for the homicide." Graves's role in the affair was minimized — he was described as Wise's pawn. Wise was condemned because he had agreed to serve as Graves's second in spite of his animosity toward Jonathan resulting from their confrontations in the House. On the field it was this animosity that supposedly drove Wise to demand multiple shots be fired, well past the point where, given the minor point of honor involved, honor had been satisfied.

The press wrote that Jonathan had been put "into a position from which no other egress for escape should be left him than one of ignominy, which would blight his present standing in the House utterly and forever, and destroy him in his own district, where he stood in the delicate and critical position of being elected on the strength of personal popularity." While this accurately expressed Jonathan's thinking with regard to his position, given the Wise-bashing intent of the article, no attempt was made to critically explore Jonathan's actions or those of the men who advised him. As with all newspapers at the time, the purpose was damage control and finding ways to blame the other party.

In early March, O'Sullivan engaged Nathaniel Hawthorne to write a biography of Jonathan. Hawthorne quickly jumped into the task and sent letters out to people he believed could fill in details about Jonathan's life. For instance, he wrote to the postmaster of Thomaston and asked for information about Jonathan's life in Thomaston. He urged the postmaster to respond in two days or sooner because he was under a deadline to finish the biography. Jonathan's biography came out in the *Democratic Review* in September.

Wise quickly understood that he was the target of most of the blame for Jonathan's death, so he wrote a letter to be distributed to his constituents in Virginia. He allowed that they had a right to judge his actions, but in no way should he be considered a murderer. He reminded them that Jones, through their joint statement, had no reservations about Wise's handling of the affair. He wrote that his role was to first attempt to reconcile the differences, and further to protect Graves's honor. He acknowledged that there were those who said he should not have agreed to be Graves's second because of his animosity and hostility toward Jonathan. Wise allowed that there had "been a slight misunderstanding be-tween us in debate which passed off with the moment and left not the trace of animosity behind." Knowing that he was from Virginia, where dueling was an acceptable mode for settling personal difference, Wise asked "that you judge me fairly, according to that public sentiment which prevails among yourselves."

Williams was targeted in the Whig press for knowing about the duel but doing nothing to stop it, and furthermore approving of Jonathan's course. It was reported that he, as well as Benton, watched Jonathan practice shooting. His complicity was said to have been exposed in a letter he wrote to his son in Maine before the duel, in which it was allegedly stated that Jonathan was to be involved in a duel and was sure to be victorious. The content of the letter was purportedly seen when someone was looking over the son's shoulder in the local post office. Williams was surprised when he heard from Ruggles that the Maine Whigs had singled him out as someone who should have prevented the duel. In his letter Williams was said to have told his son that Jonathan, after dispatching Graves, would be the most famous New Englander in Congress. He always asserted that he had never encouraged Jonathan to fight, and even tried unsuccessfully to discourage him from accepting the challenge. He said he was the only one in the Maine delegation who knew of the upcoming duel; however, he did not enlist the help of others in dissuading Jonathan. In subsequent letters to friends and family in Maine, Williams urged them to be careful not to let others see what he'd written.

Pierce, too, was attacked in the press—depicted as one who had en-couraged Jonathan to fight, and who had expressed confidence that Jona-than would kill Graves. He was also accused of bringing Benton into the conflict, with allegations flying that he and Jonathan had followed Ben-ton's advice. Pierce responded to the charges by writing an open letter denying the accusations. The letter was published throughout the coun-try. Pierce, aware that the charges against him would likely reach Tho-maston, wrote to Hezekiah Prince to refute what had been written about him. He additionally told Prince that Jonathan took "no advice but acted upon his own fixed determination," and that "he considered himself lit-erally hunted and forced into combat." He said Jonathan believed he would be attacked by Webb, but Pierce failed to mention that he was the one who initially warned Jonathan that Webb could be a threat and told Jonathan that he should consider arming himself.

A few days after the duel, Pierce wrote his friend, political ally, and fellow Bowdoin graduate John Hale to relate some of his thoughts about what had occurred in Washington. From his point of view, it was evident that there had been a fixed plan to harm Jonathan. He based his thinking on the revelations in the press about Webb's intention to injure Jonathan. He saw the political climate in Washington and the level of violence deteriorating to the point that honorable men would be required to arm themselves for their own protection. He was indirectly critical of Webster for having men such as Webb as an honored guest at the Whig dinner the night before Webb wrote his note to Jonathan. Pierce never mentioned his role in the whole affair but chose to portray Jonathan as a martyr, dying for his family name and the honor of New England. Hale later went on to represent New Hampshire in Washington in both the House and the Senate. His relationship with Pierce fell apart over the slavery issue.

It took five days for the news of Jonathan's death to reach Thomaston. On March 2, those close to Deborah, knowing what had occurred, decided that her minister, Reverend Washburn, should be the one to break the tragic news to her. Washburn took his wife Sarah with him to offer some feminine support. It was an unquestionably gut-wrenching task for them. Sarah, so disturbed by the ordeal, felt Graves should know about the anguish he had caused. That evening she wrote a letter to him "from a deep sense of duty, and with ardent desire that the hand which struck the fatal blow, at the peace and tranquility of an amiable and interesting family, may never more be stained with the blood of a fellow mortal." She described for him the scene when Deborah was first told: "One shriek of horror, burst from her anguished heart, which must bleed, bleed forever, over the memory of his premature death—the oldest child [Greenleaf, then nine] feels deeply—his little heart is rent with sorrow, while he weeping stands with his head resting on the bosom of his widowed mother, on kissing the tears from her cheek as they flow from her bursting heart." According to her, Graves should only hope that God would show him mercy. There is no record of Graves receiving the letter.

Family, friends, and the whole town were in shock. Fortunately for Deborah and the three children, they were not alone through the ordeal and the struggle forward with their lives. Deborah's family was close by to provide comfort and support, and to share in her grief. Jonathan's family in New Hampshire was also quick to reach out to her. For a woman who was always insecure and filled with self-doubt, and who regularly reached out to Jonathan for love and validation, Deborah found within herself the strength and courage to cope with her own life and that of her children. Her faith was put to the test, and she relied on it heavily. There would be many days and nights of anguish and tears ahead.

Jonathan's brother Joseph rushed to Maine, and others from New Hampshire followed. Rumor in the capital held that Joseph was headed to Washington to extact revenge. Joseph later wrote to Deborah that his first impulse was indeed to go to Washington and shoot them all from one hundred yards. On second thought, however, he believed he had too great a responsibility to his large family to put his life at risk. He also had written to Pierce and others he knew in Washington to explore ways to hold those he saw as culpable for his brother's death legally responsible, although it was not likely that any jury in South-leaning Maryland would convict anyone. He also told Deborah that he was certain that any results from the congressional inquiry would go nowhere.

Throughout Maine meetings were held in local communities to express their grief and sympathy to Jonathan's family. Resolves were approved in opposition to dueling, and anti-dueling petitions were sent to the Maine representatives in Congress. In Thomaston, on March 7, a bipartisan meeting was held to remember Jonathan. Both political friends and foes offered tributes and recollections. Whig William Farley recalled that he and Jonathan had come to Thomaston at about the same time and, in spite of their political differences, had become close friends. He remembered that he stood up for Jonathan when he was being slandered by his political foes. Farley informed the audience that while he deeply lamented the loss of his friend, he was disappointed in the choices Jonathan had made and that Jonathan had sadly misjudged what the sentiment at home would be regarding his choice to accept the duel challenge.

On March 9, a meeting of Democrats from around the state was held in Augusta. The purpose of the meeting was "to notice in a suitable manner, the atrocious murder of the Hon. Jonathan Cilley . . . and to adopt such appropriate measures in reference to the subject as its importance demands." Undoubtedly, in private, his political friends were shocked and dismayed that Jonathan had allowed himself to be goaded into a duel. It was easier for them to view Jonathan's death as a political murder, as something he was lured into, with no way to extricate himself, rather than publicly question his decisions and actions. While the group certainly wanted to pay tribute to Jonathan and his service to the state, they also wanted to use Jonathan's death to political advantage. One man was said to have commented that the party ought to get at least a thousand sympathy votes.

The *Waldo Patriot*, always looking for an opportunity to turn anything the Democrats did into something negative, wrote that it was shocked by the blatantly political purpose of the meeting. The paper saw it as "the most atrocious libel on the character of Mr. Cilley . . . the most deliberate insult to his memory, which could have been offered. What a precious consolation it must be to his afflicted wife and fatherless children, to find a public meeting called, not to sympathize with her, not to condemn the barbarous custom of dueling." The *Patriot* also commented, "The idea of turning the affair to political account, too, is as stupid as it is profligate. What man who has as much brains as an oyster, cannot perceive that there is no just connection whatever between the political questions of the day and this personal quarrel between half a dozen hotspurs in Congress."

By April the ground in Thomaston had thawed, and Jonathan's body was on its way back home. Prince was not certain whether there could be an open casket at the funeral and was going to wait until the day before to look. Jonathan's funeral took place on April 19. Thomaston Democrats held a meeting at which plans were made to erect a monument in Jonathan's memory, and a committee was established to raise the necessary money. It was not until 1841 that the project was completed and the seventeen-foot monument placed over Jonathan's grave in the Elm Grove Cemetery.

Still reeling from the loss of a congressman who, through his personality, had reached across party lines to win his seat, the men in Jonathan's district now faced the challenge of electing his replacement. Farley had hoped to be the Whig candidate, but his failing health concerned the voters, and he lost out to Captain Edward Robinson in the Thomaston polls. Jonathan's old adversary McCrates won the Democrat vote. When the entire district voted, Robinson, who had served two terms in the Maine Senate, was the winner and immediately headed off to Washington to complete Jonathan's term. He was not reelected in 1839.

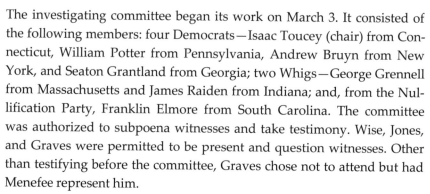

The investigating committee began its work on March 3. It consisted of the following members: four Democrats—Isaac Toucey (chair) from Connecticut, William Potter from Pennsylvania, Andrew Bruyn from New York, and Seaton Grantland from Georgia; two Whigs—George Grennell from Massachusetts and James Raiden from Indiana; and, from the Nullification Party, Franklin Elmore from South Carolina. The committee was authorized to subpoena witnesses and take testimony. Wise, Jones, and Graves were permitted to be present and question witnesses. Other than testifying before the committee, Graves chose not to attend but had Menefee represent him.

One of the first tasks before the committee was to assemble a list of witnesses. In addition to those directly involved in the duel, their list included anyone they believed to have information relevant to their inquiry. All those on the list were required to provide, before they appeared as witnesses, a written response to the following: "Please state what you know in regard to the causes which led to the death of the Hon. Jonathan Cilley, late a member of the House of Representatives, and the circumstances connected therewith, and if present on the field, state, further, all that transpired in the order in which it occurred: what were the propositions made for settling the differences, and what was said and responded to on each proposition, in order of the person speaking."

Jones and Wise provided all the written correspondence between the parties involved. The record also included the findings of the 1832 congressional committee that looked into Webb's dealings with the Bank of the United States. All the men subpoenaed appeared, and, in addition to their written responses, the witnesses answered questions from committee members as well as Wise, Jones, and Graves's surrogate. A question put to most of the witnesses addressed a suspicion by the committee members that an unmentioned reason behind Graves's challenge was that his veracity had been called into question. They asked, "Did Mr. Graves or his second, at any time before Mr. Cilley fell, communicate to Mr. Cilley, his second, or attendant friends, that a question of veracity between Mr. Graves and Mr. Cilley was a point of difficulty to be adjusted." After seven weeks the committee completed its work. Their reports were presented to the full House at the end of April.

Even before the House committee had completed its work, the Senate was debating a bill that would prohibit giving or accepting challenges to duels in the District of Columbia. About one hundred petitions and memorials, signed by close to twenty thousand people, flooded into Congress, mostly from the Northeast, urging an end to dueling and asking that those involved in duels be expelled from the House. There was, however, a law already in place that prohibited dueling in Washington — thus the trips to Maryland. In light of the recent event, there was little serious objection to the bill, but given the nature of partisan politics, each party had to make its points.

The Whigs were unconvinced that an anti-dueling law would stop the practice, believing that those inclined to fight would find a way around the law. For example, rather than write a traditional formal challenge, they might frame it in terms of an invitation to a tea party. They also objected to the strong criminal penalties in the bill, as it would put gentlemen in jail with common criminals. They asserted that the focus should be on broadening public opinion against dueling so that a man who declined a challenge would be held in higher esteem than the man who accepted it. Clay, in his brief comment on the bill, urged a change in public opinion.

Perry Smith from Connecticut, and a housemate of Ruggles, told the Senate an anti-dueling law was necessary to protect men from the North from being intimidated by Southerners. This would prevent men such as Webb, portrayed by Smith as "a man whose character was not worth a pinch of snuff," from using Southerners to do their dirty work.

Pierce took exception to Smith's comment. He believed the purpose of the bill was to suppress dueling everywhere. As for the people from New Hampshire whom he represented, they had always been very capable of protecting themselves and the country. Pierce, however, did not think any law would prevent unprincipled men (e.g., Webb) from preemptively attacking others. Obliquely referring to Webb's published plan to deal with Jonathan, he stated that anyone could be assaulted in their private lodging by armed assassins, have their limbs broken, or be killed in the streets.

William Preston from South Carolina reminded the Senate that even if a gentleman from the North were challenged, he had the choice of whether to accept, and if he chose to decline the challenge, he would have public opinion on his side. He added that the one challenged had a distinct advantage when he entered the field, for he chose the time, place, weapon, and distance. So if a Northerner who was pushed into a duel was injured or killed, it would be under circumstances that he had believed to be to his own advantage.

The only strong objection came from Arkansas's Ambrose Sevier, whose pathway into Congress came when his cousin Henry Newton was killed in the duel with Robert Crittenden in 1827. Sevier asserted that the bill would prevent those who were offended in Congress from getting satisfaction. He thought the bill was not really related to the overall problem with dueling, but only designed to protect congressmen. If the Senate really cared about dueling, he said, they would also ban dueling in the Florida and Wisconsin territories, as well as in federal forts. After Sevier's comments, one senator suggested that if Sevier saw dueling as so important, he would propose an amendment that would exclude Sevier from the law's restrictions. On April 9, the dueling bill came to a vote in the Senate and passed 34–1, with Sevier casting the only negative vote.

On April 21, the committee completed its work, and its greatly anticipated reports were presented to the House. As was expected, the committee members held different opinions, and they produced three separate reports. The four Democrats wrote the majority report, and there was a dissenting report by the two Whigs, while the gentleman from South Carolina offered a third opinion. However, the three reports concurred that, through their involvement in the duel, Graves, Wise, and Jones had breached the constitutionally granted privilege of the House. The Democrats saw the breach as serious enough to warrant Graves's expulsion from the House, and they also recommended that Wise and Jones be censured. They found no fault with Jonathan's negative comments about Webb, especially since the 1832 House committee that investigated Webb's loans from the Bank of the United States had found that Webb's newspaper had changed its editorial political leanings after he had received the loans. They also decided that Jonathan was wholly justified in refusing any communication from Webb without needing to give a reason. They concluded that because Graves knew the contents of the Webb note he had agreed to deliver to Jonathan, and that it was related to words spoken in House debate, Graves had (perhaps innocently) breached the privilege of the House. However, they held that Graves had overstepped his responsibilities to the House by pushing Jonathan to comment on Webb's character.

The report of the two Whigs, while agreeing that there had been a breach of privilege, did not believe any form of punishment was warranted. They pointed out that the House had never before punished duelists, and since all those involved participated voluntarily, it was not within the province of the House to issue consequences. Given that all those involved, including Jonathan, had breached the House privilege, it would be hypocritical to hold a public funeral for the deceased and then punish the survivors. They believed that the committee should have only presented the House with the facts and let that body interpret the information it had received.

Elmore, who also believed the privilege of the House was breached, took a position somewhere between the Democrats and the Whigs. He wrote at length on the importance of House privilege and its importance to the legislative process. He did believe that some sort of penalty should be imposed on Graves, Wise, and Jones. But he sided with the Whigs in stating that it was not the role of the committee to suggest a punishment. He did not believe that Graves intended to violate privilege, but that he was in error to question Jonathan about anything related to what had been said in the House. For Elmore, while the House had never set any precedent for penalties for breach of privilege, the issue was not one of vengeance, but rather the establishment of appropriate penalties. He suggested that in the present case penalties should be light but harsher for future violators.

With regard to Webb, none of the reports had anything positive to say. Not much credence was given to the after-the-fact letters and comments by Webb and his associates concerning their intentions to do harm to Jonathan, seeing them as bravado. All agreed that Webb's actions through the whole affair were reprehensible but concluded the House had no jurisdiction with regard to him.

The House debated until May 10 about what to do with the committee's reports. There was not much enthusiasm to rush to expel or censure, or to discuss the circumstances that precipitated the duel. The majority committee members were criticized for overstepping their mandate by offering analysis of the facts and suggesting consequences. Samson Mason from Ohio said that the report overly praised Jonathan to the exclusion of positive comments about anyone else involved. The majority report, he said, "was more like an electioneering document than anything else, endeavoring to prove one party flagrantly guilty, and the other purely innocent."

There was considerable discussion about whether the reports should be printed and distributed. While there were those who wanted the printing delayed, both Wise and Graves wanted the reports printed. Bynum and Duncan, aware that their involvement was questioned at home, wanted the reports printed so that those at home would have all the facts. John Quincy Adams advocated that any printing of the reports be postponed until they were condensed to contain only the facts.

Graves initially did not want the reports printed. While he believed the public had the right to see the testimony collected by the committee, he strongly "object[ed] and protest[ed] most solemnly against having this report printed, and spread upon the records of the House; because it contains an unfair, partial, and garbled statement of the evidence, upon which it is hypothecated to do great injustice to me in public estimation: and, if placed upon the journals of this house there to remain as long as this Government continues, it will do me gross, yea, cruel injustice." He wanted the report sent back to the committee and returned only when it contained just the facts. As time passed he became aware that only the majority report was being circulated, and he then requested twenty thousand copies of the entire report be printed. Fairfield himself told the House that he had sent a few hundred copies of the majority report to Maine and hoped to send many more.

At the same time, Graves offered an explanation of his involvement in the duel and what led him to issue his challenge: "I was involved in the commencement of this unfortunate affair innocently. I never conceived it possible that such consequence would have devolved on me, when I consented to bear that ill-fated note, other wise I should never have taken on myself the task. I am not, and never been the advocate of the anti-social and unchristian practice of dueling." He then attempted to deflect responsibility for his actions by saying he had no choice other than to act in order to avoid the wrath of public opinion. "Public opinion," he said, "is practically the paramount law of the land; every other law, both human and divine, ceases to be observed, yea, withers and perishes, in contact with it. It was this paramount law of this nation and of this House that forced me, under the penalty of dishonor, to submit myself to the code which impelled me unwillingly into this tragical affair."

In some ways, similar to Jonathan, Graves wanted to believe that his actions would be condoned by the public and also by the men in the House. The Louisville *Public Advertiser* correctly pointed out that the public in general abhorred dueling, and only a small segment of society stubbornly adhered to the fading code of honor. "He was impelled," the paper stated, "to commit the fatal deed rather than hazard his reputation with that portion of his fellow citizens who approve the barbarous practice." The article acknowledged, however, that it was "difficult in the south or west for men to exert sufficient moral courage to do right when impelled by the laws of honor to commit an outrage."

Wise was much more contemptuous, particularly of the majority report. He told the House that if they were going to call him a murderer, then they should try him. He said his involvement in the affair was in a dispute between two men and had nothing to do with the House. He threatened that if they did not try him, he would "drag from their seats here and in the other House the real culprits. The very wretches who instigated that duel, who wept crocodile tears over the bier of poor Cilley, and who got up excitement the most loathsome, for no end whatever of religion or morality, but for the vilest of political purposes." He further reminded the House that if they chose to expel him, he was certain his constituents would return him in the next election.

Wise also added his opinion that the formal funeral accorded to Jonathan was inappropriate. He said that if a member of the House ever killed him in a duel, he would want to be buried privately and without ceremony, "without the gelded Congressional coffin, the silk velvet, the armorial bearing, the crape, the honorable funeral, the mock mourning."

In the end, on May 10 the House voted to table the committee reports, never to be brought to the floor of the House again. They did, however, approve the printing of the reports. The Senate's anti-dueling bill was sent to the House, but it was not until February 20, 1839, that the House finally passed the bill. No consequences were ever issued to Graves, Wise, or Jones. The whole affair faded away, only to be resurrected in 1842, when Wise, as promised, implicated others.

Even with Jonathan's death, Ruggles's bitterness toward him continued to fester. Not only did Deborah have to cope with the loss of her husband and the responsibility of caring for three young children, but she also had to deal with lawsuits by Ruggles. Ruggles alleged that Jonathan had cheated him out of money during the years Jonathan had worked under him, and he was now, in the latter part of 1838, suing Jonathan's estate to recoup the money he insisted Jonathan had pocketed. He said the amount was $1,000, and he added $500 in interest. Given that Ruggles was a wealthy man, the amount of money he was after was trivial. According to Nealley, who had worked in Jonathan's office, Jonathan kept meticulous records of any money he took in when Ruggles was out of the office.

At one point, Jonathan had filed a suit against Ruggles; yet Prince, now acting as the administrator of Jonathan's estate, was unable to find copies of the suit in court. The suspicion was that Ruggles, who was known to have been in the court, took them. Ruggles also asserted that Jonathan had sold two rifles for him and never gave him the money. The two men who bought the rifles, however, when deposed, both said they had given the money to Ruggles, and Jonathan had not been involved.

Deborah wrote to Edward and Lucy in November 1838 to tell them of Ruggles's suit. She was very concerned that Ruggles, whom she called "the author of all our troubles," would spread his accusations about Jonathan in Washington in a deliberate attempt to tarnish Jonathan's character and honor. She wanted Edward to write to the men he knew in Washington to warn them of Ruggles's intentions. It is not known how all these legal actions turned out, but it appears from the information we have that Jonathan did not cheat Ruggles.

Hawthorne's biographical sketch was published in the *Democratic Review* in September with little fanfare. In contrast, to some degree, with his comments in 1837 after his meeting with Jonathan in Thomaston, Hawthorne focused on the softer side of Jonathan's character and his attachment and commitment to his family and the people he served.

> Mr. Cilley's domestic habits were simple and primitive to a degree unusual, in most parts of our country, among men of so eminent a station as he had attained. It made me smile, though with anything but scorn, in contrast to the aristocratic stateliness which I have witnessed elsewhere, to see him driving home his own cow after a long search for her through the village.
>
> His manners had not a fastidious polish, but were characterized by the simplicity of one who had dwelt remote from cities, holding free companionship with the yeomen of the land. I thought him as true a representative of the people as ever theory could portray. His earlier and later habits of life, his feelings, partialities, and prejudices, were

those of the people: the strong and shrewd sense which constituted so marked a feature of his mind was but a higher degree of the popular intellect. He loved the people and respected them, and was prouder of nothing than of his brotherhood with those who had entrusted their public interests to his care.

I glance at these minute particulars of his daily life, because they form so strange a contrast with the circumstances of his death. Who could have believed that, with his thoroughly New England character, in so short a time after I had seen him in that peaceful and happy home, among those simple occupations and pure enjoyments, he would be stretched in his own blood,—slain for an almost impalpable punctilio!

In the end Hawthorne found it very difficult to understand and accept Jonathan's course of action and lamented his lost potential.

Alas that over the grave of a dear friend my sorrow for the bereavement must be mingled with another grief, that he threw away such a life in so miserable a cause! Why, as he was true to the Northern character in all things else, did he swerve from his Northern principles in this final scene? But his error was a generous one, since he fought for what he deemed the honor of New England; and, now that death has paid the forfeit, the most rigid may forgive him. If that dark pitfall—that bloody grave—had not lain in the midst of his path, whither, whither might it not have led him! It has ended there: yet so strong was my conception of his energies, so like destiny did it appear that he should achieve everything at which he aimed, that even now my fancy will not dwell upon his grave, but pictures him still amid the struggles and triumphs of the present and the future.

# SIXTEEN
## Wise and Clay

It was not long before the infamous Cilley/Graves duel faded from peoples' minds, and politics in Washington went on as usual. Graves was reelected to the House one more time. His popularity at home had dipped, and he had to work to salvage his image. In a speech to a group of constituents in Louisville in the summer of 1839 he again explained his involvement in the duel. He told the audience that he had innocently agreed to deliver Webb's note to Jonathan and was taken aback by Jonathan's refusal to accept it. He continued—as he had done at the time—to assert that Jonathan told him that he meant no disrespect to him or Webb, but that he would stand behind his debate privilege. Graves said he was relieved, until he learned that some of Jonathan's "most politically violent" associates had impeached his truthfulness and were denying that Jonathan said what Graves had claimed. Graves believed that when he then asked Jonathan to put his explanation in writing, Jonathan intentionally impugned Graves's veracity. With this, Graves's personal honor had now been questioned. He additionally suggested to the audience, as a way to boost his reelection chances, that the honor of Kentucky had been challenged. He told them that while he thought the odds had been against him, he was ready to lay down his life in defense of his honor and the honor of Kentucky. Of note in this speech was his specific mention of veracity as the real basis behind his challenge. He also mentioned for the first time that he had help in writing the challenge note but did not say from whom. That wouldn't come out for three more years.

In 1840 the Whigs finally gained the White House with the election of William Henry Harrison. He died, however, just thirty-two days after his inauguration, and John Tyler became the first vice president to succeed a serving president. Wise continued to be reelected to Congress. Now, in the 27th Congress, he was the only remaining House member involved in the duel. None of the men who had served on the investigating committee were still in office. But John Quincy Adams, now seventy-five years old, and labeled by Wise as the "hissing serpent of Braintree," continued to be a tormenting thorn in the sides of those who represented Southern slaveholders. Adams was the one who resurrected the duel, and in doing so brought forth previously undisclosed information about the involvement of others in the duel's preliminary stages.

It all started in January 1842, when Adams introduced in the House a petition from a group in Haverhill, Massachusetts, calling for the dissolution of the Union. Even though Adams recommended that the request be rejected, Wise and his friends saw the petition as an opportunity to silence Adams. They held that it was treasonous for Adams to bring the petition to the House, and he consequently deserved censure. A wily politician, Adams was eager to take on the challenge, even voting against a motion offered by his friends to table the motion for censure.

In spite of Wise's tarnished reputation due to his role in Jonathan's death, he did not back off from his duelist orientation. Even as he was plotting against Adams, in the House he took offense to a comment by Edward Stanley of North Carolina and wrote a letter of inquiry to Stanley. The duel was averted, but the animosity continued. In May, while they were both at the racetrack, Stanley bumped into Wise, and Wise responded by hitting Stanley in the face with a horsewhip. A challenge quickly followed, but a duel was once again avoided when Wise was arrested. He was quickly released after posting a cash bond with its return contingent upon the settlement of their differences.

The proceedings against Adams filled the gallery. Members of the Senate even took time away from their proceedings, primarily to watch Adams in action. Thomas Marshall from Kentucky presented the motion for censure. Marshall, who had been defeated in 1837 by Graves for a seat in Congress, was the nephew of longtime Supreme Court chief justice John Marshall. After Marshall came Wise, and he talked for five-and-a-half hours over two days. Wise tore into Adams, whom he characterized as a tool of the English and a disgrace to the name of his presidential father, for consistently challenging the gag rule and for his abolitionist position on slavery.

Adams held his tongue through Wise's attack, but he was ready to respond when Wise finally finished. Adams said "he had desired to give the gentleman from Accomac an opportunity to poor out the vials of his wrath, and disgorge, to the fullest extent, his bile, which had been accumulating for three years." He told the House they had no right to try him, and reminded them that he had made the identical point in 1838, when the Democrats wanted to punish Wise, Graves, and Jones for their role in Jonathan's death. While he believed Wise was responsible for Jonathan's death, and that Wise had come to the House at the time "with his hands and face dripping with the blood of murder, the blotches of which were yet hanging upon him," Adams contended the House had no right then to punish Wise or the others, and now, four years later, an ungrateful Wise intended to prosecute the man who likely "saved this blood stained man from censure of the House."

Wise had been dogged for four years by charges that he was solely responsible for plotting Jonathan's "murder." Two days after Adams spoke, Wise responded. He opened by stating how pleased he was that he "now had an opportunity of saying what he had long wished to say. He thanked God that there was a large assembly here to hear it. An opportunity had at length arrived for him to vindicate himself, now and forever from the charge of instigating and advising the duel of Graves and Cilley."

He told the packed House chamber, which included Clay and Crittenden, that he was glad that the two senators from Kentucky were present. Looking at them, he said he would "appeal to them as his witness, that his advice was not the advice relied upon or followed in the preliminaries of that duel, it was the advice of another, higher, better, more distinguished man which was relied on." This was the first time that Clay's involvement in the duel was publicly mentioned. Needless to say, neither Clay nor Crittenden said anything, even though everyone present knew that Wise was referring to Clay. A few weeks later Clay wrote to Wise, "During all these proceedings, without any appeal to you, I remained passive and silent, suffering under conscious justice, but abiding in undoubting confidence that in this, as in other instances, truth would ultimately triumph."

Over the next few weeks Wise laid before the public what he saw as Clay's significant involvement in the affair leading up to the duel. Wise asserted that Graves had consulted Clay on Thursday, February 22, and that Clay was the one who encouraged Graves to get Jonathan's reply in writing. Wise wrote that he disagreed with this, but Graves chose to follow Clay's advice. On Friday, Graves brought Wise to Clay to get Clay's opinion on the challenge note Graves had written. Wise claimed that Clay told them Graves had no other choice but to issue the challenge. Clay, however, did not like Graves's phrasing and wrote out a different wording, which he believed would better facilitate an adjustment and prevent a duel. Wise alleged that Graves's original challenge centered around the veracity issue and in it Graves cited Jonathan's refusal to put in writing what he had spoken to Graves as the reason for the challenge. Clay, however, according to Wise, preferred to base the challenge on Jonathan's unwillingness to acknowledge Webb as a gentleman; thus Graves's honor was being called into question because he bore the note of a man not considered a gentleman. Unlike Clay, Wise believed the veracity issue was much more amenable to reconciliation, while Clay's wording closed the door to an amicable settlement. Wise charged that Clay was privy to the terms of the duel and believed they were acceptable.

Wise was hoping to regain favor with the Democratic Party, so he no longer needed to stay in Clay's good graces and had nothing to lose by bringing Clay's name into the picture. Graves, Wise, and their friends had previously made a concerted effort to keep Clay's involvement out of the public sphere. Clay must have been stunned by Wise's public charges, but he did have some involvement with the duel. Though at the time Clay certainly appreciated that his name had not surfaced, now he had no choice but to respond. What followed were a series of letters, most of which were published in newspapers throughout the country.

Clay initially wrote to Webb looking for help to refute some of Wise's charges. He wanted someone else to defend him rather than give credence to Wise's allegation by responding to him personally. He particularly wanted Webb to say that Clay had attempted to stop the duel when he found out that Graves was on his way to it. Webb did publish an editorial that supported Clay's stance.

After a blistering attack on Clay appeared in a Boston newspaper, Clay wrote to Graves asking him to come to his defense. Graves was quick to respond, and for the first time he acknowledged that he and Wise had gone to Clay that Friday morning for advice, but that he had not previously discussed the matter with Clay, although in a letter to Wise, Clay said that Graves had told him about the controversy on Thursday and that in fact Clay had urged Graves to get Jonathan's response in writing. Possibly still attempting to minimize Clay's involvement, Graves later wrote that he had not talked to Clay before Friday. Graves also wrote that Clay had only given him advice about the phrasing of the challenge and that he had used Clay's wording.

Wise wrote directly to Clay insisting that Clay admit he advised Graves before Friday and that he had written the challenge note. In an open letter to Graves, Wise asked him to confess that veracity was the primary reason for the duel, and that Wise had objected to Clay's rewording of the challenge, and thus it was Clay, not Wise, who had set the grounds for the duel. Wise suggested that Clay chose the course he took in order to garner Webb's editorial support in the upcoming presidential election.

In the end, neither Graves nor Clay supported any of Wise's charges, but the affair did take some unwarranted blame off Wise's back. If Wise hoped to improve his political image within the Democratic Party by bringing the duel back, he succeeded. The Democratic press relished in the opportunity to put Clay in an unfavorable light. O'Sullivan's *Democratic Review*, which had heaped all the blame for Jonathan's death on Wise in 1838, now, in May 1842, came to Wise's defense. The *Review* was full of regret for how it had unjustly treated Wise, and it accepted without question Wise's version of Clay's involvement. While the paper still deplored the barbarian, foolish, and dreadful code of honor, it excused Wise from guilt because he had only followed the honor code that was part of his upbringing and culture. They suggested that if Clay had not removed veracity from the challenge, it was much more likely the duel would have been avoided. The paper now recognized that the primary issue came from Graves's misunderstanding of Jonathan's reason for not accepting Webb's note. Clay was castigated for keeping his involvement secret and not coming to Wise's defense.

Again, as with most issues in Washington, the controversy over the duel faded. Adams escaped censure when, after two weeks of debate, the House tired of the whole thing and voted to table the motion.

In March, just as the accusations against him began to subside, Clay, now sixty-five, resigned his seat in the Senate, stating that he longed to return to private life. Clay's seat went to Crittenden. Crittenden had given up his original seat in 1840 to become Harrison's attorney general, but when Harrison died Crittenden was unwilling to serve under Tyler. Menefee, who did not return after the 25th Congress, had been in the running for Crittenden's seat, but his health was poor and he died in February 1841.

With his return to private life, Clay focused on the presidential election coming up in 1844. Tyler did not have the support of his party, and the Whigs turned to Clay to run against James Polk. The campaign again brought back the Cilley/Graves duel. While the Democratic press hammered Clay for his role in Jonathan's death, the Whig press blamed Jonathan's friends for pushing him into the duel and doing nothing to prevent it from taking place.

Clay was also pushed to renounce dueling and to state that he would never issue or accept a challenge. In the past Clay had been involved in two duels, but what resurfaced now was a more recent conflict. In March 1841, William King took offense to some personal comment Clay made about him in the Senate. King issued a challenge, Clay accepted, and seconds were selected. The Senate sergeant at arms had both men arrested. Clay posted a $5,000 bond to ensure he would keep the peace.

Polk ultimately won the election. Had Clay won, Graves would have been one of his electors in the Electoral College. In the end, it was unlikely that the duel issue had any effect on the election results except maybe in Thomaston, Maine, where the historically Whig-leaning community overwhelmingly supported Polk. With Clay's defeat, the Cilley/Graves duel disappeared from American politics.

# SEVENTEEN

## Mistaken Sense of Honor

Jonathan Cilley was a young man from a noble and honorable New Hampshire family whose men had distinguished themselves in service to their community, state, and country. In his adopted state of Maine, Jonathan followed his family's tradition. He served admirably and with distinction in the Maine legislature and won the respect of his community, which carried him, in the footsteps of his uncle, to the U.S. House of Representatives. He was devoted to his wife and children, relishing time at home with his family and the bees that he kept. He had a promising future, only to have it cut short on the dueling grounds. At the time of his death and over the ensuing years, the lingering question has been: How could this have happened?

From a twenty-first-century perspective, when we attempt to explain a death in a duel between two members of the House of Representatives in 1838, it is difficult to fathom what could promote two men to stand in a field, eighty yards apart, on a cold February day, and shoot at each other with rifles. It was a time, however, when the now archaic "code of honor" was in some areas of the country still strictly adhered to. Looking at all that has been written about the Cilley/Graves duel, and contrary to the political rhetoric of the time, which sought to label Jonathan's death as an intentional murder and part of a political conspiracy, there is no hard evidence to support that conclusion. Jonathan's unfortunate death, just as he was stepping onto the national stage, can only be attributed to a mistaken sense of honor, faulty thinking, and impulsive decision making on the part of the principals, neither of whom had experience with dueling protocol. Additionally, both received bad advice from the men they chose to consult and had seconds who did not live up to their responsibilities.

Jonathan's untimely death was truly a tragedy, not only for his family and friends but also for the country. It brought into national focus the senselessness of these affairs of honor and heightened the resolve of most Americans to put an end to dueling. Looking at the totality of what transpired between Jonathan and Graves, it simply should not have happened.

The House committee charged with investigating the causes that led to Jonathan's death collected a significant amount of evidence that would have allowed it to offer an informed opinion about the reasons for the duel. However, given the mandate to only address possible breaches of privilege, the committee never seriously dealt with the causes.

Although the committee took the time to ask most of its witnesses about whether an impugning of Graves's veracity was an unexpressed cause behind his challenge, the majority report only mentioned it briefly, stating that veracity was an issue, and that Jonathan never knew what Graves had said to others or understood that there was disagreement about what he had said to Graves. The committee, however, concluded that while Graves believed his veracity had been questioned, it had not been serious enough to create sufficient animosity to warrant his duel challenge (even though being called a liar had always been considered a serious affront to a gentleman's honor).

Both Wise and Menefee had stated on more than one occasion that veracity was an issue. Wise specifically told the committee that Graves insisted that what he had claimed Jonathan had said was in fact the words Jonathan had spoken to him in their conversation on February 21. Menefee replied that while veracity was never mentioned to Jonathan or Jones, he understood Graves was looking for Jonathan to publicly confirm Graves's version of what he'd said. Jones, however, told the committee that at no time had the issue of veracity been mentioned to him. The information that surfaced in 1842 reinforced the notion that veracity was in fact at the core of Graves's original challenge but had been removed by Clay. It was Wise's opinion that because it was not mentioned at the time of the duel, the discussion on the field was limited to topics that were not really the major issue, thus pushing the affair to three shots and resulting in a tragic death that could have been avoided.

Graves had allowed himself to be put in a position he had not antici-pated when he innocently agreed to deliver Webb's note. When Jonathan refused the note, Graves was quickly cognizant that Jonathan had put him in a difficult position and looked for a quick way out. Rather than simply returning the note to Webb, he consulted with Wise. Then, after his second private conversation with Jonathan, he was satisfied by what he thought Jonathan had said, believing he had been relieved of his re-sponsibility. However, when he asked Jonathan to put in writing what he'd heard Jonathan say in their first meeting, he was shocked by Jona-than's reply. Not knowing what Graves had told others, Jonathan merely repeated what he had previously said. Graves compounded the situation by believing that he had been intentionally set up by Jonathan to be humiliated. Unfortunately for Graves, all those he talked with accepted without question his recollection of his conversations with Jonathan, which reinforced Graves's belief that Jonathan's letter was designed to humiliate him. When he got Jonathan's last note declining any further response, Graves saw his veracity as irreparably attacked and felt com-pelled to issue a challenge.

From the moment Jonathan was presented with Webb's note, he per-ceived a problem brewing. His initial reply to Graves was appropriate; he had no obligation to accept the note. After his first conversation with Pierce, Jonathan regarded the ongoing events as a significant threat to his integrity, honor, and political future. Pierce failed his friend, first by framing the initial note from Webb in the context of the Southern code of honor, and second by raising Jonathan's anxiety, without any evidence, through his implication that Webb might physically assault him. When presented with the issue, Pierce, rather than consult with Northerners who might have been able to help Jonathan, went immediately to men who had been duelists; by doing so, he foreclosed any options other than dueling. He also accepted without question Jonathan's conspiracy theory. There is no evidence that Pierce attempted to talk Jonathan out of the direction he was headed in or apprised him of the implications, personal and political, of engaging in a duel. He accepted Jonathan's determina-tion and enabled it. He found a second for Jonathan and then walked away, leaving Jonathan's fate to others.

In the end, Pierce let Jonathan and the values of New England down by not trying to stop the duel. He could have informed the authorities but chose not to. Nor did he enlist the help of anyone else to stop Jonathan.

Instead, he stayed home anxiously awaiting Jonathan's return, only to find out his friend had been killed. In his correspondence after the duel he focused on Jonathan's fixed determination and how upset he was about Jonathan's death. He never talked about his own actions and what he might have done differently.

There were those who suggested that Jonathan, during his brief time in the House, purposefully attempted to gain favor with Southerners in order to enhance his status. Adams characterized Jonathan as "an ambitious Northern young man, struggling to rise on a Southern platform." Adams also saw Jonathan as deliberately provoking Graves as a way "to display to the South and West how high he soared above the region of Yankee prejudices." While Jonathan had garnered some praise from the likes of Thompson, there is no evidence that he had intentionally sought out favor from Southerners.

Jonathan put up a number of roadblocks to any reconciliation. He was resolute in his unsubstantiated belief that the whole conflict was part of a conspiracy to humiliate him and negate his influence in Congress. It had occurred in Maine, and he believed history was repeating itself, so he was determined not to talk to anyone who did not agree with him. He believed he was being coerced into a position of dishonor and mistakenly convinced himself that public opinion at home would support his actions. Unfortunately, throughout the entire affair he and his friends were never made aware of the real reason—veracity—for Graves's challenge. If he had been, the duel could have been averted.

Very early on Jonathan had made up his mind that, if challenged, he would accept. He would not allow those out to get him to humiliate him again. But would he have been humiliated in the eyes of his peers? With a little thought, Jonathan and his "real" friends could have diverted the whole issue to his advantage. Given Webb's negative reputation, had Jonathan taken the note, he could then have refused to deal with Webb. It was unlikely that Webb would have posed any real physical threat to Jonathan. Webb might have attacked him in his newspaper, but the Democratic press would have supported Jonathan, and because he'd stood up to Webb, it would likely have enhanced his standing within his party and with those opposed to dueling.

In addition, when presented with the challenge, he could have declined to accept it. It was not unheard of for a Northerner not to fight. When Daniel Webster received a challenge in 1816, he declined by saying, "It is enough that I do not feel myself bound, at all times and under any circumstances, to accept from any man, who shall choose to risk his own life, an invitation of this sort."

Jonathan could have told Graves he would not fight someone for whom he had no ill will, and that it would prove nothing for either of them to put their lives at risk. It is unlikely that Graves would have challenged Jonathan based on Jonathan's refusal to acknowledge Webb as a gentleman. In such a case, Webb would have insisted he be the one to deal with Jonathan.

Once the challenge had been issued, with Jonathan's determination to accept and get the duel over with as soon as possible, he shut others out and took control of a situation in which he had no experience. Tragically, his friends allowed this to happen. His ill-advised choice of rifles, a more lethal weapon than the traditional dueling pistol, reinforced Graves's notion that Jonathan intended to go for the kill, and this also served to solidify his determination to fight to require Jonathan's acknowledgment of what he insisted Jonathan had said to him previously.

The role of the seconds in an affair of honor is vital in guiding their principals. Jones and Wise, in their joint account from the day after the duel, wrote, "We endeavored to discharge our duties according to that code under which the parties met, regulated by magnanimous principles, and the laws of humanity." The question, though, is whether they in fact followed the code or violated it in ways that facilitated the fatal result. The code of honor was not merely an excuse for men, angry with one another, to go out and attempt to kill each other. The duel itself was the end result that followed only after attempts to reconcile differences had failed. Through this process the role of the second was primary, and there were protocols dictating the responsibilities of the seconds. When these responsibilities, with regard to Jones's and Wise's courses of action, are examined, both men were significantly lacking.

John Lyde Wilson, once governor of South Carolina, published a small book in 1838 that detailed the roles and responsibilities of both the principals and the seconds in affairs of honor. Wilson's guidelines are very useful as a reference point to examine Jones's and Wise's conduct.

Initially, even before a second took on the responsibility, the code required that he make it clear to the gentleman requesting his involvement "that you will be governed only by your own judgment, that he will not be consulted after you are in full possession of the facts." There are no records of any discussion of this nature occurring on either side. Since neither Jonathan nor Graves had experience with affairs of honor, and Jones and Wise did, before either of them took on the responsibility of being a second, they should have clearly apprised their principals of a second's role and responsibilities. Jones was rushed into the affair by Pierce and Jonathan, and he should have insisted that the duel be delayed until he had time to fully gather all the facts and had an opportunity to communicate with Wise.

There was concern at the time that Wise, because of his debate confrontations with Jonathan, carried animosity toward Jonathan into the duel, which compromised his objectivity and biased him to push the duel to multiple shots. While Wise tried to minimize the presence of any animosity, Jonathan had fearlessly opposed him, and it would be hard to imagine that Wise harbored no ill will, and that it did not influence his judgment. This alone should have been sufficient reason for Wise to decline to be Graves's second.

The urgency on Wise's and Jones's part to get the terms specified and procure a rifle for Graves sidetracked them from any discussion of ways to avoid the necessity of a duel. Jones, however, in his role of second, had the authority to slow things down. He should have known that his primary function was first to attempt to mediate the dispute and reconcile the differences. Nowhere is there any mention of an attempt by either Wise or Jones to discuss the points of honor that precipitated the challenge. They never recognized that the challenge was based on a misunderstanding of what words transpired between Jonathan and Graves.

The code also dictated that the second "use every effort to soothe and tranquilize your principal to not see things in the same aggravated light in which he views them, extenuate the conduct of his adversary whenever you see clearly an opportunity to do so." Recognizing that the combatants are agitated and angry and not looking at the issues with a clear head, a second must "use your utmost efforts to allay all excitement which your principal may labor under: search diligently into the origins of the misunderstanding." Gentlemen who get embroiled in affairs of honor, Wilson said, "seldom insult each other, unless they labor under some misapprehension or mistake." It then becomes the seconds' charge to look for these errors and "endeavor to persuade him that there must have been some misunderstanding in the matter." Again, Jones and Wise shirked their responsibility in this regard.

The entire disagreement between Jonathan and Graves escalated because of misunderstandings about what had been said and beliefs about unnamed others who were urging and promoting the conflict. Jones took Jonathan's version of the events at face value and never inquired or investigated the issue or engaged Wise, prior to the duel, in any discussion to explore alternative ways of viewing the conflict. Wise, rather than being any kind of arbitrator, accepted without question Grave's memory of his conversations with Jonathan and never made an attempt to explore possible misunderstandings or miscommunication.

Wise's most significant and ultimately fatal failure occurred on the field, when he insisted on more than one shot. In line with what others said at the time, Wilson's rules stated that "if the meeting be of no serious cause or complaint, where the party complaining had in no way been deeply injured, or grossly insulted," it is the responsibility of the challenging second to terminate the duel after the first shot. Wise, given the minor point of honor in question, had no right, according to the code, to require further concession or explanation from Jonathan. He should have terminated the duel.

Unfortunately, what should have occurred did not, and "thus died the brave and gifted Jonathan Cilley. To our regret for the loss of that splendid genius must be added another grief, that he threw away his life for so senseless a cause. True to his New England blood and training, he was ever staunch and steadfast until he swerved in this final scene. If he had a mistaken sense of honor he paid the forfeit, and we may now well spread garlands above his grave." Jonathan's definition of honor was closely tried to his own personal and political aspirations, his sense of family tradition, and his place in family lore. His personal honor allowed him to erroneously distort his issue with Graves into a larger planned attack that heightened his resolve not to give in or concede anything that could have been used by his "enemies" to discredit him or impugn his sense of honor. He also mistakenly convinced himself that those at home would agree that it was necessary for him to fight in order to defend his own as well as their honor.

> If that dark pitfall, that bloody grave, had not lain in the midst of his path, wither, wither might it not have led him! It has ended there: yet so strong was my conception of his energies, so like destiny did it appear, that he should achieve everything at which he aimed, that,

even now, my fancy will not dwell upon his grave, but picture him still amid the struggles and triumphs of the present and the future.

# Epilogue

Sadly for Jonathan's family, he left nothing that explained his thinking, motivation, or reasons for accepting a duel challenge. Deborah was left with no explanations, no direction, failing health, and three children to raise. Jones had seen him writing to Deborah and encouraged him to complete his letter, but Jonathan told him he would do it later. Later never came, and Deborah had to muster all her strength to move forward. At the time of Jonathan's death, Greenleaf was eight, Jonathan Prince was two, and Julia was only nine weeks old.

One of Deborah's early priorities was to ensure that Greenleaf received a good education. She arranged for a boarding placement in southern Maine. She worked and succeeded, with help from Duncan and Pierce, in obtaining an appointment for Greenleaf as a midshipman in the navy. In the meantime, Deborah taught school to help make ends meet. By September 1844 she had lost both parents and her brother Hezekiah. Tuberculosis had finally drained her of all her strength, and she died on September 24 at age thirty-eight.

After Deborah's death, Jonathan's sister, Elizabeth Ann Burley, and her husband raised Jonathan Prince and Julia in New Hampshire. Following in his father's footsteps, Jonathan Prince graduated from Bowdoin College and became a lawyer. When the Civil War broke out he organized the First Maine Cavalry, and by March 1862 the now Captain Cilley was in Washington and part of the Army of the Potomac. During the course of the war he was wounded three times and briefly held prisoner. At the conclusion of the war he held the rank of brevet brigadier general. He returned to the Thomaston area and resumed his law practice. He died in 1920, at age eighty-four.

Greenleaf entered the navy at the age of fourteen and was soon sailing off to the Mediterranean. He served in both the Mexican and Civil wars. He had command of a number of vessels, including the ironclad *Catskill*. He ended the Civil War as a lieutenant commander. He was passed over for promotion to commander, because earlier in his career he had been court-martialed for intoxication. This possibly occurred around 1861, because in a letter from Jonathan Prince to his sister he mentioned that Greenleaf was not going to resign from the navy. Without the active-duty promotion, he was relegated to the retired list (albeit with the rank of commander).

True to the character of his father, who would not let an injustice go unchallenged, Greenleaf, likely with the help of his brother, appears to have pushed to have his lack of active-duty promotion and placement on the retired list overturned. Petitions from citizens of Maine were submitted to Congress. The records of the 45th, 46th, and 47th Congresses show that bills were introduced in both the House and the Senate for relief. The Committee of Naval Affairs investigated the matter three times, and on each occasion their reports concluded that Greenleaf had been unjustly denied his promotion. By 1884 he had collected recommendations from a former secretary of the navy and four retired admirals who vouched for his character and lack of issues with alcohol.

The report of the 1884 committee, ironically presented by Representative George Wise of Virginia, nephew of Henry Wise, concluded that Greenleaf should be restored "to the active list from which he was only withdrawn by a so-called moral disqualification that has not existed" and restored to the active list as a captain.

During his naval travels Greenleaf had met and married the daughter of the former governor of the then Argentinian Falkland Islands. After the Civil War he settled in Argentina, dying there in 1898.

Henry Wise resigned his seat in the House in February 1844, when he was appointed the U.S. minister to Brazil. He held that post until 1847. In 1856 he was elected governor of Virginia. During Wise's term as governor, John Brown carried out his infamous raid at Harper's Ferry. Brown was sentenced to death. It was within the province of Wise's office to commute Brown's sentence, and many, particularly from the North, urged him to do so. At one point Wise looked to have Brown's sanity evaluated. If Brown had been declared insane, there would be no execution. Wise had mixed feelings about Brown. He admired Brown's principles and boldness, but in the end he decided to let the execution go forward. In later life Wise voiced regret that he did not stop Brown's hanging.

With the presidential election of 1860 looming, Wise explored a possible Democratic nomination. The party was splintered, and he thought he might be able to convince the convention that he would be a good compromise candidate. It did not work out, and in the end the Republican candidate Abraham Lincoln was elected president. With the outbreak of the Civil War, Wise served as a brigadier general in the Confederate army. He served through the entire war and was at Appomattox for the surrender.

His controversial involvement in the Cilley/Graves duel followed him to the end of his life. Both he and Jones, who had remained friends over the years, were regularly required to defend their actions. In 1873, Wise wrote a lengthy explanation and, as he had consistently done, laid the blame on Clay. Wise died at age seventy-five in 1876.

James Watson Webb continued with the *Courier and Enquirer* until it folded in 1861. His conflict with Jonathan did not do much to further tarnish his already shady reputation. In 1842 he relentlessly attacked Representative Thomas Marshall of Kentucky for coming to New York to act as a defense attorney for a man accused of swindling New York merchants. (This was the same Marshall who attempted to censure Adams.) Marshall ultimately challenged Webb to a duel. They met in Delaware on June 25. On the second shot Webb was hit in the hip; because he could not stand for a third shot, the affair was terminated.

Ironically, with Marshall's challenge of Webb, he did what Jonathan had refused to do: he recognized Webb as a gentleman. Newspaper editors typically were not thought to be on the same social level as members of Congress and thus not worthy of a challenge.

In New York it was against the law to leave the state to fight a duel. When Webb returned to the city the district attorney, a Democrat, indicted Webb and put him in jail. He was found guilty and sent to Sing Sing to serve a two-year sentence. Fortunately for Webb, he had the governor of New York, William Seward, on his side. Webb and his newspaper had supported Seward's run for governor. A petition requesting a pardon, with fourteen thousand signatures, was sent to Seward and the pardon was granted, with a promise from Webb that he would never again participate in a duel.

In 1861 Seward, having lost the Republican presidential nomination to Lincoln, was now Lincoln's secretary of state. At the start of the Civil War, Webb, who had prior military experience, believed Lincoln should commission him as a major general. When Lincoln came back with an appointment as a brigadier general, Webb turned it down. For a number of years Webb had sought a diplomatic post, and in 1849 he had been appointed minister to Austria but was not confirmed by the Senate. In 1861 Seward appointed Webb to be the minister to Brazil. He held the position for eight years with mixed reviews. At one point he was accused of taking money from a settlement he had negotiated. He died in New York in 1884 at age eighty-two.

George W. Jones lost his bid for reelection in 1839. He settled in Iowa, and in 1848 he was elected to the U.S. Senate as one of the first senators from the new State of Iowa. He served in the Senate until 1859. President James Buchanan appointed him minister to New Granada (now Colombia). Under the new Lincoln administration, Jones was recalled and returned in December 1861 to the (now at war) United States. On his return, Secretary Seward had him arrested for disloyalty, because Jones had corresponded with Jefferson Davis, the president of the Confederacy. After Jones had served sixty-four days in jail, Lincoln had him released with a promise not to conspire with the enemy. Jones then returned to Iowa, but his leanings were with the Confederacy. Two of his sons served as officers in the Confederate army. Jones died at the age of ninety-two in Dubuque, Iowa, in 1896. He was always willing to talk about the long-past Cilley/Graves duel, but with age he at times got his facts confused.

Jonathan's older brother Joseph, who never fully recovered from war injuries, continued his life as a Nottingham farmer. Unlike Jonathan, politically he was a Federalist and then a Whig. He periodically ran for state offices but was not elected. In 1846 the Whig Party in New Hampshire wanted him to run for governor, but by that time he had shifted his allegiance to the Liberty Party, which was founded as an anti-slavery organization. He was twice a Liberty Party candidate for the U.S. House of Representatives. In 1846, when Levi Woodbury resigned his U.S. Senate seat to become an associate justice of the Supreme Court, the New Hampshire legislature sent Joseph to Washington to complete Woodbury's term.

It has been said that Joseph was the first openly anti-slavery member of the Senate. Much to the displeasure of some, he regularly presented petitions from constituents urging the abolition of slavery. During his time in Washington, the country was fully engaged in a war in Mexico.

Like many Northern abolitionists, he opposed the war, believing it a scheme to expand slavery. In January 1847, he told the Senate that "the constitution of the United States has made no provision for our holding foreign territory, still less for incorporating foreign nations into our union." He then offered a resolution "That the President of the United States be requested to order the army of the United States, now in Mexico, to someplace in the United States, near the frontier of the two counties." As a result, he was vilified in the Democratic press as a traitor and accused of not supporting the troops and wanting Mexico to win the war. On the contrary, Joseph, being a man with a distinguished military background, was concerned that the army was overextended and that new recruits, part of a much-needed increase in manpower, would be rushed into combat without adequate training. In the end, the resolution was tabled.

Joseph's term in the Senate was short, only ten months. Having lost his wife in 1843, he returned to Nottingham to the house he built in 1824 to live out his years surrounded by the Cilley family. He died in 1887, at age ninety-six, outliving all but three of his nine children.

Even though William Graves returned to Congress in 1839, it was undoubtedly an uncomfortable experience for him. In circles outside the traditional Southern code of honor states, those who killed an opponent in a duel, ostensibly in defense of their honor, were scorned by most in the world of public opinion. He chose not to run in 1841 and opened a very profitable law practice in Louisville. He remained active in Whig politics, and during Clay's 1844 presidential campaign he traveled throughout Kentucky speaking on behalf of Clay. In 1848 there was talk of Graves being a candidate for Kentucky governor, but he died in September of bladder cancer at age forty-four.

Family and friends of Jonathan believed Graves died a broken man, his death hastened by his guilt over Jonathan's death. According to his physician and neighbor, Samuel Gross, Graves did suffer a very painful death. There is no concrete evidence, however, to suggest that Graves outwardly or inwardly manifested any anguish or remorse. Gross, in his frequent contact with Graves, never saw any inner turmoil, and he claimed that Graves "had long ago made up his mind that the combat was one of necessity, and that he could not, as the 'code' was then interpreted, have avoided it without a sacrifice of honor, which, to a man of his gallant nature, is always more precious than life itself."

# Notes

## INTRODUCTION

Page 2—*"My name must not"*: "The Martyrdom of Cilley," *Democratic Review*, March 1838, p. 502.

Page 3—*"The most unpleasant thing"*: Jonathan to Deborah, February 26, 1832, *Breach of Privilege*.

## CHAPTER 1

Page 8—*"an undivided interest in the welfare"*: L. O. Williams, *A New Hampshire Hilltop*, p. 68.

Page 11—*"In the American Revolution"*: *New Hampshire Patriot*, November 28, 1820.

Page 12—*"Thus may the British army"*: J. Scales, *Life of Gen. Joseph Cilley*, p. 30.

Page 12—*"waved his sword over his head"*: J. Scales, *Life of Gen. Joseph Cilley*, p. 36.

Page 13—*"Colonel Cilley's regiment"*: J. Scales, *Life of Gen. Joseph Cilley*, pp. 39–40.

Page 14—*"Colonel Cilley was accustomed to say"*: J. Scales, *Life of Gen. Joseph Cilley*, p. 50.

Page 16—*"He was a man of good judgment"*: W. Plumer, *Sketch of Maj. Gen'l Joseph Cilley*, p. 10.

Page 17—*"protect citizens' political freedom"*: L. O. Williams, *A New Hampshire Hilltop*, p. 91.

Page 17—*"the godlessness of New Hampshire"*: L. O. Williams, *A New Hampshire Hilltop*, p. 96.

Page 17—*"His religion consisted more"*: W. Plumer, *Sketch of Maj. Gen'l Joseph Cilley*, p. 12.

## CHAPTER 2

Page 23—*"quiet as a church mouse"*: New Hampshire Patriot, August 2, 1814.

Page 23—*"Moderate salaries, no unnecessary Taxes"*: New Hampshire Patriot, October 29, 1816.

Page 24—*"to write Latin grammatically"*: Bowdoin College Catalog, 1822.

Page 25—*"To him I owe almost as much"*: Jonathan to Ann, June 10, 1821, *Breach of Privilege.*

## CHAPTER 3

Page 29—*"by strong, spirited horses"*: H. Bridge, *Personal Recollections,* p. 3.

Page 30—*"there must have been"*: F. P. Stern, *The Life and Genius of Nathaniel Hawthorne,* p. 67.

Page 30—*"Cilley is also a fine fellow"*: G. W. Pierce to Josiah Pierce, November 30, 1821. Maine Memory Network, Maine Historical Society.

Page 30—*"probably derived all"*: "Biographical Sketch of Jonathan Cilley," *Democratic Review,* September 1838, p. 69.

Page 30—*"as a young man of exceeding"*: R. Harwell, *Hawthorne and Longfellow,* p. 60.

Page 30—*"possessed a remarkable"*: N. Hawthorne, "Biographical Sketch of Jonathan Cilley," *Democratic Review,* September 1838, p. 70.

Page 31—*"a hideously ugly college"*: E. Mather, *Nathaniel Hawthorne: A Modest Man,* p. 37.

Page 31—*"one of the most pleasant"*: Jonathan to Ann, July 7, 1822, *Breach of Privilege.*

Page 32—*"rather too young to encounter"*: R. Harwell, *Hawthorne and Longfellow,* p. 8.

Page 32—*"uniformity and sameness"*: Jonathan to Ann, March 14, 1825, *Breach of Privilege.*

Page 33—*"sleeping at public worship"*: Faculty Records Bowdoin College, September 1, 1823.

Page 33—*"walking unnecessarily"*: Faculty Records Bowdoin College, September 17, 1824.

Page 33—*"heart sick"*: Jonathan to Ann, March 1825, *Breach of Privilege.*

Page 34—*"irregularity of eating and drinking"*: Faculty Records Bowdoin College, March 30, 1823.

Page 34—*"that students be prohibited"*: Faculty Records Bowdoin College, July 21, 1823.

Page 34—*"whereas there exists in College"*: L. Hatch, *History of Bowdoin College*, p. 323.

Page 34—*"We the undersigned subscribers"*: Hawthorne's *"Pot-8-O Club,"* at Bowdoin College.

Page 35—*"dedicated to card playing"*: B. Wineapple, *Hawthorne: A Life*, p. 47.

Page 35—*"between forty and fifty fish"*: Jonathan to Ann, May 25, 1824, *Breach of Privilege.*

Page 36—*"procured a school"*: Jonathan to Ann, December 8, 1823, *Breach of Privilege.*

Page 36—*"elocution was practiced"*: D. W. Howe, *What Hath God Wrought*, p. 371.

Page 36—*"free and natural"*: N. Hawthorne, "Biographical Sketch of Jonathan Cilley," *Democratic Review*, September 1838, p. 70.

Page 38—*"then a poet of no mean"*: R. Harwell, *Hawthorne and Longfellow*, p. 60.

Page 38—*"unquestionable genius"*: G .L. Austin, *Henry Wadsworth Longfellow*, p. 67.

Page 38—*"barrel of the best"*: Hawthorne's *"Pot-8-O Club,"* at Bowdoin College.

Page 40—*"vehicle of truth"*: J. Cilley, "Fictional Writing," Bowdoin College Archives.

Page 40—*"the strongest barrier"*: J. Cilley, "Satirical Composition," Bowdoin College Archives.

Page 41—*"wait if not too impatient"*: Jonathan to Ann, March 1825, *Breach of Privilege.*

Page 42—*"many hundred had collected"*: A. G. Spear, ed., *Journals of Hezekiah Prince Jr.*, p. 252.

Page 43—*"a young man of quick"*: N. Hawthorne, "Biographical Sketch of Jonathan Cilley," *Democratic Review*, September 1838, p. 70.

## CHAPTER 4

Page 47—"*considerable excitement in this*": A. G. Spear, ed., *Journals of Hezekiah Prince Jr.*, p. 89.

Page 47—"*which his political*": C. Eaton, *History of Thomaston*, Vol. 1, p. 338.

Page 48—"*thus is this subject*": A. G. Spear, ed., *Journals of Hezekiah Prince Jr.*, p. 177.

Page 48—"*for purposes of improvement*": A. G. Spear, ed., *Journals of Hezekiah Prince Jr.*, p. 56.

Page 48—"*Is the great influx*": A. G. Spear, ed., Journals *of Hezekiah Prince Jr.*, p. 171.

Page 48—"*Are the miseries*": A .G. Spear, ed., *Journals of Hezekiah Prince Jr.*, p. 155.

Page 48—"*Which is the most*": A. G. Spear, ed., *Journals of Hezekiah Prince Jr.*, p. 123.

Page 48—"*under the editorial care*": C. Eaton, *History of Thomaston*, Vol. 1, p. 349.

Page 49—"*clerking in the office*": D. M. Gold, "John Appleton and the Practice of Law," p. 132.

Page 49—"*too much pomp*": Jonathan to Ann, February 10, 1826, *Breach of Privilege.*

Page 50—"*Mr. Cilley frequently calls*": A. G. Spear, ed., *Journals of Hezekiah Prince Jr.*, p. 271.

Page 50—"*Are the mental capacities*": A. G. Spear, ed., *Journals of Hezekiah Prince Jr.*, p. 278.

Page 51—"*was breeding*": Jonathan to Ann, April 2, 1826, *Breach of Privilege.*

Page 51—"*No American feelings*": Jonathan to Uncle, date unknown, *Breach of Privilege.*

Page 52—"*mindful of a gallant people*": "Fiftieth Anniversary Oration," July 4, 1826, Thomaston Historical Society.

Page 53—"*'Tis a vexatious life*": Jonathan to Ann, February 10, 1826, *Breach of Privilege.*

Page 53—"*a pretty, really pretty girl*": Jonathan to Ann, February 10, 1826, *Breach of Privilege.*

Page 54—"*that at the present*": Jonathan to Ann, April 2, 1826, *Breach of Privilege.*

Page 54—*"I am a modest youth"*: Jonathan to Ann, July 6, 1826, *Breach of Privilege.*

Page 54—*"where I should hear"*: Jonathan to Ann, April 2, 1826, *Breach of Privilege.*

Page 54—*"We poor mortals"*: Jonathan to Ann, July 6, 1826, *Breach of Privilege.*

Page 55—*"I never was in love"*: Jonathan to Ann, July 7, 1826, *Breach of Privilege.*

Page 55—*"I am in love"*: Jonathan to Ann, August 31, 1827, *Breach of Privilege.*

Page 55—*"I told you I was in love"*: Jonathan to Ann, August 31, 1827, *Breach of Privilege.*

Page 56—*"the ten thousand false"*: Jonathan to Cousin, January 11, 1828, *Breach of Privilege.*

Page 56—*"younger man stronger"*: Jonathan to Ann, August 31, 1828, *Breach of Privilege.*

Page 56—*"What a damnation fuss"*: Jonathan to Ann, January 11, 1828, *Breach of Privilege.*

Page 56—*"how slick and cunningly"*: Jonathan to Ann, February 6, 1828, *Breach of Privilege.*

Page 57—*"they were informed"*: A. G. Spear, ed., *Journals of Hezekiah Prince Jr.*, p. 414.

Page 57—*"the poor old gentleman"*: A. G. Spear, ed., *Journals of Hezekiah Prince Jr.*, p. 414.

Page 58—*"restore you to health"*: Deborah to Jonathan, August 13, 1828, *Breach of Privilege.*

Page 59—*"not be afraid by reading"*: Deborah to Jonathan, August 27, 1828, *Breach of Privilege.*

Page 60—*"a rose and a lily"*: Jonathan to Ann, March 15, 1828, *Breach of Privilege.*

Page 60—*"I love to look"*: Jonathan to Ann, February 14, 1830, *Breach of Privilege.*

Page 60—*"a very tolerable sum"*: Jonathan to Ann, March 15, 1829, *Breach of Privilege.*

Page 61—*"old friends would assemble"*: *Congregationalist*, June 24, 1886.

Page 61—*"turned fed"*: Jonathan to Uncle, February, 1828, *Breach of Privilege.*

## CHAPTER 5

Page 64—*"worth making a long"*: Jonathan to Deborah, February 26, 1832, *Breach of Privilege.*

Page 65—*"Gross misrepresentations"*: Jonathan to Deborah, February 26, 1832, *Breach of Privilege.*

Page 66—*"dirt farmers and down-east"*: C. A. Jellison, *Fessenden of Maine*, p. 19.

Page 68—*"to draw up a full"*: "Thomaston Election," Maine Historical Society.

Page 72—*"to destroy my political"*: Jonathan to Dunlap, November 3, 1832, Cilley Letters, Thomaston Historical Society.

Page 74—*"as a federalist"*: Ruggles to Albert Smith, December 6, 1832, Fogg Collection, Maine Historical Society.

Page 74—*"the first act and declaration"*: N. Hawthorne, "Biographical Sketch of Jonathan Cilley," *Democratic Review*, September 1838, p. 71.

## CHAPTER 6

Page 76—*"continual misrepresentation"*: Jonathan to Deborah, January 13, 1833, *Breach of Privilege.*

Page 77—*"the low cunning of mere"*: Portland Advertiser, January 13, 1833.

Page 77—*"useful to the cause"*: Jonathan to Deborah, January 13, 1833, *Breach of Privilege.*

Page 77—*"was slow to withdraw"*: N. Hawthorne, "Biographical Sketch of Jonathan Cilley," *Democratic Review*, September 1838, p. 72.

Page 78—*"had the independence"*: Portland Advertiser, February 22, 1833.

Page 80—*"are shoving jack planes"*: Kennebec Journal, July 3, 1833.

Page 80—*"I must act for myself"*: Kennebec Journal, July 3, 1833.

Page 81—*"the Judge was bitter"*: Deborah to Jane Cilley, June 24, 1833, *Breach of Privilege.*

Page 82—*"was of insane mind"*: Bradbury Cilley Will, New Hampshire State Archives.

Page 82—*"unquestionably a gentleman"*: Eastern Argus, July 5, 1833.

Page 82—*"abuse and ingratitude"*: Samuel Smith to Samuel Upton, June 11, 1833, Samuel E. Smith Papers, Bowdoin College.

Page 83—*"I regret that I cannot"*: *Eastern Argus*, July 31, 1833.

Page 83—*"as a deceived man"*: *Eastern Argus*, July 31, 1833.

Page 84—*"long winded harangue"*: *Eastern Argus*, August 19, 1833.

Page 84—*"This is the name"*: *Eastern Argus*, August 23, 1833.

Page 85—*"to know by what"*: *Eastern Argus*, September 6, 1833.

Page 86—*"this man will yet learn"*: *Jeffersonian*, August 26, 1833.

Page 87—*"If the private character"*: *Kennebec Journal*, August 28, 1833.

Page 88—*"Webster, by his unrivalled"*: *The Farmers' Cabinet*, October 18, 1833.


## CHAPTER 7

Page 91—*"have a pleasant session"*: Jonathan to Deborah, January 1, 1834, *Breach of Privilege*.

Page 91—*"his enemies have not"*: *Portland Advertiser*, January 13, 1834.

Page 91—*"that they might undertake"*: N. Hawthorne, "Biographical Sketch of Jonathan Cilley," *Democratic Review*, September 1838, p. 72.

Page 92—*"effectively condemn any man"*: F. O. J. Smith to G. W. Pierce, January 10, 1834, Maine Memory Network, Maine Historical Society.

Page 92—*"for an alleged injury"*: *Eastern Argus*, January 3, 1834.

Page 92—*"persecuted by Ruggles"*: Jonathan to Deborah, January 13, 1834, *Breach of Privilege*.

Page 92—*"drawn into any schemes"*: Deborah to Jonathan, January 3, 1834, *Breach of Privilege*.

Page 92—*"My enemies have gone too"*: Jonathan to Deborah, January 7, 1834, *Breach of Privilege*.

Page 94—*"You need not fear"*: Deborah to Jonathan, January 3, 1834, *Breach of Privilege*.

Page 94—*"enemies, enemies"*: Deborah to Jonathan, January 6, 1834, *Breach of Privilege*.

Page 94—*"Why in the world"*: Jonathan to Deborah, January 7, 1834, *Breach of Privilege*.

Page 94—*"there is quite a reformation"*: Deborah to Jonathan, February 5, 1834, *Breach of Privilege*.

Page 95—*"How thankful we ought"*: Deborah to Ann, March 27, 1834, *Breach of Privilege*.

Page 95—*"not religious"*: Jonathan to Deborah, January 1, 1834, *Breach of Privilege.*

Page 95—*"enquire and know"*: Deborah to Jonathan, February 5, 1834, *Breach of Privilege.*

Page 96—*"feels happier in an open"*: Jonathan to Deborah, February 10, 1834, *Breach of Privilege.*

Page 96—*"I am thought"*: Jonathan to Deborah, January 10, 1834, *Breach of Privilege.*

Page 96—*"a much injured man"*: *Portland Advertiser*, January 13, 1834.

Page 97—*"by acting the part"*: *Eastern Argus*, January 20, 1834.

Page 97—*"most odious and malicious"*: *Jeffersonian*, February 3, 1834.

Page 98—*"the gentleman from Portland"*: *Kennebec Journal*, January 22, 1834.

Page 99—*"an individual who"*: *Portland Advertiser*, February 8, 1834.

Page 99—*"a virulent and unprovoked"*: *Portland Advertiser*, February 10, 1834.

Page 99—*"he would respect"*: *Portland Advertiser*, February 8, 1834.

Page 99—*"a station for which"*: *Thomaston Republican*, February 28, 1834.

Page 100—*"It is right"*: Deborah to Ann, March 27, 1834, *Breach of Privilege.*

Page 101—*"I am satisfied"*: Hamlet Bates to Jonathan, September 5, 1834, Cilley Letters, Thomaston Historical Society.

Page 101—*"Judge Ruggles is not"*: Deborah to Ann, October 1, 1834, *Breach of Privilege.*

Page 102—*"The poison was intended"*: Letter of Leonard Jarvis to his Constituents, Maine Historical Society.


CHAPTER 8

Page 106—*"unfortunate for you"*: Charles Jarvis to Josiah Pierce, January 24, 1835, Maine Memory Network, Maine Historical Society.

Page 106—*"amusing the boys"*: *Eastern Argus*, January 28, 1835.

Page 107—*"F.O.J. Smith, L.S.C."*: *Portland Advertiser*, March 24, 1835.

Page 108—*"Your friends"*: Ira Berry to Smith, December 14, 1834, F. O. J. Smith Collection, Maine Historical Society.

Page 108—*"Mr. Cilley is a man"*: *Portland Advertiser*, March 26, 1835.

Page 108—*"let all minor causes"*: *Eastern Argus*, March 1835.

Page 109—*"probably destined"*: Prince Jr. to Jonathan, March 8, 1835, *Breach of Privilege*.

Page 110—*"Cilley is resolved"*: G. W. Pierce to Josiah Pierce, February 7, 1835, Maine Memory Network, Maine Historical Society.

Page 110—*"always made strong"*: G. W. Pierce to Josiah Pierce, March 8, 1835, Maine Memory Network, Maine Historical Society.

Page 111—*"deep regret that"*: Pierce to G. W. Pierce, October 2, 1835, Maine Memory Network, Maine Historical Society.

Page 112—*"calculated to strike"*: *American Advocate*, January 7, 1835.

Page 114—*"It appears to me"*: Fairfield to wife, December 22, 1935.

Page 114—*"Slavery is a question"*: *Eastern Argus*, January 19, 1836.

Page 115—*"The truth is"*: *Oxford Democrat*, April 6, 1836.

Page 115—*"thrive only in commotion"*: *Eastern Argus*, May 3, 1836.

Page 117—*"who in his first"*: *Eastern Argus*, April 9, 1836.

Page 117—*"damned little rascal"*: *Alexandria Gazette*, March 31, 1836.

Page 118—*"drunk on slavery"*: C. F. Adams, ed., *Memoirs of John Quincy Adams*, Vol. 9, p. 294.

Page 118—*"a real fighter"*: Fairfield to wife, January 13, 1836.

Page 118—*"Mr. Bynum comes off"*: *Torch Light*, June 23, 1836.

Page 119—*"What a farce"*: Fairfield to wife, June 14, 1836.

Page 120—*"He is running"*: Bridge to Hawthorne, November 17, 1836, In H. Bridge, *Personal Recollections*, p. 143.

Page 121—*"behaved in this matter"*: F. P. Stern, *The Life and Genius of Nathaniel Hawthorne*, p. 94.

Page 121—*"I doubt whether"*: Bridge to Hawthorne, December 25, 1836, In H. Bridge, *Personal Recollections*, p. 147.

Page 121—*"where we would"*: Jonathan to Hawthorne, November 17, 1836, In H. Bridge, *Personal Recollections*, p. 145.


CHAPTER 9

Page 123—*"the Democracy of the County"*: *Age*, February 15, 1837.

Page 123—*"in spite of the"*: C. Eaton, *History of Thomaston*, p. 382.

Page 124—*"Saw my classmate"*: N. Hawthorne, *Passages from the American Note-book*, pp. 75–76.

Page 126—*"I cannot help"*: Jonathan to Deborah, October 1, 1837, *Breach of Privilege*.

Page 127—*"you make me say"*: Jonathan to Deborah, October 7, 1837, *Breach of Privilege*.

Page 127—*"It will not do"*: Jonathan to Deborah, September 24, 1837, *Breach of Privilege*.

Page 128—*"but organize and quarrel"*: Davee to Josiah Pierce, September 20, 1837, Maine Memory Network, Maine Historical Society.

Page 128—*"of an utter destitution"*: *Daily National Intelligencer*, September 12, 1837.

Page 129—*"I cannot resist"*: *Daily National Intelligencer*, September 12, 1837.

Page 130—*"I claim no privilege"*: *Oxford Democrat*, September 26, 1837.


## CHAPTER 10

Page 133—*"Death to me"*: Jonathan to Deborah, December 15, 1837, *Breach of Privilege*.

Page 134—*"the looks of dear"*: Jonathan to Deborah, December 18, 1837, *Breach of Privilege*.

Page 136—*"I regretted the occurrence"*: G. L. Prentiss, *Memoir of S.S. Prentiss*, p. 134.

Page 137—*"Wise is an impudent"*: Jonathan to Deborah, February 9, 1838, *Breach of Privilege*.

Page 138—*"was impelled to say"*: *Daily National Intelligencer*, January 25, 1838.

Page 139—*"utterly annihilated before"*: "The Martyrdom of Cilley," *Democratic Review*, March 1838, p. 495.

Page 139—*"Indian hater"*: *Waldo Patriot*, February 23, 1838.

Page 139—*"no sympathies for Indians"*: Adams to Charles Adams, March 19, 1838, *Proceedings of the Massachusetts Historical Society*, p. 292.

Page 139—*"If you could see"*: Jonathan to Deborah, February 9, 1838, *Breach of Privilege*.

Page 140—*"a direct and unequivocal"*: *Congressional Globe*, 25th Cong., 2nd sess., p. 173.

Page 140—*"as an act of justice"*: *Courier and Enquirer*, February 13, 1838.

Page 140—*"things do not go"*: *Courier and Enquirer*, February 12, 1838.

Page 141—*"That as the course"*: *Congressional Globe*, 25th Cong., 2nd sess., p. 173.

Page 142—*"he trusted that"*: *Congressional Globe*, 25th Cong., 2nd sess., p. 174.

Page 142—*"But what's the use"*: *Memoirs and Service of Three Generations*, p. 13.

Page 142—*"employed for the purpose"*: *Congressional Globe*, 25th Cong., 2nd sess., p. 175.

Page 142—*"black, base, and foul"*: *Congressional Globe*, 25th Cong., 2nd sess., p. 176.

Page 143—*"Ruggles gets deeper"*: Jonathan to Deborah, February 14, 1838, *Breach of Privilege*.

Page 143—*"Ruggles's character is gone"*: Jonathan to Deborah, February 18, 1838, *Breach of Privilege*.

Page 144—*"disgrace the lowest brothel"*: *Courier and Enquirer*, February 16, 1838.

Page 144—*"Things do not go"*: *Waldo Patriot*, March 2, 1838.

Page 145—*"I see in the Globe"*: Deborah to Jonathan, February 18, 1838, *Breach of Privilege*.

## CHAPTER 11

Page 148—*"To the Hon. Jonathan Cilley"*: Webb to Cilley, *Report of the Select Committee*, 25th Cong., 2nd sess., no. 825, p. 3.

Page 148—*"merely a note"*: *Daily National Intelligencer*, July 24, 1839.

Page 149—*"that he had learned"*: *Report of the Select Committee*, 25th Cong., 2nd sess., no. 825, p. 127.

Page 149—*"an embarrassing situation"*: *Report of the Select Committee*, 25th Cong., 2nd sess., no. 825, p. 119.

Page 151—*"there was no necessity"*: *Report of the Select Committee*, 25th Cong., 2nd sess., no. 825, p. 128.

Page 151—*"that he hoped"*: *Report of the Select Committee*, 25th Cong., 2nd sess., no. 825, p. 127.

Page 151—*"that his friends"*: *Daily National Intelligencer*, July 24, 1839.

Page 152—*"In the interview which I had"*: Graves to Cilley, February 21, 1838, *Report of the Select Committee*, 25th Cong., 2nd sess., no. 825, p. 3.

Page 152—*"that he should not"*: *Report of the Select Committee*, 25th Cong., 2nd sess., no. 825, p. 103.

Page 153—*"The note which you just"*: Cilley to Graves, February 21, 1838, *Report of the Select Committee*, 25th Cong., 2nd sess., no. 825, p. 4.

## CHAPTER 12

Page 155—*"highly incensed"*: *Report of the Select Committee*, 25th Cong., 2nd sess., no. 825, p. 56.

Page 155—*"Sir, Your note of yesterday"*: Graves to Cilley, February 22, 1838, *Report of the Select Committee*, 25th Cong., 2nd sess., no. 825, p. 4.

Page 156—*"would perceive the propriety"*: *Report of the Select Committee*, 25th Cong., 2nd sess., no. 825, p. 77.

Page 157—*"he saw in the note"*: *Report of the Select Committee*, 25th Cong., 2nd sess., no. 825, p. 104.

Page 157—*"Sir, Your note of this date"*: Cilley to Graves, February 22, 1838, *Report of the Select Committee*, 25th Cong., 2nd sess., no. 825, p. 5.

Page 158—*"determined character"*: *Report of the Select Committee*, 25th Cong., 2nd sess., no. 825, p. 125.

Page 159—*"not much"*: R. Williams, undated note, likely February 23, 1838, Reuel Williams Papers, Maine Historical Society.

Page 159—*"I did not write you"*: Jonathan to Deborah, February 22, 1838, *Breach of Privilege*.

## CHAPTER 13

Page 161—*"confidence in the weapon"*: *Report of the Select Committee*, 25th Cong., 2nd sess., no. 825, p. 124.

Page 162—*"caused me so much"*: R. Williams, undated note, likely February 23, 1838, Reuel Williams Papers, Maine Historical Society.

Page 162—*"As you have declined"*: Graves to Cilley, *Report of the Select Committee*, 25th Cong., 2nd sess., no. 825, p. 5.

Page 163—*"that his mind"*: R. Williams. undated note, likely February 23, 1838, Reuel Williams Papers, Maine Historical Society.

Page 163—*"he should go out"*: *Report of the Select Committee*, 25th Cong., 2nd sess., no. 825, p. 121.

Page 166—*"that James Watson Webb"*: Report of the Select Committee, 25th Cong., 2nd sess., no. 825, p. 86.

Page 167—*"Your note of this morning"*: Cilley to Graves, *Report of the Select Committee*, 25th Cong., 2nd sess., no. 825, p. 5.

Page 167—*"Mr. Cilley proposes to meet"*: Jones to Wise, *Report of the Select Committee*, 25th Cong., 2nd sess., no. 825, p. 5.

Page 168—*"was either to make"*: Report of the Select Committee, 25th Cong., 2nd sess., no. 825, p. 57.

Page 168—*"The terms arranging the meeting"*: Wise to Jones, *Report of the Select Committee*, 25th Cong., 2nd sess., no. 825, p. 6.

Page 169—*"that he must fight"*: R. Williams, undated note, likely February 23, 1838, Reuel Williams Papers, Maine Historical Society.

Page 169—*"I have had an exciting day"*: Jonathan to Deborah, February 23, 1838, *Breach of Privilege*.

Page 170—*"But what is it I hear"*: Deborah to Jonathan, March 1, 1838, *Breach of Privilege*.

## CHAPTER 14

Page 171—*"There was an agitation"*: Adams to Charles Adams, March 19, 1838, *Proceedings of the Massachusetts Historical Society*, p. 289.

Page 172—*"I will receive at Dr. Reilly's"*: Jones to Wise, *Report of the Select Committee*, 25th Cong., 2nd sess., no. 825, p. 6.

Page 172—*"I have called at this place"*: Wise to Jones, *Report of the Select Committee*, 25th Cong., 2nd sess., no. 825, p. 6.

Page 173—*"Your note, dated at ten o'clock"*: Jones to Wise, *Report of the Select Committee*, 25th Cong., 2nd sess., no. 825, p. 7.

Page 173—*"Through the politeness of my friend"*: Jones to Wise, *Report of the Select Committee*, 25th Cong., 2nd sess., no. 825, p. 7.

Page 174—*"never dishonor the name"*: Report of the Select Committee, 25th Cong., 2nd sess., no. 825, p. 49.

Page 175—*"desired them to conduct"*: Report of the Select Committee, 25th Cong., 2nd sess., no. 825, p. 129.

Page 175—*"That, in declining"*: Report of the Select Committee, 25th Cong., 2nd sess., no. 825, p. 59.

Page 176—*"give my compliments"*: Report of the Select Committee, 25th Cong., 2nd sess., no. 825, p. 133.

Page 178—*"assign some reasons"*: *Report of the Select Committee*, 25th Cong., 2nd sess., no. 825, p. 45.

Page 178—*"I am authorized by"*: *Report of the Select Committee*, 25th Cong., 2nd sess., no. 825, p. 46.

Page 179—*"I am authorized by Mr. Cilley"*: *Report of the Select Committee*, 25th Cong., 2nd sess., no. 825, p. 46.

Page 180—*"my friend, in coming"*: *Report of the Select Committee*, 25th Cong., 2nd sess., no. 825, p. 46.

Page 180—*"Gentlemen, we have come"*: *Report of the Select Committee*, 25th Cong., 2nd sess., no. 825, p. 69.

Page 181—*"does not require"*: *Report of the Select Committee*, 25th Cong., 2nd sess., no. 825, p. 46.

Page 181—*"a chance shot"*: *Report of the Select Committee*, 25th Cong., 2nd sess., no. 825, p. 137.

Page 182—*"that they were merely"*: *Report of the Select Committee*, 25th Cong., 2nd sess., no. 825, p. 138.

Page 182—*"You do not allow"*: *Report of the Select Committee*, 25th Cong., 2nd sess., no. 825, p. 138.

Page 182—*"they must thirst"*: *Report of the Select Committee*, 25th Cong., 2nd sess., no. 825, p. 71.

Page 182—*"they better give up"*: *Report of the Select Committee*, 25th Cong., 2nd sess., no. 825, p. 90.

Page 182—*"I am shot"*: *Report of the Select Committee*, 25th Cong., 2nd sess., no. 825, p. 90.

Page 182—*"My friend is dead"*: *Report of the Select Committee*, 25th Cong., 2nd sess., no. 825, p. 47.

Page 182—*"Mr. Cilley is killed"*: *Report of the Select Committee*, 25th Cong., 2nd sess., no. 825, p. 135.

Page 183—*"A challenge was never"*: N. Hawthorne, "Biographical Sketch of Jonathan Cilley," *Democratic Review*, September 1838, p. 75.


CHAPTER 15


Page 185—*"Mr. Cilley has a wife"*: *Journal of Commerce*, February 25, 1838.

Page 185—*"Webb is truly"*: B. Tuckerman, ed., *The Diary of Philip Hone*, p. 295.

Page 186—*"Such is the naked"*: Report of the Select Committee, 25th Cong., 2nd sess., no. 825, p. 47.

Page 186—*"An event has occurred"*: Congressional Globe, 25th Cong., 2nd sess., p. 199.

Page 187—*"the ceremonies"*: Adams to Charles Adams, March 19, 1838, Proceedings of the Massachusetts Historical Society, p. 290.

Page 187—*"the parties who engage"*: Funeral Oration Delivered at the Capitol, p. 7.

Page 188—*"some of the Gentlemen"*: Adams to Charles Adams, March 19, 1838, Proceedings of the Massachusetts Historical Society, p. 290.

Page 188—*"Graves I have not seen"*: Fairfield to wife, March 7, 1838.

Page 188—*"That a committee"*: Congressional Globe, 25th Cong., 2nd sess., p. 201.

Page 189—*"giving to Mr. Cilley"*: Adams to Charles Adams, March 19, 1838, Proceedings of the Massachusetts Historical Society, p. 290.

Page 189—*"Some of the vile"*: B. Tuckerman, ed., The Diary of Philip Hone, p. 296.

Page 190—*"A great crime has been"*: "The Martyrdom of Cilley," Democratic Review, March 1838, p. 493.

Page 191—*"into a position from"*: "The Martyrdom of Cilley," Democratic Review, March 1838, p. 499.

Page 192—*"been a slight misunderstanding"*: Daily National Intelligencer, March 16, 1838.

Page 192—*"no advice but acted"*: Pierce to Hale, March 2, 1838, Hale-Chandler Papers, Rauner Special Collections Library, Dartmouth College.

Page 193—*"from a deep sense"*: Sarah Washburn to Graves, March 2, 1838, Breach of Privilege.

Page 194—*"to notice in a suitable"*: Waldo Patriot, March 9, 1838.

Page 196—*"Please state what"*: Report of the Select Committee, 25th Cong., 2nd sess., no. 825, p. 55.

Page 196—*"Did Mr. Graves"*: Report of the Select Committee, 25th Cong., 2nd sess., no. 825, p. 78.

Page 197—*"a man whose character"*: Congressional Globe, 25th Cong., 2nd sess., p. 283.

Page 199—*"was more like"*: Congressional Globe, 25th Cong., 2nd sess., p. 362.

Page 200—*"object[ed] and protest[ed]"*: Public Advertiser, May 18, 1838.

Page 201—*"he was impelled"*: *Public Advertiser*, May 18, 1838.

Page 202—*"the author of all"*: Deborah to Nealleys, November 18, 1838, *Breach of Privilege*.

Page 202—*"Mr. Cilley's domestic habits"*: N. Hawthorne, "Biographical Sketch of Jonathan Cilley," *Democratic Review*, September 1838, p. 74.

Page 203—*"Alas that over the grave"*: N. Hawthorne, "Biographical Sketch of Jonathan Cilley," *Democratic Review*, September 1838, p. 75.

## CHAPTER 16

Page 205—*"most politically violent"*: *Daily National Intelligencer*, July 24, 1839.

Page 206—*"hissing serpent of Braintree"*: C. Simpson, *The Good Southerner*, p. 43.

Page 207—*"he had desired"*: *Congressional Globe*, 27th Cong., 2nd sess., p. 176.

Page 207—*"now had an opportunity"*: *Congressional Globe*, 27th Cong., 2nd sess., p. 194.

Page 207—*"During all these proceedings"*: Clay to Wise, February 28, 1842, *Papers of Henry Clay*, Vol. 9, p. 661.

## CHAPTER 17

Page 214—*"an ambitious Northern"*: Adams to Charles Adams, March 19, 1838, *Proceedings of the Massachusetts Historical Society*, p. 289.

Page 215—*"It is enough that"*: G. W. Curtis, *Life of Daniel Webster*, Vol. 1, p. 155.

Page 215—*"We endeavored to discharge"*: *Report of the Select Committee*, 25th Cong., 2nd sess., no. 825, p. 47.

Page 215—*"that you will be governed"*: J. L. Wilson, *The Code of Honor*, pp. 6–7.

Page 217—*"thus died the brave"*: *Memoirs and Service of Three Generations*, p. 29.

Page 217—*"If that dark pitfall"*: N. Hawthorne, "Biographical Sketch of Jonathan Cilley," *Democratic Review*, September 1838, p. 75.

## EPILOGUE

Page 220—*"to the active list"*: *Committee Report*, 48th Cong., 1st sess., no. 691, p. 2.

Page 223—*"the constitution of the United States"*: *Congressional Globe*, 29th Cong., 2nd. sess., p. 231.

Page 223—*"had long ago"*: S. Gross, *Autobiography of Samuel D. Gross, M.D.*, p. 107.

# Bibliography

Adams, Charles Francis, ed. *Memoirs of John Quincy Adams, Comprising Portions of the Diary From 1795 to 1848.* 12 vols. Philadelphia: J. B. Lippincott, 1876.

Anderson, Eve, ed. *A Breach of Privilege: Cilley Family Letters, 1820–1867.* Rockland, ME: Seven Coin Press, 2002.

Austin, George Lowell. *Henry Wadsworth Longfellow: His Life, His Works, His Friendships.* Boston: Lee & Shepard, 1883.

Bradbury Cilley Will. Probate Records, New Hampshire State Archives, Concord, New Hampshire.

Bridge, Horatio. *Personal Recollections of Nathaniel Hawthorne.* New York: Harper and Brothers, 1893.

Cilley, Jonathan. "Fictitious Writing." Class Records: Class of 1825. Bowdoin College Archives, Brunswick, Maine.

Cilley, Jonathan. "Satirical Compositions." Class Records: Class of 1825. Bowdoin College Archives, Brunswick, Maine.

Cole, Donald B. *Jacksonian Democracy in New Hampshire, 1800–1851.* Cambridge, MA: Harvard University Press, 1970.

Crouthamel, James L. *James Watson Webb: A Biography.* Middletown, CT: Wesleyan University Press, 1969.

Eaton, Cyrus. *History of Thomaston, Rockland and South Thomaston, Maine.* Vol. 1. Hallowell, ME: Masters, Smith & Co., 1865.

Freeman, Joanne B. *Affairs of Honor: National Politics in the New Republic.* New Haven, CT: Yale University Press, 2001.

*Funeral Oration Delivered at the Capitol in Washington Over Body of Hon. Jonathan Cilley.* New York: Wiley Putnam, 1838.

Gaffney, Thomas L. "Maine's Mr. Smith: A Study of the Career of Frances O. J. Smith, Politician and Entrepreneur." PhD dissertation, University of Maine, 1979.

Gold, David M. "John Appleton and the Practice of Law in 19th Century Maine." *Maine Bar Journal* (May 1986): 132–38.

Goldman, Perry M., and James S. Young, eds. *The United States Congressional Directories, 1789–1840.* New York: Columbia University Press, 1973.

Gross, Samuel D. *Autobiography of Samuel D. Gross, M.D.: with Sketches of His Contemporaries.* Philadelphia: George Barrie, 1887.

Harwell, Richard. *Hawthorne and Longfellow: A Guide to an Exhibit.* Brunswick, ME: Bowdoin College, 1966.

Hatch, Louis C. *The History of Bowdoin College.* Portland, ME: Loring, Short & Harmon, 1927.

Hatch, Louis C. *Maine: A History.* Somersworth: New Hampshire Publishing Company, 1974.

Hawthorne, Julian. *Nathaniel Hawthorne and His Wife.* Boston: J. R. Osgood, 1885.

Hawthorne, Nathaniel. "Biographical Sketch of Jonathan Cilley." *United States Magazine and Democratic Review* 3 (September 1838): 69–77.

Hawthorne, Nathaniel. *Passages from the American Note-Books.* Boston: Houghton, Mifflin, 1892.

"Hawthorne's 'POT-8–O-Club' at Bowdoin College." Essex Institute Historical Collection, July 1931.

Hay, Melba Porter. "Compromiser or Conspirator? Henry Clay and the Graves-Cilley Duel." In *A Mythic Land Apart: Reassessing Southerners and Their History,* edited by Thomas H. Appleton Jr. and John David Smith. Westport, CT: Greenwood Press, 1997.

Hazlett, Charles A. *History of Rockingham County New Hampshire and Representative Citizens.* Chicago: Richmond-Arnold, 1915.

Holland, Barbara. *Gentlemen's Blood: A History of Dueling from Swords at Dawn to Pistols at Dusk.* New York: Bloomsbury, 2003.

Holt, Michael F. *The Rise and Fall of the American Whig Party: Jacksonian Politics and the Onset of the Civil War.* New York: Oxford University Press, 1999.

Howe, Daniel Walker. *What Hath God Wrought: The Transformation of America, 1815–1848.* New York: Oxford University Press, 2007.

Jellison, Charles A. *Fessenden of Maine: Civil War Senator.* Syracuse, NY: Syracuse University Press, 1962.

Jones, George W. "Jonathan Cilley of Maine and William J. Graves of Kentucky, Representatives in Congress: An Historical Duel." *Maine Historical and Genealogical Recorder* 6 (1889).

King, Horatio. "History of the Duel Between Jonathan Cilley and William J. Graves." *Collections and Proceedings of the Maine Historical Society,* 2nd series, 3 (1892): 127–48, 393–409.

"Letter of Leonard Jarvis to His Constituents of the Hancock and Washington District, in Maine." 1835. http://www.archive.org/details/letterofleonardj00jarv.

Maine State Bar Association. *One Hundred Years of Law & Justice.* 1991.

Marr, Harriet Webster. *Atkinson Academy: The Early Years.* Edited by Mary Alice Weaver. Springfield, MA: John E. Stewart, 1940.

"The Martyrdom of Cilley." *United States Magazine and Democratic Review* 1 (March 1838): 493–504.

Mather, Edward. *Nathaniel Hawthorne: A Modest Man.* New York: Thomas Y. Crowell, 1940.

Meacham, Jon. *American Lion: Andrew Jackson in the White House.* New York: Random House, 2008.

*Memoirs and Services of Three Generations.* Reprinted in *The Courier Gazette* (1909).

Miller, William Lee. *Arguing About Slavery: John Quincy Adams and the Great Battle in the United States Congress.* New York: Vintage Books, 1995.

"Mr. Henry A. Wise and the Cilley Duel." *United States Magazine and Democratic Review* 10 (May 1842): 483–87.

Nylander, Jane C. *Our Own Snug Fireside: Images of the New England Home, 1760–1860.* New Haven, CT: Yale University Press, 1993.

Parsons, Lynn Hudson. *The Birth of Modern Politics.* New York: Oxford University Press, 2009.

Plumer, William. *Sketch of Maj. Gen'l Joseph Cilley.* Manchester, NH: Thomas H. Tuson, 1891.

Prentiss, George L., ed. *A Memoir of S. S. Prentiss.* New York: Scribners, 1879.

*Proceedings of the Massachusetts Historical Society*, 2nd series, Vol. 12, *1897–1899*. Boston: Massachusetts Historical Society, 1899.

Remini, Robert V. *The House: The History of the House of Representatives*. New York: HarperCollins, 2006.

Reynolds, David S. *Waking Giant: America in the Age of Jackson*. New York: HarperCollins, 2008.

Ring, Elizabeth. *Maine in the Making of the Nation, 1783–1870*. Rockport, ME: Picton Press, 1996.

Sabine, Lorenzo. *Notes on Duels and Dueling, Alphabetically Arranged, with Preliminary Historical Essay*. Boston: Crosby, Nichols, 1859.

Scales, John. *Life of Gen. Joseph Cilley*. Manchester, NH: Standard Book Company, 1921.

Schlesinger, Arthur M., Jr. *The Age of Jackson*. Boston: Little, Brown, 1946.

Seitz, Don C. *Famous American Duels*. New York: Thomas Y. Crowell, 1929.

Simpson, Craig M. *A Good Southerner: The Life of Henry A. Wise of Virginia*. Chapel Hill: University of North Carolina Press, 1985.

Smith, Frances O. J. *Mr. Smith's Review of the "Letter of Leonard Jarvis, to His Constituents of the Hancock and Washington District, in Maine."* Maine Historical Society, 1835.

Spear, Arthur, ed. *Journals of Hezekiah Prince, Jr., 1822–1828*. New York: Crown, 1965.

Staples, Arthur G., ed. *The Letters of John Fairfield*. Lewiston, ME: Lewiston Journal, 1922.

"Statement of Henry Jones." *Niles National Register*, March 3, 1838.

"Statement of Thomas Hart Benton." *Niles National Register*, March 10, 1838.

Stearns, Franklin Preston. *The Life and Genius of Nathaniel Hawthorne*. Philadelphia: J. B. Lippincott, 1906.

Stewart, Frank Henderson. *Honor*. Chicago: University of Chicago Press, 1994.

*Thomaston Election*. Maine Historical Society, 1832.

Tuckerman, B., ed. *The Diary of Philip Hone*. New York: Dodd, Mead, 1889.

U.S. Congress. House of Representatives. Committee Report. 22nd Cong., 2nd sess., no. 460.

U.S. Congress. House of Representatives. Committee Report. 45th Cong., 3rd sess., no. 150.

U.S. Congress. House of Representatives. Committee Report. 46th Cong., 2nd sess., no. 1777.

U.S. Congress. House of Representatives. Committee Report. 47th Cong., 1st sess., no. 2066.

U.S. Congress. House of Representatives. Committee Report. 48th Cong., 1st sess., no. 691.

U.S. Congress. House of Representatives. *Report of the Select Committee Appointed to Investigate the Causes Which Led to the Death of the Hon. Jonathan Cilley*. 25th Cong., 2nd sess., no. 825.

Votes of the Executive Committee. Faculty Records (1821–1825). Bowdoin College Archives, Brunswick, Maine.

Wallner, Peter A. *Franklin Pierce: New Hampshire's Favorite Son*. Concord, NH: Plaidswede, 2004.

Wheelan, Joseph. *Mr. Adams's Last Crusade*. New York: Public Affairs, 2008.

Williams, Jack K. *Dueling in the Old South: Vignettes of Social History*. College Station: Texas A&M University Press, 1980.

Williams, Leon Oscar. *A New Hampshire Hilltop*. Nottingham, NH: John R. Williams, 2005.

Wilson, John Lyle. *The Code of Honor, or Rules for the Government of Principals and Seconds in Dueling.* Charleston, SC: 1838.

Wineapple, Brenda. *Hawthorne: A Life.* New York: Alfred A. Knopf, 2003.

Wise, Barton H. *The Life of Henry Wise, 1806–1876.* New York: Macmillan, 1899.

Wyatt-Brown, Bertram. *Southern Honor: Ethics and Behavior in the Old South.* New York: Oxford University Press, 1982.

Young, James Sterling. *The Washington Community, 1800–1828.* New York: Columbia University Press, 1966.

## NEWSPAPERS

*Age* (Augusta, ME)
*American Advocate* (Hallowell, ME)
*Charleston Courier* (Charleston, SC)
*Congregationalist* (Boston)
*Courier and Enquirer* (New York)
*Daily National Intelligencer* (Washington, DC)
*Daily Whig & Courier* (Bangor, ME)
*Eastern Argus* (Portland, ME)
*Farmers' Cabinet* (Amherst, NH)
*Jeffersonian* (Portland, ME)
*Journal of Commerce* (New York)
*Kennebec Journal* (Augusta, ME)
*Maine Enquirer* (Bath, ME)
*Maine Workingmen's Advocate* (Belfast, ME)
*New Hampshire Patriot* (Concord, NH)
*Niles National Register* (Baltimore, MD)
*Oxford Democrat* (Norway, ME)
*Portland Advertiser* (Portland, ME)
*Public Advertiser* (Louisville, KY)
*Recorder* (Thomaston, ME)
*Republican* (Thomaston, ME)
*Torch Light* (Hagerstown, MD)
*Waldo Patriot* (Belfast, ME)